Additional Praise for
American Gridlock

"Woody Brock's writings are often the first place I encounter issues that soon become central debates within public policy. He is prescient, penetrating, broad, surprising and wise. Some writers illuminate yesterday's news, a few may shed light on tomorrows. But very few thinkers can help you to understand the issues that will shape not only next year, but also the next decade. As America faces a pivotal election, his book could not be more timely."

—Edward Smith, *The Times* (London)

"The events of the past several years have clearly exposed the faults in standard economic and financial analysis. And the economics profession currently seems at a loss to provide credible and practical policy prescriptions for the current malaise facing the U.S. and other major countries. In this fascinating book, Woody Brock stands above the crowd with his original and well thought out plans for a sensible way forward to a brighter future. It is a welcome counter to the widespread gloom that surrounds most of the discussion of the outlook."

—Martin Barnes, Chief Economist, BCA Research

"The world is bogged down by incremental thinking and yearns for some "big ideas" to liberate us from the serial crises that confront us. Over the years "Woody" Brock has proven himself as an original thinker whose solutions to problems often turn out to be right. Now, in this book, we have a set of recommendations that may put us on the right course."

—Byron R. Wien, Vice Chairman, Blackstone Advisory Partners LP

"Woody Brock tackles America's big problems at a breathtaking scale. No small ideas here. And no flinching from the conclusions which follow from the fierce logic he applies. Read this book to find a way forward out of the broken politics and doctrinaire policies that leave so many disgusted and depressed to the prospect of a genuine prosperity."

—Joseph Dear, Chief Investment Officer, California Public Employees Retirement System (CalPERS)

"Woody thoughtfully addresses the critical issues facing our country and shows how they can be resolved using a different analytical approach. A must read for any serious market participant."

—Susan E. Manske, Vice President and Chief Investment Officer, The John D. and Catherine T. MacArthur Foundation

"Woody Brock is an American masterpiece. There is no one like Woody. No one is able to think as broadly as Woody, while simultaneously thinking so deeply. No one is as amusingly insightful, witty and provocative as Woody. Woody's economics are a blend of deep, revolutionary, insight and common sense. I will never know how he does it, but I deeply appreciate that he does it. No one is a better catalyst for my own thinking than Woody. Read *American Gridlock*. Savor *American Gridlock*. Allow yourself to be provoked and prodded by *American Gridlock*. Then put it down, go fishing, then reread a month later. You will be deeply and lastingly rewarded for your efforts."

—Richard N. Foster, Investment & Advisory Services; former Managing Director, McKinsey & Company; author of *Creative Destruction*

"For decades Woody Brock has enlightened a select audience with his logically rigorous, factually impeccable analyses of past developments and future trends. Time and again I have seen his insights prove true, especially in cases where he has challenged the prevailing wisdom of the era. Now for the first time he addresses a general readership, with a comprehensive assessment of how to cope with the most intractable public problems of our time. I don't agree with every one of his prescriptions, which is why I am all the more sincere in recommending the thoroughness and rigor of his logic."

—James Fallows, *The Atlantic*

"*American Gridlock* is a major endeavour containing deeply profound insights. It requires the courage to see that economics has largely failed and must be replaced as the master discipline by political theory and science, and with a new emphasis on fairness and justice in the distribution of benefits and rewards. Woody Brock is one of the few thinkers of our times who can tackle this mountainous task and unlock the paralysis in which the increasingly muddled debate about Capitalism has plunged us."

—Lord Howell of Guildford, Minister of State, Foreign and Commonwealth Office, UK

"If Woody Brock did not exist, God would have had to invent him. He is a unique, challenging thinker who makes most conventional economic forecasters look like trend-followers. Serious investors and students of public policy should be delighted that he has finally written a book in which his renowned analytical approach focuses on public policy. This is badly-needed fresh air in a seriously polluted environment."

—Don Coxe, Chairman, Coxe Advisors LLP

"*American Gridlock* provides a compelling framework for citizens, policymakers and market participants to overhaul their views on many important issues of the day. The power of Woody Brock's approach—emphasizing deductive reasoning and eschewing information overload—makes this elegantly written book a must read for those who value understanding over data. I would suggest burying oneself in *American Gridlock* before occupying Wall Street, the executive suite or public office."

—Scott Bessent, Chief Investment Officer, Soros Fund Management

"H. Woody Brock is one of the few leading economists who can combine high-powered theory and deductive logic to yield practical solutions to real-world issues. He constantly surprises and inspires with new creative inputs and insights. In his latest book, he provides thought-provoking ideas on how to get a polarized and gridlocked America on the path to progress."

—Christian Casal, Office Manager McKinsey & Company, Switzerland

"If you can handle the truth about America's Lost Decade, Phiberalism, Leverage, Thugocracies, and Distributive Justice then *American Gridlock* is a must read. You will leave behind today's heads I win, tails you lose mentality. No more repetitive talking heads, know it all politicians and tired academics. Woody offers up common sense solutions based on sound reasoning to today's pressing problems. Finally, the TRUTH!

—John H. Carlson, Fidelity Investments, Boston

"*American Gridlock* delivers desperately needed fresh air and sunlight, dispelling the funk and gloom that are dampening the American spirit. Woody Brock defines five critical problems confronting the US today and leads the reader to compelling win-win policies that will break the current gridlock and put America on a path to sustainable prosperity. His work is original and of critical importance. The clear thinking and optimism of one of the world's great thinkers obviates the need to contemplate writing America's obituary. Anyone with a vested interest in our future should place *American Gridlock* at the top of his reading list."

—Jan L. Yeomans, Vice President and Treasurer, 3M

"Woody is a paragon for prosperity, and he is a master of truth and its processes—something our postmodern age has let drift out of the public discourse. He must be read by politicians, policymakers, CEOs and advisers, and by everyone concerned with today's problems and building a sustainable and prosperous future. He shows how it can be done without unnecessary pain, making this book the antidote to the current global economic and financial malaise. His new book is a must read for every politician, policymaker, adviser, CEO, and everyone concerned with today's problems and building a sustainable future."

—Michael Roux, Chairman, Australian Davos (ADC) Forum

"If ever there was a time when a fresh, original approach to understanding the challenges facing democratic capitalism was needed, it is surely now. This book offers such an approach, and provides novel answers to wickedly difficult questions about the sustainability of our way of life in the 21st Century. I have admired Woody Brock's creative strategies to address complex issues for decades, and rank this book as his greatest, and most important effort yet."

—Keith Ambachtsheer, Director, Rotman International
Centre for Pension Management, Rotman School of Management,
University of Toronto

"*American Gridlock* surpasses the lofty expectations of a long-standing client. To provide 'win-win' solutions to our most vexing economic problems, Woody employs commonsense coupled with profound and not often cited academic principles. His analysis addresses the challenges—deficits, entitlements, financial meltdowns, dealing with China, and Distributive Justice—that must be confronted to arrest the decline of the West. Most impressively, his is a refreshingly independent and optimistic voice in an era of partisanship and pessimism."

—Ed Sullivan, Ph.D., CFA, Managing Director,
General Motors Asset Management

"*American Gridlock*, the new book by Woody Brock, should be required reading in Washington. First, because it is offers real solutions to many of today's biggest problems that are based on solid grounding in economic and political theory. Secondly, because it offers real hope that there is a way out if only folks will start to think differently and creatively."

—Will McLean, Vice President and Chief Investment Officer,
Northwestern University

"I have known Woody for many years and have always admired his brilliance on economic issues. He has advised many of us on looming economic disasters including his prediction of the crash in 2008. Not surprisingly, in *American Gridlock: Why the Left and Right are Both Wrong,* Woody, like only he can do, diagnoses the persistent problems in today's economy then sets his sights on prescriptions for fixing them—prescriptions that others are unable or unwilling to see. This stunning work is wholly different than anything that has come before it, with invaluable insights for policymakers, businessmen, and everyday citizens alike. This book is a must read for anyone who longs for Washington D.C. to stop the shouting and start addressing our nation's problems in a real and meaningful way."

—J. Pepe Fanjul, Vice Chairman, President, and Chief Operating Officer of Fanjul Corp., and Florida Crystals Corp.

"*American Gridlock* provides the first optimistic analysis suggesting how the United States can recover its leadership position and solve its strategic financial dilemmas. The U.S. has lost its moral and political compass. Woody Brock suggests it can be regained by using an approach to the issues based on reasoning from first principles, clear definition and consistent logic. Everyone interested in the future of American leadership must read and study this book. It is hard work but worth it."

—Sir Roderick Carnegie AC, Chairman, Pacific Edge Group

"Across the years, the noted decision theorist Dr. H. Woody Brock has advised a global clientele of public and private sector leaders faced with crucial challenges. Thanks to this deeply intelligent, clearly written, and heartfelt book, the commonsensical wisdom of a legendary advisor to investors, corporations, republics, kingdoms, foundations, and NGOs, now comes home to the USA, where it is sorely needed."

—Kevin Starr, University Professor and Professor of History, University of Southern California. author of *Americans and the California Dream, 1850–1915*

"Woody's writings including his new book, *American Gridlock,* should be required reading for all current and aspiring members of Congress and the White House. He always provides well founded and insightful commentary that identifies and explains complex developments in economics and finance and provides practical solutions to the enormous challenges facing the United States and the world economy."

—Dennis Schwartz, Vice President, Pension Fund & Investments, Deere and Company

"Woody Brock presents a powerful and provocative explanation of a public choice system that has lost its way. Through compelling logic and lucid narrative, he offers a bold solution to the current crisis and paints a picture of an economic future that can be salvaged. This book is compulsory reading for anyone with a serious interest in public policy."

—Peter Crone, Chief Economist, Business Council of Australia and former Senior Economic Adviser to the Prime Minister of Australia, the Honourable John Howard

"Woody Brock is a master at explaining complex, highly mathematical and often overlooked economic theories in terms anyone can understand. In *American Gridlock,* he uses new and sophisticated economic theory to derive win-win solutions to five of America's most pressing problems. His focus on deductive logic provides clarity of thought that should serve as a standard for economic and financial writers everywhere."

—Chris Doheny, Associate Director of Asset Allocation and Risk, The Ford Foundation

American Gridlock

American Gridlock

WHY THE RIGHT AND LEFT ARE BOTH WRONG

COMMONSENSE 101 SOLUTIONS
TO THE ECONOMIC CRISES

H. Woody Brock

WILEY

John Wiley & Sons, Inc.

Published by John Wiley & Sons, Inc., Hoboken, New Jersey.
Published simultaneously in Canada.

For general information on our other products and services or for technical support, please contact our Customer Care Department within the United States at
(800) 762-2974, outside the United States at (317) 572-3993 or fax (317) 572-4002.

Wiley also publishes its books in a variety of electronic formats. Some content that
appears in print may not be available in electronic books. For more information
about Wiley products, visit our web site at www.wiley.com.

Library of Congress Cataloging-in-Publication Data:
Brock, H. Woody.
    American gridlock : why the right and left are both wrong commonsense 101
solutions to the economic crises / H. Woody Brock.
       p.   cm.
    Includes index.
    ISBN 978–0–470–63892–7 (hardback); ISBN 978–1–118–23462–4 (ebk);
    ISBN 978–1–118–22079–5 (ebk); ISBN 978–1–118–24122–6 (ebk)
       1. United States—Economic policy—2009–   2. Right and left (Political
science)—United States.   3. Capitalism—Social aspects—United States.
    I. Title.
    HC106.84.B76   2012
    330.973—dc23
                                                      2011039260

Printed in the United States of America
10 9 8 7 6 5 4 3 2 1

"I have little patience with scientists who take a board of wood, look for its thinnest part, and drill a great number of holes where drilling is easy."

—Einstein

■ ■ ■

Dedicated to Kenneth Arrow, the late Horace Brock, Sir Roderick Carnegie, the late John Harsanyi, Mordecai Kurz, Mendel Sachs, and Lloyd Shapley. Mentors all.

Contents

Preface

Keep it simple. But not too simple.

—Einstein

Pessimism is ubiquitous throughout the Western world today. Whether today's anxiety stems from the inability of politicians in Washington, DC, to fund the U.S. welfare state, or from the intractable euro crisis in Europe, there is a rising sense of gloom and helplessness on both sides of the Atlantic. I am an optimist, and this book is offered as an antidote to this contagion of gloom. It proposes solutions to many seemingly insoluble problems, for example, the prospect of a Lost Decade, and ballooning U.S. health-care spending. I believe these to be novel solutions, and in arriving at them, I have drawn upon new and quite sophisticated theories that are based upon deductive logic. These are the levers and pulleys that make it possible to identify new policy solutions.

This book has three goals. The first is to identify five important problems confronting the United States that must be addressed and solved. The second goal is to champion the role of deductive as opposed to inductive logic in arriving at solutions to these problems. Deduction yields much better results, particularly in policies that are win-win in nature. By way of review, "deductive logic" in this context is the process of laying down some Basic Assumptions or axioms, and then deducing the desired policies from those axioms—when possible. This process is much less prone to bias than that of "inductive logic," where policy solutions are sought from the analysis of real-world data.

The third goal is to demonstrate how this discovery of win-win policies makes it possible to tone down today's Dialogue of the

Deaf—that Left-versus-Right shouting match that has resulted in American gridlock. A far greater consensus is possible than is now recognized, and gridlock can be broken on issue after issue. This book should be read at these three different levels of analysis corresponding to these three different goals.

Identifying Five U.S. Challenges

Each of the following challenges confronts the United States now, and will do so for years to come. Resolving them is fundamental to the nation's future.

1. **The Threat of a Lost Decade:** There is a very real possibility that the decade of 2011–2020 will be one of slow growth, very high unemployment, rising federal debt of the wrong kind, an accelerating loss of bond market credibility, and an end to U.S. economic leadership for the first time in a century. Can we prevent a Lost Decade of this kind? Yes, we can. There is a unique solution to the nation's current economic crisis, a particular type of U.S. Marshall Plan. This conclusion is deduced from first principles utilizing a branch of advanced macroeconomic theory that is not familiar to most economists and policy analysts.

2. **The Entitlements Crisis:** Polls make clear that the American public is finally aware that today's welfare state is in terminal decline. My favorite indicator of this reality is the poll in which more young Americans under 30 believe they will see flying saucers than believe they will ever receive Social Security checks. Additionally, people are beginning to understand the role that has been played by "phliberals" (phony liberals) in causing this state of affairs. A phliberal is a well-meaning person who blindly endorses a flawed concept of equality between people. "I believe that a woman is equal to a man. That a gay person is equal to a straight person. That a poor person is equal to a rich person. That a white person is equal to a black person. But that an old person today is four times superior to an old person of the next generation, and should therefore receive a return on lifelong Social Security contributions four times greater than will be received by a retiree in the next generation." A genuine liberal would insist that "an old person today is equal to an old person tomorrow, and

both should receive the same return on their contributions." Phliberalism is to liberalism what the Tea Party is to conservatism: an embarrassment.

Phliberalism must be exposed for what it is, and the welfare state must be rationalized so that tomorrow's elderly will get a fair shake. In the case of the United States, this implies a complete rethink of ballooning Medicare and Medicaid spending, the heart of the entitlement crisis. At the policy level, might it be possible to significantly increase access to health care for millions while at the same time driving *down* total health-care spending as a share of GDP? Yes, this is in fact possible, and there is a unique solution to this problem that is deduced from three simple axioms. Regrettably, this solution was not known and was thus never considered during the 2008–2010 debate over U.S. health-care reform.

3. **The Risk of Future Financial Market Meltdowns:** Capitalism has egg all over its face, largely because of the global financial crisis of 2007–2009. But what exactly was the cause of this? Was capitalism itself to blame? Or was it particular abuses within the mortgage and housing sector? And what about greed and self-dealing on Wall Street? Were these also to blame? While these frequently cited causes certainly exacerbated the Perfect Storm, the true causes ran much deeper. As will be shown utilizing the new theory of "endogenous risk" recently developed at Stanford University, the true culprit was excess leverage legitimized by the U.S. government. And because excess leverage has not been suitably curbed since the crash, there will be future Perfect Financial Storms, even if no one is greedy. These must be prevented, and fortunately they can be.

4. **The Need to Learn How to Bargain Effectively with Thugocracies:** The rise of China has been one of the biggest stories on Planet Earth since 1980. But was its astonishingly high growth rate legitimate, or did it result from predatory Chinese policies that boosted its own growth rate at the expense of its trading partners? Consider China's currency manipulation. To listen to commentators and to read the op-ed pages during the past decade, it would seem that China has finally addressed its currency issue after dragging its heels for a long time. After all, its currency has risen against the dollar by about 27 percent since 2005. But this is highly misleading: The dirty little secret

here is that, despite this recent increase, the official exchange rate of the yuan/dollar remains nearly 45 percent *below* what it was back in 1990, incredible as that might seem.

Had China not cheated its way to success by violating almost every norm of free and fair trade, the currency should have at least tripled since 1990 according to economic theory—and should certainly not have been cut in half. Had China been compelled to comply with acceptable international trade policies, millions of Western jobs that were "outsourced" would probably have been saved. But the U.S. government buckled at every stage of the way, always apologizing for China and never forcing that nation to pay any price for its unfair practices. It is time for the U.S. government to stand up for its citizens, earning an A rather than a D in Bargaining Theory 101. Drawing upon groundbreaking work by mathematician John F. Nash Jr. (who is most well known from the book and movie about his life, *A Beautiful Mind*), we show how this can be achieved.

5. **The Need to Salvage Capitalism, and to Confront "Distributive Justice":** What kind of an economic system is the best one, and what exactly does that mean? Today's debate about the pros and cons of "capitalism" are inevitably muddled, and riddled by confusion about what Adam Smith and his descendants actually believed in. But if the status of capitalism is problematic, consider the plight of anyone attempting to understand the issue of distributive justice, the subject of who should receive how much of the "pie," and why. This is arguably the most important and least discussed issue in all of public affairs. As the Nobel laureate economist Kenneth Arrow tellingly pointed out in a 1987 interview with the economic historian George Feiwel: "If one asks, 'What does the economic system produce?,' the answer is that it produces a distribution of income." Slam dunk.

Who really does owe how much to whom, and why? Being either for or against "the Bush tax cuts" may be a litmus test of party loyalty in the United States, but having a position on this matter falls far short of possessing a proper theory of distributive justice. Yet Democrats, Republicans, op-ed writers, and bloggers never come clean on this issue. It is politely sidestepped. In contrast, Harvard philosopher Michael Sandel does confront it, and in doing so he has become *the* global rock star of international academia amongst students worldwide. Maybe the young evince a deeper understanding of what really matters in life than we more cynical older guys do. Given growing outrage over today's inequality of wealth and income, we must at long last start addressing the thorny issue of fair shares. The final chapter of this book explains how to do so.

Solutions to all five of these problems are proposed in Chapters 2 through 6. These solutions are somewhat original, and this brings me to the second goal of this book.

Finding Win-Win Solutions via Deductive Logic, Not via Data Crunching

One main reason for today's gridlock is that we do not think correctly about policy problems and how to solve them. Because of this, we end up deadlocked, arguing at cross purposes. In the philosophy of science, we learn that there are two principal routes for arriving at solutions to problems of most any kind. We can utilize the logic of induction (think data crunching), or else the logic of deduction (think reasoning from first principles). The history of science makes clear that most important problems have been solved over the ages by deductive logic. Students first come into contact with this type of thinking when they study Euclid's geometry. Some 300 years before Christ, Euclid showed how the truths about plane geometry could be deduced as theorems in a step-by-step manner following from precise definitions, and from Basic Assumptions or axioms. This is known as the axiomatic method, and it can be utilized either formally or somewhat informally.

Did you know that this is the same way John F. Nash Jr., solved the problem of how two people bargaining over a pie would reach an agreement on how to split it? Or that this is the way Einstein arrived at his theory of general relativity? Did you know that this is the way Peyton Young arrived at his formula for measuring "to each according to his contribution" in ethics—and proved there could be no other solution? Or that "to each according to his needs" has been clarified in a similar fashion? Did you know that this is the way in which Claude Shannon discovered the true meaning of "information" required for the modern computer revolution? Or that this is also the way the great mathematician John von Neumann discovered the correct way for people to make a rational decision in the face of uncertainty? And finally, did you know that this is the way to determine a solution to the U.S. health-care spending crisis? (See Chapter 3.)

Most people do not understand this point. They incorrectly assume that, with enough data, scientists can "crunch" their way to the truth. In reality, data almost always underdetermine the truth, and that partly because of this reason, inductive logic alone has led to the discovery of very few important scientific truths. This is not to suggest that data are unimportant in scientific discovery, for they certainly are. To begin with, real-world experience and the information we acquire get us thinking about problems, and play a role in suggesting axioms, or first principles. But the solutions to problems that we seek are then deduced from these axioms, with the assistance of little or no data. Information reenters the picture in the final stage of the scientific discovery process known as "confirmation." Data-gathering experiments are run to test the hypotheses that have been deduced.

Why do I stress this point? A principal reason why is that today's young people are completely unfamiliar with the logic of deduction, much less aware of its power. Even Euclidean geometry is no longer studied. But should we be surprised? After all, this is the age of the Internet, and we are all inundated with "information" purporting to reveal this or that, but which in reality reveals little. This is the era of spreadsheets, of data mining, of tweets, and of econometrics. Give a smart Ivy League investment banking intern an Excel spreadsheet, give him access to the wealth of data on the Internet, and he will data-mine his way to the truth—or so he thinks.

The first mistaken assumption here is the belief that truth *can* be identified in this manner. But it almost never can be, as can be shown formally. The second erroneous assumption is that someone is actually interested in discovering the truth from the data. The intern's boss wants those results by 6 p.m. today, and he wants them to support his view that the deal he is working on is a winner. How interested is he in the truth? What about politicians? Do they and their Left-wing/Right-wing think tanks really want to know the truth about, say, the impact of different tax rates on GDP? Or do they merely wish to bolster their ideological prejudices?

Regrettably, data are increasingly cherry-picked for precisely this purpose. In banking, the intern may be told to identify data lending support to a project his boss already likes. In politics, you need only contrast the op-ed articles in the conservative *Wall Street Journal* and the liberal *New York Times* to witness the same phenomenon in spades. Each side searches for and cites facts that support ideological positions arrived at long before—positions that are prejudiced in the true sense of that word: *pre*-judged.

All this leads to an amplification of today's Dialogue of the Deaf, in which there is neither an interest in truth nor a logical method for discovering it, if and when it is sought. But this is precisely where the opportunity lies. For the use of deductive logic leads to better and more compelling policy solutions than does today's bastardized logic of induction. In particular, it leads to *win-win* solutions that have a much greater chance of gaining bipartisan support than the win-lose policies that dot newspaper headlines. But why is this the case?

The answer is seductively simple. In applying deduction to topics ranging from public policy analysis to pure mathematics, the same two-step process takes place. First, it is necessary to specify a set of Basic Assumptions that, by their very nature, should be "transparently true." In number theory, we must accept: "For any integer n, there is always a next bigger integer, $n + 1$." Seems reasonable to me. Or in plane geometry: "Between any two points on a plane, there will exist one and only one straight line connecting them." Seems reasonable. Or in health-care reform, "A satisfactory health-care system must first provide universal coverage, and second cause total health-care spending eventually to *shrink* as a share of GDP." Don't these two assumptions seem as desirable as apple pie and motherhood?

Second, solutions to problems can often be deduced from simple axioms of this kind, and when this is the case, disagreement can be quelled. For if simple and compelling axioms logically imply a set of policies consistent with them, then who can disagree with such policies? If there is a health-care system satisfying these two appealing axioms, who would reject it? What remains for the Right and the Left to bicker about? In accepting the axioms, you accept the conclusions. The Dialogue of the Deaf thus can be dampened. Indeed, the conclusions arrived at what seem like lessons from the syllabus of Common Sense 101. Whether mathematics is needed to proceed from axioms to conclusion, or not, makes little difference. What matters is the quality of reasoning involved, and whether the axioms are compelling to any reasonable person, regardless of his or her political leanings.

Can this elegant approach work in the case of the real-world challenges identified previously? Yes—much more so than you might imagine. In this vein, the second goal of this book is to convince you of this by applying deductive logic to our five problems and hopefully deducing better solutions to each than have hitherto been proposed.

Dampening the Dialogue of the Deaf

Reasoned debate about important policy issues has morphed into a shouting match in which there is no recognition that win-win solutions exist. But they do exist, and they are exactly what the doctor ordered. Such policies are needed to build bipartisan support on issues, and thus to terminate gridlock here in America, and gridlock elsewhere for that matter. My third goal is to demonstrate that the win-win solutions I deduce for the five problems analyzed are neither Right wing nor Left wing in nature. Because of this, a genuine consensus becomes possible, one that should help rid the nation of gridlock.

Interestingly, Plato anticipated Euclid's achievement in his celebrated Socratic *Dialogues* characterized by their dialectical method. The goal was for everyone to reason his way through to a conclusion. Unlike Euclid who restricted himself to geometry, Plato covered a broad range of philosophical subjects, and utilized an elementary and informal type of deductive logic. In reviewing two of his dialogues for this book, the *Crito* and the *Apologia*, I was surprised at how many steps were involved in his logic, and how much hard work was required by the participants in order to reach conclusions. There was a commitment to civilized debate. Sound bites played no role. The ancient philosophers understood much better than we do that issues worth debating are complex, and require multiple steps of logic to reach a solution: chains of deduction, as it were. The idea that an eight-second sound bite from some cable news "expert" could settle some important issue would have struck them as risible. And how right they would have been.

If I had one wish in this regard, it would be that prominent figures in today's media would assume the role of Platonic critics, and target politicians' policy illogic more than their sexual and financial peccadilloes. In this vein, I want to help create a new game of "Gotcha" to be played throughout the media community. This game could impart a new dimension to political discourse throughout the media, a dimension that might render deduction-based policy analysis as hip as Michael Sandel at Harvard is rendering moral theory. This too can be done, and I shall sketch how.

Summary of Chapters

Chapter 1 reviews the issues of deductive and inductive logic, and relates them to today's Dialogue of the Deaf. I stress how there are many different forms of deductive logic relevant to problem solving, and that some of the most useful of these are quite new. These include the logic of game theory, of risk assessment theory, of the economics of uncertainty, of incentive structure theory, and of axiomatic moral theory where issues of justice and fairness are finally being demystified. Today's growing problem of information overload is also discussed. I argue that this burden can be lifted by a greater reliance on deductive logic—since it usually turns out that very few variables end up mattering in theories that are derived from first principles. In this regard, the phrase "information overload" is a much better descriptor than people realize.

For example, suppose you were attempting to determine a solution to Nash's celebrated bargaining problem: How will two different players with different tastes and endowments agree to divide a pie? You seek a formula that can predict what the division of the pie will prevail in any situation. Just think of the vast amount of data you might want to crunch to determine which of 40 possible "factors" best explain bargaining behavior. Think of all the experiments you could conduct to discover the dozen or so variables that really matter! In doing so, however, you would never possibly conceive of what Nash discovered via axiomatic deduction: There is only *one* variable that matters to the outcome—the degree of risk aversion of Player 1 compared to that of Player 2. No information overload here!

Analogously in physics, recall two of the most famous formulas in the history of science: Newton's $F = ma$ and Einstein's $E = mc^2$. There are only three variables in each. Surprisingly often in the history of science, the deeper the truth, the fewer the number of variables or "factors" that matter—and the less the information needed. The Good Lord was indeed parsimonious and elegant, as philosophers of science like to say. Who is revealing this to today's students? Do they understand that the great problem with information lies not in its quantity or quality, as is commonly supposed, but rather in its irrelevance in helping us unearth the truth?

My final and favorite example is the Birthday Paradox from probability theory. Suppose you are at a dinner party of 50 people, and you are asked to bet on the probability that some two people present share a common birthday. What should your betting odds be? Using informal induction, you could survey hundreds of college graduates to arrive at a consensus probability. In doing so, you will discover that there is a 7.5 percent chance of a common birthday. But don't use this result as it is wrong, and will be bad for your wallet! But how then do you learn the truth? Using more formal inductive logic, you could organize and pay for one hundred similar dinner parties of 50 people, and discover empirically how many times two people share a common birthday. But that would be very expensive. Happily there is an inexpensive shortcut. You simply deduce the answer from the laws of probability theory in a few minutes, starting with the only "information" needed: the odds are 1 in 365 that any person present at the party is born on any given day of the year. In this manner, you learn via deduction that the true probability of a common birthday is 97 percent. Virtually no data were involved, you saved a lot of money, and by making the appropriate bet, you will make a lot of money. You see, better thinking pays.

Chapter 2 focuses on how to salvage the Lost Decade we have entered. I first propose four macroeconomic objectives, namely, more rapid growth, much lower unemployment, much smaller fiscal deficits so as to placate bond markets, and massive infrastructure investment. I then argue that there exists a single macroeconomic solution that is consistent with all four of these goals, and that satisfies an associated set of constraints. This is a Marshall Plan of sorts. In demonstrating that all this is possible, the crucial point is that the word "deficit" as currently used turns out to have no meaning at all. For there are good deficits, and bad deficits, and only the latter trouble the bond markets. Sloppy definitions have always been a problem in theory construction. Recall the fate of the "phlogiston" in chemistry—the alleged source of fire. Once Joseph Priestley discovered oxygen in the eighteenth century, it was realized that there was no phlogiston. The same fate befell the concept of the "ether" in electromagnetic theory once Einstein showed that it did not exist. My own focus will be on dispelling widespread confusion about the term "deficit."

A principal source of inspiration in this reformulation of the meaning of deficits was the treatise *Public Investment, the Rate of Return, and Optimal Fiscal Theory* published in 1970 by Kenneth Arrow and Mordecai Kurz at Stanford University. Their work is completely deductive in nature. Regrettably, this book never gained a wide audience, primarily because it was very mathematical. Nonetheless, it never got any better. Given today's crisis four decades later, the

Arrow-Kurz theory encourages a complete rethink of the meaning, the proper role, and the correct size of fiscal deficits. It implicitly suggests that we need a domestic Marshall Plan, one that I flesh out. As is consistent with the third goal of this book, my conclusions about what the United States must do to avoid a Lost Decade are neither Left wing nor Right wing. Rather, they are win-win in nature, should generate consensus, and should thus dampen today's Dialogue of the Deaf.

Chapter 3 addresses the explosion of future spending on "entitlements." The chapter principally addresses the gargantuan problem of health-care spending, a funding problem that dwarfs that of Social Security. At the end, I briefly tackle Social Security, if only to demonstrate that this is an easy problem to resolve as many policy analysts already appreciate.

In addressing runaway health-care spending, I start from scratch, utilizing the deductive logic of supply/demand analysis in economics. The basic result is a theorem: Under eminently reasonable assumptions, the United States will see the quantity of health care *increased*, yet health-care spending *decreased* as a share of GDP, if and only if the "supply curve" of health-care services shifts outward faster than the "demand curve." Conversely, I prove that if the reverse occurs, with the demand curve shifting out faster than the supply curve (which under ObamaCare may well shift backwards), the nation will go bankrupt. Additionally, the analysis demonstrates that the kinds of "cost controls" (a term with no meaning, it turns out) fashionable within the Washington Beltway are, in most cases, counterproductive, and end up driving total expenditure higher. These are not my opinions—they are theorems that hold true under reasonable assumptions.

The main results here are proven schematically using simple supply/demand graphs within the text. But because of their crucial importance to the nation's future, the results are proven formally in Appendix B. Imagine my editors' shock: "Equations? My God, we must hide these. What will a reader think?" Well, relax, as these equations are hidden at the end of the book, and they are primarily included for the benefit of skeptics who are curious about how such a felicitous health-care outcome is possible. Once again, the health-care solution I arrive at cannot be defined as Left wing or Right wing. Instead, it is win-win in the extreme. This should further dampen today's Dialogue of the Deaf.

Chapter 4 confronts the issues of Perfect Financial Storms such as the crash of 2007–2009. What really causes such storms, and once this is understood, what can be done to prevent them in the future? In engineering, it is well known that "state" and "control" variables must never be confused. The former are states of the system, for example, the way waves break on the shoreline. The latter are those decision variables that can be manipulated to prevent the waves from doing damage, for example, constructing seawalls. According to legend, King C'nut of Denmark had to make this distinction clear to his courtiers.

In the case of the recent global financial crisis, most explanations feature the role of "irrationality," "greed," and "stupidity" in generating Perfect Storms. Excuse me, but aren't these characteristics of human beings mere state variables? Do we really think we can legislate greed away, or that there is more greed today than ever before? We might as well be so arrogant as to think we can legislate teenager horniness away. Reread your Aristophanes!

The true control variable that is the culprit is excess leverage. Unlike greed, this can and should be controlled much more than it has been. This point is deduced from first principles. In doing so, I utilize a very new form of deductive logic developed at Stanford University in the past 15 years. This is the theory of endogenous risk developed by Mordecai Kurz, the same professor who wrote the book with Kenneth Arrow on fiscal theory mentioned earlier. This new theory represents a true milestone in our understanding of risk, and in particular those "fat tail" risks that Nassim Taleb describes so well, but fails to explain from first principles, in his highly readable book, *The Black Swan*.

In particular, the theory makes it possible to really understand the sources of Perfect Storms without invoking vacuous concepts such as greed, the phlogiston of financial theory. Because I have benefited from many years of Mordecai Kurz's assistance in extending his theory to the field of investment management, and thus know it very well, I am able to make his results seem like additional lessons from Common Sense 101. But there is nothing obvious about the difficult chains of deductions that Kurz had to make in order to obtain his results.

Chapter 5 is entitled "Bargaining Theory 101: How *Not* to Deal with China." The chapter conveys two quite different messages. In the first half, I argue that the most important domestic and international problems of our time are becoming ever more political.

Therefore, it should not be surprising that economists who are not trained in political science and political theory have less and less to say, despite the ubiquity of economic commentators, and the annoying frequency of their *pronunciamenta*. The lack of serious discussion about the coming collapse of welfare states throughout the West offers a case in point. To be sure, this development has important economic consequences, but not causes. The distinction here is fundamental.

The most fundamental cause—wherein the cure—lies deep within political theory, not economics: The "incentive structure" underlying capitalist democracies encourages politicians seeking election and reelection to continually promise constituents far more benefits than can ever be paid for in the future. The result has been a wholesale mortgaging of the future over many decades. And now the bill is coming due. The late Mancur Olson was a political theorist who developed the kind of logic needed to redress this development. But he is gone, and no one has replaced him, in my opinion. Alas, we do not live in the Age of Mancur Olson as we should, but rather in the Era of Larry Summers. Economists rule supreme, and students flock to economics courses as their meal ticket to a good future. But neither Larry nor his colleagues have said anything of interest about how to redress the incipient collapse of the welfare state. What we need is a veritable rebirth of political theory, a field that has been moribund.

Accordingly, this chapter proposes a strategy whereby political theory and political science can supplant economics as the master discipline. More specifically, my proposal is that the theory of multilateral bargaining developed originally by John Nash and extended by John Harsanyi should be placed at the core of a new discipline of political science. Incidentally, both these scholars won the Nobel Memorial Prize together for their work, along with Reinhard Selten. One reason why political science is often dismissed as "mushy" is that there is no core model underlying it. All we get are a pastiche of unrelated results. It is as if we were to study Econ 101 without ever learning about the law of supply and demand, or the role of perfect competition.

The Nash-Harsanyi theory should play precisely this role in political science and political theory, and I show why at considerable depth. In particular, I show how Harsanyi's work made possible for the first time a precise meaning of "power" and how to measure it.

Doing so presupposed the existence of his bargaining model. Not surprisingly, both Nash's and Harsanyi's work is completely deductive, in fact axiomatic in nature. Neither relied upon data to arrive at their theories of bargaining and of power.

In the second half of this chapter, I apply the Nash-Harsanyi theory to China and its trade policies. Utilizing Harsanyi's concept of relative power, I show how the United States has had far greater power than China along four of the five dimensions of power that Harsanyi isolated. Yet in almost every conflict, we have backed down, and watched China walk away with all the spoils. I conclude that most U.S. administrations have been either risk-averse to a completely inappropriate degree, or else just plain incompetent when bargaining with their antagonist. In either case, it was average Americans who got hurt for no valid reason.

Some readers may find my views here somewhat hawkish. This is partly because I stress the importance of using threat power during negotiations, precisely as the Nash-Harsanyi theory prescribes. In today's environment, the word *threat* is politically incorrect in the extreme. But excuse me. Even if you are a full-fledged pacifist, you had better understand what Nash and Harsanyi deduced from first principles: It is precisely the articulation of credible threats that obviates conflict, that motivates cooperation, and that ultimately secures peace. The U.S. Cuban Missile Crisis of the early 1960s is a case in point. Threat power is precisely what defused thermonuclear war. But is anything really new? Didn't the ancients say, *"Si pacem vis, bellum parare,"* which translates to, "If you wish for peace, prepare for war." So once again, my proposals of how to negotiate with the Chinas of the world are neither Left nor Right wing, even if they might appear hawkish on the surface.

Chapter 6, the final chapter, fleshes out the concept of an idealized political economy, and what this concept implies for making life better for us all. With Anglo-Saxon capitalism in the doghouse, and communism discredited everywhere, it is time to ask: What properties do people really want from their resource allocation systems? Is "economic efficiency" enough? What about stability? Privacy? Decentralization? Freedom? And last but not least, distributive justice? I review what classic economic theory has to say about all this, and in particular what the late economist Leonid Hurwicz contributed to the subject. He was a former teacher of mine at Harvard, and the best teacher I ever had. He was a notoriously "big" thinker who extended the criteria for good resource allocation systems to include numerous societal norms other than economic efficiency, norms like freedom and privacy. For this work and for his related theory of mechanism design, he too went on to win the Nobel Memorial Prize.

But what about the norm of distributive justice? Doesn't this highly "moral" norm lie well *outside* the province of economics? No, in fact, it does not. A commitment to true Adam Smith capitalism logically entails a serious commitment to redistribution. This point is virtually unknown, and I devote considerable attention to setting the record straight. Ignorance of this reality has permitted self-styled conservatives to believe they can comfortably ignore the troublesome issue of redistribution. But if they are true capitalists, they cannot, as it turns out. In one of the greatest theorems in the history of economic theory established back in 1953, we learned that true capitalism and redistribution from the lucky to the unlucky go hand in hand. They represent two sides of the same coin.

Nonetheless, despite the strong implications of economic theory for distributive justice, economists have largely sidestepped this controversial issue, preferring instead to focus on the non-controversial norm of economic efficiency. But there was always a moral in addition to an economic case for fair shares. The good news in this regard is that moral theorists have revitalized interest in distributive justice by utilizing new insights from decision theory and game theory. Indeed, during the past half-century, three comprehensive theories of distributive justice have been set forth: one by John Rawls at Harvard, one by utilitarian philosophers including John Harsanyi, and one by myself.

My own contribution was to insist that any satisfactory theory of justice must include two distinct distributive norms: to each according to his needs *and* to each according to his contribution. Starting with Karl Marx's *Communist Manifesto* of 1848, these two norms were usually considered to be incompatible, and a widespread prejudice in the philosophical community emerged favoring needs-justice. Contribution-justice on the other hand has been ignored. But this is not satisfactory. Imagine operating a sports team without an ability to identify and appropriately reward MVPs. In the real world, "fairness" requires paying appropriate respect to both concepts in their respective habitats. A proper theory of justice must respect this.

These three theories are reviewed and contrasted in the final portion of Chapter 6. For once, the *moral* dimension of fair distribution is squarely confronted, not circumvented. Once again, the solutions arrived at cannot be dismissed as Left wing or Right wing. This is particularly true of my own theory, which integrates the needs-norm associated with liberal redistributionism and the contribution-norm usually associated with capitalism. This final portion of the book is demanding, but it is arguably the most profound and intrinsically interesting part of the book.

Intended Readership

This book has been written for anyone troubled by the decline of the United States, and indeed of the West, for anyone who seeks compelling solutions to today's policy challenges, and for anyone sick and tired of pessimism and gridlock. No mathematics has been used, except in Appendix B where the health-care spending theorems are proven from first principles. Nonetheless, the arguments are from time to time logically dense, even if clear, and perseverance will be required. No pain, no gain.

It has always been my penchant to talk up to an audience, not down. If a difficult theoretical point arises that is important to an argument, my instinct is to explain it clearly, to assume people *want* to understand it, and never to gloss over it "because it is too difficult for average people." For those readers who are more analytical and seek back-up material, extensive endnotes are grouped at the back of the book. I have included these both for the sake of completeness and to encourage younger readers to pursue the topics involved at greater depth.

There is, of course, a risk in writing a book that covers six different topics. The risk is that experts in each field will find many faults with the analysis. The truth is that a book doing full justice to each of the topics would need to be 10 times longer. But I have not attempted definitive analyses. Rather, my more modest goal has been to illustrate how deductive logic can help us identify win-win solutions to problems that must be solved, solutions that dampen the Dialogue of the Deaf and break American gridlock. The substantive policy issues involved are best understood as case studies for the application and appreciation of this logic.

A Personal Odyssey

This book represents the summit of a personal odyssey of sorts, which is one reason I have taken the liberty to use the first person. My interest in "how to think" stemmed from my late father's insistence that one's quality of thought is what matters, and not what one knows. He was a pioneer aviator in the 1930s, but he had previously attended Harvard Law School, where he said he learned how to think.

Though influenced by my father, I ended up following my own course. I started reading ancient Greek literature at a very young age, and began writing on various philosophical and political topics as a graduate student at Princeton. Looking back, I now see that by 1985 I had caught the bug that would result in the contents of this book, especially its emphasis on the power of deductive logic in a wide variety of fields. My obsession had become the importance of clear thinking, and my first two publications addressed this topic: one in the "liberal" *New York Times*, the other in the "conservative" *National Review*. By way of background, I had passed my undergraduate years at Harvard studying history and economics. I only began to get serious about my studies during a gap year when I went to work in the interior of Papua, New Guinea. There, in the jungle, I began to read mathematics on my own. One thing led to the next, and by the mid-1970s, I completed my PhD thesis at Princeton applying game theory to foundational issues in political and moral theory.

My great good fortune was to have chosen as my thesis topic the problem of distributive justice, that is, the issue of who owes how much to whom, and why. This topic had been moribund for decades until the 1971 publication of the magisterial *Theory of Justice* by John Rawls. This treatise made the subject red hot, and catalyzed my own interest at the time. But I had a lucky break. I had been exposed to a close circle of mathematical economists under whom I had studied while an applied mathematics graduate student at Harvard, as well as to the great West Coast game theorists Lloyd Shapley at the RAND Corporation and John Harsanyi at the University of California at Berkeley. My involvement with these masters of deduction paid off in three ways.

First, I absorbed their approach to problem solving, and came to understand the power of their way of thinking. I have tried to inculcate this throughout this book, if at a very informal level. Second, I learned how stupid I was by comparison with these scholars. When you have extended discussions over several decades with someone of the stature of Kenneth Arrow, always generous with his time, you are reminded of your own limitations on every visit. Third, I gained a powerful ability to distinguish sound from unsound arguments. This was the greatest payoff, and its legacy runs throughout this text.

Unsound thinking abounds everywhere today, especially among highly prejudiced commentators who take their own views much too seriously. Rigorous thinking based upon first principles and clear definitions has become an endangered species, if not a stegosaurus. My debt of gratitude to my early mentors is very great indeed, as indicated in my dedication of this book. They, of course, bear no responsibility for the numerous mistakes and oversights in this text.

My ability to discuss the wide variety of issues analyzed in this book reflects my personal career during the past two decades. In the mid-1980s, I was invited to found a small research group that would focus on "structural changes" in the United States and the global economy. The structural changes to be analyzed could be demographic, macroeconomic, microeconomic, financial, or whatever. The range of issues was very broad, and this is reflected by the breadth of topics in this book. Since historical data and inductive logic are of limited usefulness in assessing structural changes, I became more reliant than ever upon the use of deductive logic in analyzing sundry developments across the globe.

Coming full circle, I now find that my graduate and postgraduate research on distributive justice is becoming more and more topical. Indeed, an awakening of interest in this topic worldwide may signal a change in our intellectual and moral priorities. All in all, the time seemed ripe for a book reprising all these past and present interests.

I am particularly indebted to Kevin Commins of John Wiley & Sons for approaching me to write this book in late 2009 when I had no intention of doing so, to John O'Leary for invaluable assistance with Appendix B on health care expenditure, and to Eugene Lancaric, Mary Ryan, and Charles La Rosa for indispensable editing.

H. Woody Brock
"Twin Quarries"
Gloucester, Massachusetts

1

Dialogue of the Deaf

What to Do About It

Where is the wisdom we have lost in knowledge?
Where is the knowledge we have lost in information?

—T. S. Eliot

Two decades ago, during ski season, I had the pleasure of spending a weekend in the Alpine chalet of Bill and Pat Buckley near Gstaad, Switzerland. For those of you who don't remember, the late William F. Buckley Jr. was the dean of American conservative politics, having founded the *National Review* and having hosted the conservative talk show *Firing Line* for three decades. At lunch we were joined by his close friend Ambassador John Kenneth Galbraith, the celebrated Harvard economics professor who was as liberal as Bill was conservative. Despite their sharply contrasting views on many topics, the two carried on a civilized discourse in which each put forth and defended his views intelligently and rationally. Even better, they ended up achieving a modicum of consensus in their views via the dialectic of step-by-step reasoning. Of course, such behavior was once expected, and the lack of it was seen as "bad manners." Those days are long gone.

What a contrast their dialogue offers to today's deafening Dialogue of the Deaf between Left and Right. This can take the form of shouting matches on cable news talk shows, or stale cross fire between liberal op-ed writers at the *New York Times* and conservatives at the *Wall Street Journal,* or debates in the U.S. Congress—even in the Senate, which was once known for its bipartisan courtesies. Today's Dialogue of the Deaf treats us citizens to an endless repetition of predictable views by commentators and politicians—views that rarely if ever change. The predictable partisanship of most pundits suggests that they are completely unaware of an arresting new scientific discovery:

PQ is inverse to IQ

Where PQ refers to a person's Predictability Quotient, and IQ refers to his or her "effective" Intelligence Quotient.

That's right: The more the reader can predict the conclusion of a column by reading its first two sentences, the lower the effective IQ of the columnist. The reason why is simple: The columnist stopped wanting to learn long ago, even if he is reputedly brilliant and possessed a high IQ at age six. A new Nobel Prize in Remedial Logic should be awarded to those researchers who unearthed this important new relationship.

Almost everyone in the establishment media is now assumed to be either on the Left or on the Right, in varying degrees, and their views are highly predictable. The fact that Left and Right are categories that have ceased to be meaningful does not seem to bother anyone. The possibility that a compelling middle ground might exist seems to have evanesced into thin air. And once you are tagged as on the Left, then you must remain on the Left, and vice versa. Even entire think tanks are now regularly tagged "Left of center" or "Right of center." When I made this point to the head of a very prestigious research institute, he explained to me that the identity bestowed by such labeling was "very good for the funding of contract research." To be sure, there are a number of commentators who do not fall into these categories. Nonetheless, the tenor of the times is the crossfire between Fox News and MSNBC. The result is that we are all losers.

The Price Paid: Policy Gridlock

Perhaps the most serious price we are paying for this polarization is policy gridlock on issues ranging from global warming to national energy policy, to our stance toward Islamic radicalism, and to entitlements reform—health-care reform in particular. Everyone on both sides of the aisle concedes that there is gridlock and that little, if anything, is being done about our most pressing problems. But there is widespread misunderstanding about the true cost of policy gridlock. This cost can take two very different forms.

First, it can mean that nothing is done about a problem when arriving at a consensus is impossible. Social Security reform to date offers an example of this form of gridlock. The can is forever kicked down the alley and nothing is done to improve matters. The problem with procrastination is that the longer-term cost of remedial action skyrockets.

Second, gridlock can be broken and legislation passed even when there is no consensus, provided that a veto-proof majority exists. This is exactly what happened when the Democratic majority in the House, under Nancy Pelosi's whip, rammed ObamaCare through Congress in the spring of 2010. The most significant piece of legislation in a generation passed with no Republican support whatsoever. Gridlock was broken, but watch what you wish for. Highly partisan majority rule victories of this kind can and usually do backfire. This will certainly happen in the case of the health-care reform bill, an all-important piece of legislation that was a bad one, as will be proven in Chapter 3.

To anticipate, the ObamaCare reforms are almost exclusively focused on "more demand," with little thought to "more supply." Indeed, several of the new bill's provisions will cause shrinkage of supply as doctors choose to exit a system mandated to pay them less each year for standard procedures. The point is that, while the reform bill did break policy gridlock, it did so in a very biased manner that will cause access to health care to be much more restricted than intended, and cost growth to be far higher than is necessary. My own question is: How did the level of thinking about this crucially important issue degenerate to such a point that a demand-centric set of policies could ever have been considered in the first place—by either party? My Labrador retriever knows this is the wrong way to reduce total expenditure. So did the Australians when they expanded health-care coverage in the early 1970s under Prime Minister Gough Whitlam.

How different it was when policy differences in Washington were ironed out *in camera*, and indeed in civilized discourse between such journalists of yore such as James "Scotty" Reston and Walter Lippmann. Their writings conveyed the impression that they themselves were often as confused by policy dilemmas as their readers were, and that they were attempting to discover answers for themselves as well as for their readers. Such commentators showed little interest in ridiculing the views of those who disagreed with them, as Rush Limbaugh on the Right and Paul Krugman on the Left regularly do today. Readers learned from and alongside these wiser men.

As a result, our own personal views about complex issues were forged over time via an ongoing learning process, a dialectic of the sort endorsed by Plato. And these views often changed over time. All of this went hand in hand with the reality that, while there were indeed sharp policy differences between political parties, there was little policy gridlock in today's sense. Compromises were regularly ironed out. I cannot recall either the Democratic or the Republican Party ever being described as "the Party of No," much less being proud of such a label, as many Republicans are today.

What Went Wrong: Origins of the Dialogue of the Deaf

At least five developments over the past half-century have contributed to today's Dialogue of the Deaf. These range from the culture wars of the 1960s and 1970s, to the triumph of inductive logic, to significant changes in lifestyle, and to the advent of extensive Congressional gerrymandering. It will be helpful to review the role played by each.

The Culture Wars

To a certain extent, the "culture wars" of the late 1960s and 1970s hastened the end of civilized discussion as the gulf between the Left and Right grew, and as the attacks of the one on the other grew ever more vitriolic. Much of what happened reflected the way in which political debate expanded to include very personal concerns such as the obligation to serve in a much-hated war (Vietnam); or the probity of having an abortion; or the true purpose of public education; or the rectitude of child discipline; or the validity of "deference" to any authority, whether Einstein or God; or the quest for sexual liberation; or the relativism of all forms of "morality"; or the deconstruction of reason, rectitude, and scientific truth. Given this turmoil, who could have been surprised by the infamous *Time* magazine cover in April 1966: "Is God Dead?" The absolutism of arguments in these culture wars forced many bystanders to choose sides in a binary manner, and the politics of the late 1960s and 1970s became nasty indeed. Civilized debate in this environment became almost impossible.

Decline of the Classics and of the Dialectical Method

One particular casualty of the culture wars was interest in the classics—a field of study that was already waning by 1965. After all, the authors of the great books were dead white males, so how could they be expected to lead us toward any concept of the truth? The greatest of the dead white males was arguably Plato, and the Socratic *Dialogues* that he promulgated set forth the *process* required for truth seekers to bridge their differences and arrive at the terra firma of common ground. The timeless graphic image of this particular pursuit of truth is the cave of ignorance central to Plato's *Republic*. The voyage of life was a lifelong learning process guided by deductive reasoning that gradually led us from the flickering shadows of ignorance in the interior of the cave toward the daylight of truth on the outside. To Plato, learning is a lifelong struggle in which sound bites play no role.

Indeed, the dialectical method found in Plato's *Dialogues,* such as the *Crito, requires* the participants to progress via primitive rules of deductive logic from Proposition A to B, then from B to C, and ultimately to the common ground of the conclusion Z. By contrast, in today's Dialogue of the Deaf, one side keeps repeating "It's F, idiot," whereas the other retorts "No, it's H, idiot." Note that there is no Proposition G linking F and H. Moreover, the origins of propositions F and H are never clear, much less questioned. As for the idealized terminus Z, well, it is neither sought nor reached. After all, when each side starts off knowing the truth, who needs the hassle of reasoning? This is as true on cable news as it is in Congress or at the dinner table at home. Patience, along with a belief in logic, is required for the dialectic to work, and both traits are largely absent from dialogue today.

Studying the dialectical process in classical Greek as a young person fundamental altered how I would pursue truth-seeking throughout my own life, and how I expected others to reason in attempting to convert me to their views. It was a process that required a measure of mutual respect, humility, patience, and most important, opinion modification. A commitment to reasoned debate used to be instilled at school by the teaching of the classics, ancient Greek and Latin in particular, and by instruction in those lost arts of rhetoric and debating. But most students today are not exposed to these disciplines. What they have lost is not simply the ability to reason and debate more clearly but also, and equally important, the awareness of the *fun* of doing so.

The Triumph of Inductive Logic

If the painstaking process of deductive logic enshrined in Plato's *Dialogues* has fallen into disuse, the reverse is true of the other form of logic: induction. When using the term *inductive logic* I mean the use of real-world data to arrive at a conclusion, a public policy, or whatever. Yet policy analysis today often refers to a partisan process in which those on each side of an argument cherry-pick facts to support their own case. The invention of the Internet with its voluminous and easy-to-access data has facilitated this process. This is of course a bastardization of the inductive process, which traditionally was presumed to be objective in the sense made clear by the symmetry conditions taught in any course in statistics. But when participants in a debate have never been taught to recognize and distrust the illogic of bastardized induction, inductive arguments can be very persuasive. The person with more dramatic factoids almost always wins.

Additionally, adducing supporting facts and examples is much less time-consuming than deducing truth from persuasive premises, the process of starting at A and ending at Z. No room for sound bites or tweets here! The difference between deduction and induction in a public policy context will be discussed at greater length in the next chapter, partly because this distinction is central to the argument in this book, and also because it is rarely discussed. For the moment, it suffices to acknowledge the triumph of induction in amplifying the Dialogue of the Deaf. It is a form of logic ideal for politicians and commentators who know that their audience is very impatient, and wants answers *now*. It is the ideal form of logic for a sound-bite era. This relates to my next point.

Lifestyle Changes and New Technologies

If the culture wars played a pivotal role in the advent of the Dialogue of the Deaf, so did technological change and associated changes in lifestyles. With the invention of TV and then the Internet, life sped up. Audiences exploded in size. Talk-show hosts and columnists became celebrities. And incomes exploded with audience size and with celebrity. Given ever-declining faculties of valid reasoning along with increased impatience with laborious truth-seeking, commentators and politicians now "brand" themselves by adopting increasingly polarized identities. Indeed, it was economically rational to do so. Would Rush Limbaugh be as rich as he presumably is had he adopted a Socratic approach to political discourse? Moreover, once branded, how better to preserve one's brand and augment one's income than to become ever more expert in trashing the opposition, a pastime that spectators seem to love? "Gotcha" has become the game of our times.

Congressional Gerrymandering

During the past 30 years, states have been involved in a significant effort to gerrymander a large number of congressional seats. Doing so makes them "safe seats" controlled by one party. By extension, congressmen end up being pulled to the Left if they are Democrats, and pulled to the Right if they are Republicans. This is because they are much more vulnerable to influences from the extreme flank of their own party than to the rhetoric of the opposite party. This development in turn has widened the gulf between Left and Right and thereby amplified the Dialogue of the Deaf.

Alas, the Media Was the Message

As these developments unfolded, Marshall McLuhan's perceptive prophecy was fulfilled: The media did indeed become the message. What he missed is that truth-seeking proper would become the victim of a media-centric world, and that political gridlock would emerge with all of its attendant carnage. In a world of "Gotcha" and of black-and-white truths, who has time for those fine shades of gray in which truth actually resides?

An End to the Dialogue of the Deaf and an Exit from Gridlock

There are two main problems to be solved if this nation is to get back on track. First, win-win policy solutions must be identified for the five real-world problems addressed in Chapters 2 through 6. Second, the Dialogue of the Deaf must come to an end, policy gridlock with it, and these solutions must be implemented. A central premise of this book is that one and the same approach can be utilized to resolve *both* of these problems. More specifically, by utilizing somewhat advanced forms of reasoning that have been developed during recent decades and that are not widely appreciated (e.g., game theory, the economics of uncertainty, the theory of endogenous risk, incentive structure logic, and axiomatic ethics), we can arrive at compelling bipartisan policy solutions to today's problems and mute the Dialogue of the Deaf at the same time.

The Surprise

How can it be possible to kill these two birds with one stone? The answer is that truly persuasive policy analysis will, by its very nature, narrow the divide between Left and Right, thereby forging a new middle ground. This in turn is true because the kinds of logic required to solve many important policy problems *persuasively* are all branches of deductive logic—Socratic logic in a new guise, as it were. But by its very nature, this kind of reasoning shifts disagreement back from policy *conclusions* where it is easy to disagree ("Higher taxes on the rich—yes or no?") to policy *premises* that are much less contentious, and that most everyone can find "reasonable."

It is no accident that people tend to agree on premises, when properly introduced. For throughout history, premises (axioms in science) were supposed to have the property of being transparent and noncontroversial. In mathematics, consider the axiom: For any integer n, there is a next integer, $n + 1$. Try doing number theory without this helper! Analogously, in health-care reform, consider the two premises that a good system must permit much greater access to citizens than at present, and that the growth of total expenditure must not only slow, but decline as a share of GDP. Apple pie and motherhood, anyone? Who could question the desirability of either? In political theory, consider the opening lines of the U.S. Declaration of Independence: "We hold these truths to be self-evident. . . ." Nonetheless, it can be a long way from premise to conclusion, and this is where the necessity for deductive logic enters in.

There are many forms of deduction, from sloppy to rigorous modes. In the ideal case, the logic guiding us from Basic Assumptions introduced in step A to the conclusion in step Z will be rigorously deductive in nature. If this is the case, then there will be virtually no disagreement about the outcome Z (e.g., the policies required to achieve the twin health-care goals) since, once the premises are granted, the outcome follows naturally and without disagreement. A principal goal in what follows is to demonstrate that surprisingly powerful forms of logic now exist to guide us quite noncontroversially from acceptable premises to win-win solutions across a wide array of contentious policy problems. Given the importance of the points being made here, a little history of logic should prove helpful here. Moreover, the story is interesting and not well known.

The Axiomatic Method

This refers to the idealized kind of deductive logic described previously in which theorems (conclusions) result from axioms via mathematical proof. It is known as the axiomatic method, and this is the gold standard in how to think through difficult problems and solve them. Students first encounter this when they study Euclidean geometry, to the extent that this is still taught. They witness how the ancient Greek mathematician Euclid postulated a set of "elementary truths" or "axioms" at the start of his treatise. For example, one celebrated axiom postulates that between any two points lying on a plane, there is one and only one straight line connecting them. Who will disagree with this? Well, when taken with Euclid's other simple axioms, this implies that the sum of the angles in every triangle will equal 180 degrees.

This is not someone's opinion. Rather it is an irrefutable theorem. No money need be spent by ideologically driven think tanks on studies to find counterexamples of triangles where the angles do not add up to 180 degrees. No Dialogue of the Deaf arises here, since the method of analysis puts an end to it. As a matter of interest, Euclid was so revered in the past that in America in 1900 there were reputedly as many streets named Euclid as there were streets named Jefferson or Washington. I was told this in Miami's South Beach, where I once spent a week on Euclid Avenue, a street only blocks from Jefferson and Washington avenues. Today, however, most young people have never heard of Euclid. I know this because I ask them.

Extension from Pure Mathematics to the Social Sciences

For two millennia, rigorous premise-to-conclusion reasoning was largely restricted to pure mathematics, although Aristotle's *Politics* tackled political problems in a somewhat axiomatic manner, as did Dante's *Monarchia*. But this situation changed dramatically in the twentieth century. Quite suddenly, the axiomatic method began to be used in physics in the 1920s, and subsequently in the decision sciences, starting in the late 1940s. The central figure in introducing the axiomatic method both to physics and to the social sciences was the mathematician "Johnny" von Neumann who spent the last decades of his life at the Institute for Advanced Studies at Princeton. Einstein and he were among the first permanent members of the institute, and were regarded as perhaps the most brilliant two men of their era.[1]

In 1932, von Neumann startled the physics community by showing how the new formulas of quantum mechanics could be deduced mathematically from five axioms, or "first principles." While this was hardly the first use of the axiomatic method in physics, it was perhaps the most spectacular one to date. Then in 1944, von Neumann with his Princeton colleague Oscar Morgenstern published *The Theory of Games and Economic Behavior*. The book made extensive use of axiomatics. The *American Mathematical Society Bulletin* announced, "Posterity may regard this book as one of the major scientific achievements of the first half of the 20th century." And so it was. Within a few decades, this gold standard of clear thinking would revolutionize political science, economics, sociology, evolutionary theory, and even political and moral theory.

I was trained in this area by several of the founding fathers of axiomatic social science, and I would end up using this method to help solve a very difficult problem in the foundations of ethics: What exactly do we mean when we say "to each according to his or her needs?" Is there a formula for determining a needs-based allocation in any situation? If so, is it unique, or could there be rival formulas implying different needs-respecting allocations? The answer is yes. There exists a unique allocation formula for a broad class of problems that satisfies seven reasonable axioms. The well-known attorney Kenneth Feinberg needed precisely such a formula when he was mandated by the government of New York State to allocate several billion dollars in relief money to survivors of the 9/11 disaster "in accord with families' relative needs." But no formula for doing so had been discovered at that time. All this is relevant to Chapter 6 on ideal societies.

This result drew heavily upon John F. Nash's axiomatic theory of bargaining. Nash, best known as the subject of the biography

A Beautiful Mind, had shown at Princeton in 1950 that five simple axioms imply a unique solution to the problem of which player gets how much of the pie as the result of bargaining over it. John Harsanyi, a colleague of Nash's who shared with him the 1994 Nobel Memorial Prize, would draw upon this theory and arrive at a unique formula for measuring political power in a multilateral bargaining context involving threats and coalitions (see Chapter 5). As a result, the previously fuzzy concept of "relative power" became crystal clear and quantifiable in the form of a power index.

In a third direction, Nash's Princeton colleague Lloyd Shapley laid down three simple axioms in 1953, and demonstrated the existence of a unique formula making it possible to allocate goods in accord with "to each according to this relative contribution." Years later, Peyton Young would show axiomatically that there can be no other formula than Shapley's for capturing the concept of relative contribution. These and many other advances would have startled and pleased Carl Friedrich Gauss in the early nineteenth century, arguably the greatest mathematical genius in history. He wrote:

> There are problems to whose solution I would attach an infinitely greater importance than to those of mathematics, for example touching ethics, or our relation to God, or concerning our destiny and our future; but their solution lies wholly beyond us and completely outside the province of science.

It turned out that Gauss' speculation was wrong. The all-powerful method of deduction from first principles is now as much at home in the social sciences as it is in physics and mathematics. Yet the impressive progress that has been achieved along these lines is altogether unknown by the wider public, and even by today's most thoughtful commentators.

The Illogic of Policy Analysis Today

Extremely sloppy logic is partly responsible for the Dialogue of the Deaf, as we noted previously. But let's dig deeper. Exactly how does contemporary policy analysis ride roughshod over the demands of the logical gold standard introduced previously? Exactly why is it that any high school debating coach in 1900 would be shocked by the illogic of the policy debates on cable news? What has gone wrong?

Lack of Clearly Articulated Basic Assumptions

Consider traditional textbook microeconomics, such as the study of supply, demand, and efficiency in competitive markets. The main result here is that, under particular assumptions such as perfect competition, the resulting allocation of goods and services will be efficient. This simply means that the inputs available for creating and baking the pie are transformed into the biggest pie possible. There is no waste. The "invisible hand" of the price system will magically lead to an efficient allocation of resources. This result was first conjectured in a very fuzzy manner by Adam Smith in 1776 in his *Wealth of Nations*. During the next two centuries, it was clarified, and was finally proven to be true in an axiomatic manner with all the i's dotted and t's crossed by the economists Kenneth Arrow and Gerard Debreu in their landmark 1954 paper (see Chapter 6).

We finally knew what "capitalism" really meant, and under what conditions it actually does deliver the goods. Conversely, we learned to identify those conditions under which the invisible hand of the price system will not function optimally, resulting in "market failures" requiring aggressive government intervention. The contribution of Arrow and Debreu was to clarify up front exactly what was being assumed. Their use of the axiomatic method *required* such clarity, by its nature. As a result, much of what had been viewed as contentious no longer was.

Before the true nature of capitalism was understood, it was possible for Karl Marx 150 years ago to misinterpret and refute capitalist dogma, to press the case for communism, and to win converts. This might not have happened had the remarkable virtues of *true* capitalism been understood. The same held true, but in reverse, in the case of communism. When we finally looked at communism through the prism of modern game theory, we learned theoretically what was being proven true in reality in dozens of failed political experiments worldwide: Due to "incentive structure" problems at its roots, communism was a bad form of resource allocation that would not work well anywhere (see Chapter 6). Is this merely academic? Not when over 80 million people died on the ideological altar of badly confused thinking about rival kinds of resource allocation systems, and what each kind could in fact deliver.

Another example of how a lack of clear assumptions and sloppy thinking can imperil the general welfare can be found in today's debate over how to avoid a Lost Decade in the United States between 2011 and 2020. At the time of this writing, politicians and analysts are bitterly divided over the question of whether to increase the already huge government deficit (running at about 10 percent of GDP per year), or to shrink it. This division between Right and Left has paralyzed fiscal policy and has amplified today's Dialogue of the Deaf in the process. *New York Times* columnist Paul Krugman outdid himself by deeming anyone who believes in cutting the deficit during this sputtering recovery to be "clueless and heartless." As we shall see in the next chapter, the truth is that the very concept of deficit lying at the heart of this policy divide is fundamentally misconceived. When this is clarified via superior logic, much of the disagreement between today's two camps disappears, and today's stentorian Dialogue of the Deaf on this issue can be muted.

What superior logic? Whose superior logic? In 1970, the two eminent Stanford University economists Kenneth Arrow and Mordecai Kurz revolutionized theoretical macroeconomics in a way that made this progress possible. In particular, by incorporating the theory of public finance into macroeconomics, a wholly new interpretation of government spending and of deficits became possible—one very relevant to today's deficit debate. Regrettably, their book was very mathematical and was not widely read. Yet despite its extreme importance, it is never cited within the policy community. An application of the Arrow-Kurz logic to solving the Lost Decade problem will be the subject of the final part of Chapter 2. Not surprisingly, their logic is deductive in the extreme.

Enjoining an Argument at the Wrong Stage

Another manifestation of sloppy logic practiced in contemporary policy analysis is the tendency to introduce logic of sorts at the wrong stage of the debate, typically far downstream from the initial step in which Basic Assumptions or axioms *should* have been introduced. By enjoining the debate at any arbitrary stage downstream, the step-by-step procedures required by convincing deductive logic can never materialize. The force of any logic that is brought to bear gets watered down, if not lost altogether. The more the all-important chain of reasoning from premises to conclusion breaks down, the more irrational both parties become in pressing their claims.

In practice, the further downstream politicians and their staffers enjoin the debate, the more they tend to substitute their own biased policy conclusions for proper arguments, leading to a biased conclusion. As a result, a meaningful dialectic becomes almost impossible, poor policies ultimately get adopted, and members of the Left and the Right continue to shout at each other.

Using the Wrong Kind of Logic

As was stated previously, we are living in an age when inductive logic has run amok. It is widely assumed that almost any problem can be solved by enough data crunching. Students today believe that if they are equipped with a powerful database and the appropriate spreadsheet program, the truth will reveal itself. Their belief is strengthened by the ever-increasing power of analytical models, and the ever-growing size of databases. This is as true in finance as it is in policy analysis. In economics, it has reached the point at which many students do not know the difference between economic theory proper and econometrics! To be sure, data analysis is crucially important in any scientific endeavor, but only if it is the right kind of analysis and if it is utilized at the right stage of an argument.

Traditionally, the search for scientific truth implied a two-step process. First came the development of a testable theory—preferably via the axiomatic method of deductive logic, when possible. Second came the testing of the theory via inductive logic. Thus, Newton and Einstein deduced their two theories of gravity from first principles, with data playing a surprisingly small role in their deductions. The same can be said of the theory of supply and demand in economics and its myriad implications, of the theory of multilateral bargaining and "power politics" axiomatized by John Nash Jr., and John Harsanyi, of the modern theory of information developed by Claude Shannon, and of fundamental advances in moral theory. The minimal role of data and data analysis in the derivation of these theories is truly remarkable.

Once such theories were deduced, scientists would utilize inductive logic to test and, if possible, to falsify them. Perhaps the most famous example of this two-step process was Einstein's 1916 discovery through deduction of his general theory of relativity, and its subsequent testing in 1919 by Sir Arthur Eddington. Eddington was chairman of the Royal Society in London, and held Isaac Newton's Chair in Mathematics at Cambridge University. To test Einstein's prediction that light would be bent by the gravitational force of the sun, Eddington sent an expedition to Somalia to photograph the behavior of light during the 1919 solar eclipse there.

When the photos were taken, they fully confirmed Einstein's predictions, and Einstein overnight became the most famous person on earth. When Eddington offered to send the heavy photographic plates that confirmed relativity to Einstein in Berlin, the latter politely declined the offer, given its expenses and the turmoil of the end of World War I. He is reported to have written, "You see, Sir Arthur, I do not need to see the plates. The theory had to be right, for it satisfied the principle of relativity." Such is the confidence of a genius who derived his theories and their predictions from extremely sound axioms. Were the theory not supported by the facts, then the axioms would have been wrong. But Einstein's axioms were Ivory Snow pure, and his theory proved correct.

Today, across a wide array of disciplines, the traditional emphasis favoring deductive versus inductive logic in the search for truth has been inverted. This is even true in physics where the triumph of logical positivism has sanctioned the formulation of sloppy theories created to make sense of empirical observations. Given this situation, it is no accident that, after six decades of trying, the "standard model" of quantum field theory in modern physics has still not been extended to incorporate gravity, largely for the reasons Einstein had correctly pointed out. Yet the claim that gravity must be "quantized" is still being flogged, with ever more expensive super-collider experiments ending in disappointment, like those currently being carried out at CERN in search of the Higgs Boson particle. As for the ever-so-trendy string theory, it has yet to generate a single falsifiable prediction. The little known truth is that, for all its mystique, theoretical physics is in complete disarray, as the physicist Mendel Sachs has shown mathematically, and as a millennial essay in *Scientific American* pointed out over a decade ago.[2]

Precisely the same is true in financial economics where an army of practitioners endlessly mine data to unearth statistical correlations in hopes of identifying new trading opportunities. Few such correlations endure long enough to be profitable, partly because correlation is often mistaken for causation, and partly because correlation structures change rapidly, due to ongoing structural changes in the economy and in the data it generates.

Logic of the "Is" versus the "Ought"

Interestingly, when we turn to public policy analysis, the nature of deductive logic in public policy analysis is deeper and more demanding than in many other sciences. In particular, the identification of an optimal policy requires the utilization of *two* quite different forms of deductive logic: the logic of what I shall call the "is" versus the logic of the "ought." Physics by comparison usually only requires the logic of the "is." Let me explain this important distinction.

First, there is *explanatory* deductive logic whereby we deduce how the world really works. For example, we deduce in physics that Force equals Mass times Acceleration, or $F = ma$ (Newton's second law) and that Energy equals Mass times the square of the Speed of Light, $E = mc^2$. And we deduce in game theory that two rational players in a simple bargaining game end up agreeing on a division of the pie in inverse proportion to their degrees of relative risk aversion. I call such logic the logic of the "is," as it describes and often explains reality.

Second, there is the *normative* deductive logic of the "ought." This logic focuses on what decisions we *ought* to make if our behavior is to be optimal and consistent with the laws of the "is." Consider two examples of this kind of logic at work. The first stems from engineering, whereas the second stems from public policy analysis.

In the first case, an engineer might ask: What is the best trajectory for sending a man to the moon and back—where "best" means the most fuel-efficient trajectory? The particular logic needed to answer this question is known as the calculus of variations in pure mathematics, and was discovered in the mid-eighteenth century. It permits engineers to determine the total amount of fuel required by each and every possible trajectory from the earth to the moon and back. It then identifies the particular path that is most fuel efficient. This kind of logic is completely different from the underlying logic of the "is." Yet this kind of logic *presupposes* knowledge of the "is" if it is to be successfully implemented.

For example, without first understanding that the constraint that $F = ma$ must be satisfied, rather than some erroneous constraint such as $M = fa$, there is no way to determine the least-fuel trajectory that *ought* to be selected. Note that the logic of the "is" is primary here: The physicist discovering the true laws of nature does not require the help of the engineer, whereas the engineer fully depends upon using the right laws of nature when he calculates a best policy.

The second application lies within public policy analysis. Which forms of taxation ought we to adopt in order to maximize future growth? How large a fiscal deficit ought we to run so as to restore growth? These questions about the "ought" cannot be answered without first understanding the underlying "is," in this case the true laws describing how different kinds of taxes and/or different sizes of deficits impact economic growth. Regrettably, the logic typically utilized in establishing both the "is" and the "ought" in policy analysis is sloppy in the extreme. In establishing the "is," analysts are either too lazy or too ignorant to determine the economic equivalent of whether $F = ma$ or $M = fa$ or $A = mf$. They merely cling to their prejudices. When we get such laws wrong, man does not return from the moon, and economies do not recover as they could.

As for deducing the "ought," that is an optimal economic policy that ought to be adopted, the process is usually so politicized that optimal policies rarely get adopted. For example, building upon the laws of the "is" in macroeconomics, President Obama's former White House chief economist Christina Romer had established in important research with her husband, John, that the government "ought" to cut taxes rather than increase spending as the better way to revive today's economy. Yet regardless of her position in the White House, the Obama administration increased spending and proposed back-door tax hikes for small business proprietors who already confronted soaring health-care premiums. I am not making a Right-wing versus a Left-wing point here, as Republican administrations often follow suit. Rather, I am pointing out how a simple law of the "ought" can get trampled by politics.

Using Unconditional Modes of Forecasting

One natural way to bridge policy differences is to convince people that they are not nearly as far apart in their views as they think, which is often the case. What often causes unnecessary disagreement is the failure of each side to *condition* their forecast on meaningful scenarios. For example, consider the disagreement between two economic analysts, Tim who believes inflation will run at 7 percent over the next three years, and Betty who thinks it will average only 2 percent. In making their forecasts, both know that the U.S. Federal Reserve has pursued a policy of extreme "quantitative easing" during the past three years. That is, it has "monetized" U.S. debt by buying in over $2 trillion of government and mortgage securities, and holding them on its balance sheet.

Tim views this monetization (or "printing of money" as he thinks of it) as a guarantee of future inflation. Betty does not. For she is better trained in economic theory than Tim (both admit this) and she understands that, while monetization of deficits may be a *necessary* condition for future inflation, it is certainly not *sufficient*. In particular, she knows that the large increase in bank reserves created by monetization need not trigger any inflationary growth in the money supply under certain conditions.

For example, suppose the public undergoes a shift in its belief structure from one of collective optimism about the future to one of collective pessimism (just as is happening today), and suppose as a result that people no longer want to borrow and spend as they used to. In this case, Betty knows that banks will not be able to transform their excess reserves (stemming from monetization) into new loans to you and me. Rather, banks will simply sit on their reserves. If this happens, then no new money enters the system, and the economy does not experience "a lot more dollars chasing the same number of widgets." Betty knows that, *conditioned on this scenario of household pessimism*, there will be no inflation despite monetization.

Now, Betty happens to run into Tim at a finance convention. They chat at lunch about inflation. She finds that Tim was ignorant of the various conditions (including consumer pessimism) under which quantitative easing need not result in inflation. Once she has explained these realities to him, she asks Tim for his forecast of the borrowing behavior of consumers. It turns out that they share the same view on household behavior—the role of collective pessimism in particular. As a result, they end up sharing the same forecast of inflation itself. Their initial disagreement was a bogus conflict, which disappeared when proper scenario-conditioning took place.

The more general point here is that many of today's disagreements that are contributing to American gridlock are bogus conflicts, upon closer inspection. But unless there is a person like Betty who takes the time to explain her view, these disagreements remain in place and further polarize public debate. *Who today has the incentive to play Betty's role?*

To conclude, we live in a society where faulty logic of many kinds affords policy makers much too much "wiggle room," which allows them to adopt highly partisan policies. Moreover, there is no one to expose the illogic of their policies.

What Must Be Done to Raise the Level of Debate

Let me now propose four strategies that could raise the level of national debate in a manner that facilitates the adoption of better policies.

1. Demonstrate that Win-Win Solutions Actually Exist

The remainder of this book is a step in this direction. As already indicated, higher-order levels of deductive logic are utilized to derive solutions to the prospect of a Lost Decade, to the entitlements spending crisis lying ahead, to excessive financial market instability, to the problems of dealing with thugocracies, and to the question of distributive justice—or "fair shares" of the social pie. The unfamiliar logics utilized will be the levers and pulleys used to identify new solutions to contentious issues. In all cases, it should be possible to reduce polarization and arrive at common ground.

2. Government Must Reform Itself

Can Congress credibly reform itself from within, at least to a certain extent? I am cautiously optimistic here. To begin with, politicians on both sides of the aisle are in trouble, and for the same reason: growing outrage by citizens of all political stripes at American gridlock. In poll after poll, people acknowledge gridlock to be the principal reason why government is unable to offer solutions to *any* of the principle problems impacting their lives, and their future living standards. Politicians are keenly aware of this, and will have an ever greater incentive to seek superior policies lest they be voted out of office. Necessity is indeed the mother of invention, and the policy failures resulting from today's gridlock could morph into those win-win policies I believe to exist.

Indeed, the very existence of such policies could become "answered prayers" for politicians facing the wrath of the voting public in what the historian Simon Schama has called "an age of rage." But for all this to happen, a necessary condition is that win-win policies actually exist. A principal motivation for this book is to demonstrate that they do.

3. Media Must Shame Washington into Reforming Its Modus Operandi

I want to help create a new game of "Gotcha" whereby the media expose the malfeasance of politicians to such an extent that they are shamed into changing their way of doing business. Imagine a world where the press sponsors ongoing "logic audits" aimed not only at exposing the illogical underpinnings of many proposed policies, but also of making crystal clear the price that taxpayers pay for such illogic—the price in concrete terms of foregone income and reduced living standards.

As part of such a logic audit strategy, why not introduce an "irrationality index" for scoring politicians' degree of mendacity and bad logic? Their scores should be publicized far more than their financial or sexual peccadilloes, or their rankings as "true" liberals or conservatives. Indeed, now that almost everything else has been quantified, why shouldn't costly policy illogic have *its* own index? Isn't this what really matters?

Recall how the intelligentsia laughed at the folksy presidential campaign of Texas businessman Ross Perot in 1992. Yet when Perot went on TV and held up large cards that graphically illustrated what burgeoning deficits would do to the lives of average citizens, the public responded very favorably. Indeed, Perot ended up winning a much larger percentage of the vote than most pundits expected. Why was anyone surprised? After all, most of the points he was making came right out of the Common Sense 101 syllabus.

If Perot's strategy was successful 20 years ago, when the issue of fiscal red ink was minor league compared to today's, just think of the fodder a better educated press could reap by focusing on the policy illogic of individual politicians when the nation has lost its triple-A credit rating for the first time, and when national solvency may be at stake. Once again, our new game of "Gotcha" must be designed to expose the huge costs to individuals of each politician's policy irrationality, and not to expose whether a candidate knows how to spell Vladivlostok, or once made an "inappropriate" remark. National policy should not be a game of Trivial Pursuit. We absolutely must up the ante in this new game of "Gotcha." With a push of this kind by the media, the incentive for politicians on the Left and Right to put their heads together and to identify common ground and win-win policies would be much greater than it is today.

4. The Educational System Must Perform Its Own Role in Instigating Reform

To begin with, institutions of public policy such as the Harvard Kennedy School could inaugurate programs aimed at educating both politicians and media representatives on the *meaning* of logically deduced win-win policies, on the potential role of new higher-order logics in helping us to identify them, and on how to sell them politically. Fascinating case studies of the application of new logics and of political progress would be prepared and distributed to schools nationwide. Students of such schools and programs would then go out and ensure that our new game of "Gotcha" would be constructive rather than nihilistic. For they would know what they were talking about. In some ways, this proposal reprises traditional civics courses that were designed to make students politically aware. But it goes much further.

The ultimate goal, of course, would be better policies, and who better to press for these than idealistic youths whose own futures are now being devalued at every turn? The young would join a growing chorus of people of all ages demanding serious debate about critical issues. Moreover, the students would have been trained to demand meaningful n-step arguments rather than one-step sound bites from politicians and policy wonks alike.

But why stop with schools of public policy? What about a role for departments of political science? Don't we need political scientists and theorists far more than those retreaded "administration economists" and financial pundits who dominate the news and say ever less of any value? Finally, what about the agenda of the Aspen Institute's "thinker" program, and other such high-profile venues? We need all interested parties on board. All this may sound idealistic, but the price paid by *not* attempting new approaches is rising rapidly. So is the extent of public rage, and today's angst must be channeled to drive reform.

Indeed, I want the proposed new game of "Gotcha" to become positively trendy. I want students and junior faculty to develop computer games dedicated to chastising if not ridiculing named politicians and named media figures alike for the insulting vapidity of their opinions and policy proposals, if and when this is appropriate. By extension, I want a higher level and more demanding state of national debate aimed at shunning those who indulge in bad reasoning at our expense, Amish style. And speaking of debate, I want debate *proper* to be restored to its rightful place in the high school and undergraduate curricula. Debating must become very trendy, with heaps of esteem and money bestowed on the best debaters. Cheerleaders and linebackers, move over. Make way for tomorrow's neo-rationalists.

Conclusion

The overall goal of this agenda is to shrink the wiggle room politicians currently have to dodge responsibility, to lie to us, and to further mortgage our future. The advent of cost/benefit analysis was a first step toward reducing such wiggle room. New procedures were implemented for making the stewards of the public interest more accountable to the public. Analogously in the business world, the advent of double-entry bookkeeping five centuries ago narrowed the wiggle room for business managers to embezzle money from their investors. In one form or another, it is always logic audits of some sort or another that have set us straight. After all, human beings are thinking creatures. Sadly, such audits do not exist today.

The optimism that permeates this chapter stems from my own conviction that the application of superior forms of logic really can lead us to identify win-win solutions to our most pressing problems—solutions occupying a nonpolarizing middle ground in the policy arena. In the next five chapters, I press this case strongly. If I succeed, then the first of my four strategies for muting the Dialogue of the Deaf will have been implemented. But strategies two, three, and four will remain to be addressed.

CHAPTER 2

Must There Be a Lost Decade?

A Socratic Dialogue with the President Explains Why Not

The U.S. economy faces two quite different yet interrelated challenges between 2010 and 2050. The first challenge stems from the prospect that the current decade becomes a Lost Decade. Worries in this regard center on the likelihood that subpar growth will make it difficult for the U.S. unemployment rate to fall from its current rate back to a more normal rate. The present chapter shows how a fundamental rethink of fiscal policy and of the role of government can simultaneously raise GDP growth, reduce the unemployment rate, slash the fiscal deficit thus placating bond market vigilantes, and redress the crisis of deteriorating U.S. infrastructure. A new kind of Marshall Plan is proposed for the entire decade and beyond.

The second challenge facing the nation centers around the longer-run fiscal crisis of ballooning entitlements spending on Social Security and Medicare that threaten national solvency between 2020 and 2050. Chapter 3 will propose concrete solutions to this second challenge. In the case of the all-important Medicare spending crisis, the proposed solution is original and, to the best of my knowledge, has not been proposed anywhere else up to now.

The solutions proposed to both the shorter-run and longer-run American crises are deduced from a few basic assumptions that almost anyone will find "reasonable." This being true, the resulting policy prescriptions should be compelling to citizens and policy makers of many stripes, and thus should prove win-win in nature. As a result, it should be possible to build widespread support for these policies and in doing so to dampen today's Dialogue of the Deaf about government deficits, and to break policy gridlock.

23

The U.S. economy is still recovering from its most serious slump since the 1930s. In doing so, it faces a number of unusual headwinds that have given rise to fears of a Lost Decade between 2010 and 2020. Primary concern centers on a level of economic growth inadequate to bring down the nation's unemployment rate (properly measured) to normal levels. Additionally, substandard growth will also prevent the decrease in the fiscal deficit now being demanded by the global bond market. Finally, there is the growing negative impact on GDP of the nation's deteriorating infrastructure. Just as positive infrastructure investment raises productivity and hence GDP growth (witness China), so can negative net infrastructure investment blunt productivity growth and thus economic growth. In this regard, both the United States and the United Kingdom are increasingly criticized for their dilapidated infrastructure and lack of remedial investment. Both nations need to put a new roof on their house, and to do so soon.

The principal goal of this chapter is to show how refinement of current macroeconomic policy can help to resolve all these concerns and thus avoid a Lost Decade. More specifically, policies are identified that can simultaneously reduce the fiscal deficit *and* reduce the unemployment rate *and* significantly increase economic growth and productivity *and* placate anxious bond market vigilantes and confront our infrastructure investment needs on a massive scale. In short, Mr. President, we can have our cake and eat it too. This is a view completely at odds with today's widespread assumption that we must either shrink today's deficits way down and thus impair economic and employment growth, or else continue with unprecedented large fiscal stimulus and hope against hope that bond market vigilantes will "understand." It turns out that this either/or assumption is fallacious, and has blinded us to the prospect of a brighter future.

This chapter first reviews the seven principal headwinds to a strong economic recovery to date. This review will orient the material that follows. The discussion then goes deeper. Utilizing two quite different GDP forecasting perspectives, it demonstrates why strong growth is very unlikely to materialize under current policies during the remainder of the decade. Yet very strong growth will be required to bring the unemployment rate back down to normal. The final section of the chapter sets forth the revisions in fiscal policy required to achieve all four goals identified earlier. To make the discussion more accessible to the reader, I have written this last section as a hypothetical Socratic dialogue between President Obama and myself. I have found this Q&A format to be extremely effective in simplifying the story being told, and in permitting the reader to participate by asking questions and getting timely answers as these questions unfold in a natural logical progression.

Seven Headwinds That Have Stunted U.S. Economic Recovery

Before identifying these headwinds, consider Figure 2.1. This shows the magnitude of recessions and recoveries during the past 70 years, where we measure magnitude by the percentage change in GDP.

Figure 2.1 shows the magnitude of the recession from several different perspectives. First, the total drop of output in the 2007–2009 recession was larger than in any previous recession during the past half-century. The magnitude of this drop can best be visualized as the amount of black ink lying *below* the zero growth line. Simply compare this most recent drop with those of previous recessions. Second, contrast the magnitude of the recovery (the black ink *above* the zero line from 2009 on) with the loss of output during the recession. The ratio of this recovery/recession magnitude is the smallest in recent times. This is why it is taking so long for GDP to regain its prerecession level, and why the job market recovery has been so tepid. Third, by reviewing the entire time span shown, you can glimpse one of the great macroeconomic developments of the twentieth century, namely the stabilization of life on Main Street. If you use

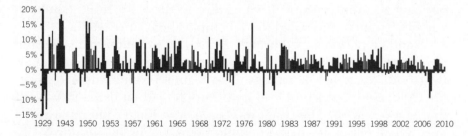

Figure 2.1   Annualized GDP Change from 1929 to 2010

Note: Data are annual from 1929 to 1946 and quarterly from 1947 to the first quarter of 2011.

Data source: Bureau of Economic Analysis, and Strategic Economic Decisions, Inc.

formal statistical analysis, you can show that the decade-by-decade volatility of GDP declined by over 75 percent over the century (earlier decades not shown). There are five interesting reasons why this occurred, and these are reviewed in note 1.[1]

The magnitude of our most recent recession represents a sharp deviation from this trend toward milder recessions, and the principal reasons for this will be discussed in Chapter 4. The principal culprit turns out to have been excessive leverage by households and banks alike. Paradoxically, the widespread willingness to assume so much leverage resulted in part from the very stability that people became used to after World War II as the great moderation of economic volatility occurred. Life simply was not as risky as it had been, for all the reasons cited in note 1.

So what were those seven headwinds that have prevented a more rapid and indeed normal recovery during the present business cycle?

1. Depressed Labor Market

There are two distinct ways in which the current U.S. labor market is the worst since the Great Depression of the 1930s. First, there is the *length* of the unemployment line, and second there is the *rate* at which the line becomes shorter during a recovery. As for the total level of unemployment, the unemployment rate reached a shocking 16 percent by late 2011, two years after the onset of a recovery boosted by the largest fiscal and monetary stimulus in half a century. I am using here the broadest possible unemployment measure known as the U6. This measure includes part-time workers along with discouraged workers who have stopped looking for jobs. The principal reason for the length of this line was the very large number of people fired during a very deep recession, along with the ongoing accumulation of new entrants to the work force (students and immigrants) who failed to find employment since 2007.

Another reason was the high growth in productivity, a blessing in all times other than a recession. During four quarters, productivity growth exceeded 4 percent. The higher productivity growth is, the easier companies find it to lay off workers when demand falls off during a recession. The result will be an even longer unemployment line. A final reason for high unemployment was the magnitude of distress in the housing industry, and also in state and local government.

The *rate* at which the unemployment line becomes shorter depends primarily upon the strength of the recovery (e.g., the rate of GDP growth), which, as we just noted, has been substandard. It also depends upon the rate of productivity growth. Fortunately, productivity growth stopped rising in 2011. This is now helping to dent the unemployment rate. Even so, the GDP growth rate in the recovery has averaged about 2.5 percent, and new entrants have continued to join the workforce every year. Accordingly, even with much lower productivity growth, companies have had little need to rehire workers. In most past business cycles, the economic growth rate was much higher during the first few years of recovery and the productivity growth rate was somewhat lower than this time around. As a result, the cyclical fall in unemployment during upturns was much more robust than it has been this time.

2. Household Spending Restraint

After over three decades of excess borrowing and binging, households are finally cutting back. Household debt is being paid off, even if mortgage foreclosure and bankruptcy is one reason why. The savings rate as computed by the Commerce Department soared to just under 6 percent from less than 2 percent before the crisis. While Americans remain American, and thus consumer spending has recovered to a certain extent, consumer sentiment is very different than it was before the recession. People have discovered the true costs of being over-leveraged, most especially in housing, but also in general.

The combination of soaring mortgage default rates, personal bankruptcies, and joblessness has been chilling to almost everyone. Additionally, Americans are aging and discovering how bleak their retirement prospects really are. The median net worth of heads of households that are 65 years old is currently *one-fourth* the level needed for people to retire as they had planned. As a result, millions will attempt to remain in the workforce into their seventies, and will be forced to cut back on their lifestyles.

Soaring medical costs are playing a role as well. Everyone has friends who find themselves crippled with astronomical hospital bills, even if they have insurance. Indeed, with insurance companies requiring ever-higher copayments, *underinsurance* is becoming as grave a problem as lack of insurance used to be before ObamaCare. Finally, the reduction in household net worth as a whole has sobered many families. An increasing number of people do not expect their net worth to bounce back. The resulting "wealth effect" is yet another headwind for the economy.

3. Housing Industry Depression

Investment in new housing has been a mainstay of the U.S. economy since 1945, but it is contributing little if anything to the current recovery. Indeed, the housing crisis worsened as 2011 unfolded, with house prices once again falling, and the inventory of unsold homes rising in many parts of the country. The number of annual housing starts fell from about 2,068,000 at the start of the bust in 2006 to only 581,000 today—over two years into the recovery. It is likely that residential investment spending will continue to prove a drag on the economy for many years to come. Perhaps the most important reason why lies in the belief of an increasing number of Americans that "our house may *not* in fact be the best investment we ever made." This represents the inversion of a basic article of faith in American life. People at long last are learning the frightening downside of leverage.

4. State and Local Government Contraction

The crisis in state and local government is the worst in over half a century, reflecting a collapse in revenues and the advent of the day of reckoning after decades of giveaways to public employees' unions. Consider the performance of the public sector during the past three recessions. In the 36 months after the start of the July 1990 recession, the net change in state and local employment was up by 678,000 jobs. In the 36 months after the start of the March 2001 recession, the net increase in jobs was 665,000. Thirty-six months after the start of the recent December 2007 recession, the number was *negative* 148,000. It would rise to over negative 600,000 by October 2011. This is as shocking as the data on housing starts. Until this recession, the public sector was regarded as a safe haven in the employment world.

There are two unusual drivers of what has happened in this sector. First, the long-predicted explosion in medical and retirement costs among public sector employees is occurring. Payment of these benefits has state-constitutional priority in many states over payment for the services (running the subways) that the public needs. So workers who provide these services have been getting laid off in record numbers. Second, tax receipts dropped more than expected. One reason why was the trend toward lower income taxes for poorer citizens and higher taxes on the rich. As it happened, the misfortunes of the rich proved highly correlated when the bust occurred, so that tax revenues collapsed more than anticipated. This further increased the need to shed jobs.

5. Lackluster Business Investment

Even though many companies are flush with cash and have had stellar earnings, their capital spending has not propelled the economy forward, as many hoped it might, and as it did in the 1995–2000 period. To begin with, businesses expected that the fears and dampened spirits of many households would contribute to a sluggish recovery, just as they did. Second, capacity utilization of the nation's capital stock has been low so there was little need to invest rapidly. Third, investment opportunities in the newly developing nations have been greater than here at home, and corporations have vigorously pursued these instead of investing at home. Fourth and finally, surges in capital spending usually occur just after some important technological breakthroughs have occurred. These tend to occur without warning, and none seem to be in sight at present.

For example, the rewiring of America during the 1995–2000 capital spending boom was largely due to the wave of Internet activity following Marc Andreessen's launch of the Netscape browser in late 1994. No one was caught off guard more than Microsoft's Bill Gates who promptly declared this browser to be the technological game-changer of our time, and who proved correct. The ensuing boom in capital spending was a record breaker. Tax receipts soared so much that a U.S. fiscal surplus was achieved, unemployment fell to under 4 percent, and productivity growth soon exploded. Alas, such investment booms are infrequent, and government policy cannot trigger the dates of their arrival.

6. Oil, Commodities, and Health-Care Price Shocks

The rise of gas prices to around $4.00 per gallon by mid-2011 had depressive effects on consumption. While no one can know how the Middle Eastern crises will play out, there is a significant probability of further turbulence—even in Saudi Arabia and Iran—such that oil could ultimately spike to price levels hitherto unknown. This would indeed prove a headwind. For the moment, today's global slump has driven prices back down.

Middle Eastern instability and supply disruptions are not the only forces impacting the oil market. There is also soaring demand from the developing economies, which is not being matched by enough new supply for prices to remain moderate in the future, except in recessions. The same is true for numerous other commodities.

The growing proportion of total world economic growth attributable to fast-growing developing countries ensures that this supply/demand imbalance will continue for several decades to come. Traditionally, increased supply would have matched or exceeded increased demand, keeping prices stable despite strong growth. The history of commodity prices in the twentieth century attests to this point. What is new is the lack of incentives for companies with the required know-how to invest in those thugocracies where so much of the world's copper, oil, and other commodities can be found. As a result, increased supplies that traditionally *would* have been forthcoming will not be. Copper offers a very good case in point.

As for health-care costs, little need be said. In poll after poll, Americans express grave concern not only over soaring health-care premiums, but also over the phenomenon of underinsurance. Who does not know someone who discovers that their insurer will cover only 65 percent of the cost of treatment? With U.S. surgery and hospitalization costs by far the highest in the world, and rising, who can afford a 35 percent copayment? This often will wipe out a lifetime of savings.

7. Inevitable Reduction in Fiscal and Monetary Stimulus

During most recoveries, interests rise and fiscal deficits fall. In principle, both developments provide a drag on recovery. The good news is that such drag is more than offset by a resurgence of pent-up demand and optimism in the household and business sectors. But this time around, the *magnitude* of the cyclical adjustment back to normalcy in the years ahead is unprecedented. Interest rates start off much lower than ever before, whereas fiscal deficits are humongous. In an era of already restrained growth, the withdrawal of such large fiscal and monetary stimulus could prove to be yet another headwind to the rapid recovery the nation needs to achieve its goals in output and employment. Yet unless great care is taken, the bond market may soon demand precisely such a reduction in stimulus.

Reasons for Lackluster Growth During the Remainder of this Decade

The headwinds we have just discussed explain why GDP growth during the current recovery has been lackluster, far below the level of growth required to reduce the unemployment rate back to normal levels. Some of these developments imply a continuation of subpar growth and hence a truly Lost Decade—for example, the need for fiscal and monetary tightening, and consumer pessimism. Yet to do justice to this risk, we must now delve deeper and look further ahead in an attempt to forecast the period 2013–2020. To do so, let me sketch two different approaches to GDP forecasting. While interrelated, they are quite different in spirit, and permit two quite different routes to a forecast. When applied to the remainder of this decade, both presage a level of growth inadequate for the nation's goals of significant deficit reduction and employment growth.

GDP Forecasting Proper

Every beginning economics student will recall the textbook definition of GDP as

$$\text{GDP} = \text{Consumption} + \text{Investment} + \text{Government Spending} + \text{Net Exports} \qquad (2.1)$$

where Consumption is household spending; Investment includes corporate investment in plant and equipment as well as household investment in housing; Government Spending represents all government spending excluding transfer payments, and Net Exports is the difference between what the nation exports versus imports. The more goods the nation makes and exports to others (compared to what it does not make and imports), the greater GDP will be. Clearly, the greater the value of each of these four terms, then the greater GDP will be.

To prepare a forecast of GDP *growth*, namely the future percentage *change* in GDP, most analysts utilize this adding-up equation and assess what the percentage change will be (positive or negative) in each of the four components. By then weighting these four subsidiary forecasts by the relative share of GDP accounted for by each component (Consumption being the largest at about 71 percent), and by adding the four results, they arrive at the desired forecast of GDP growth itself. What can we now forecast along these lines for the remainder of the decade?[2]

Keeping in mind the various headwinds detailed previously, it is reasonable to expect consumption growth to be restrained given the public's general shift toward caution, if not outright pessimism.

To be sure, consumer sentiment has improved, if unevenly, since the dark days of 2008 and 2009, and Americans are not depressive by nature. Nonetheless, the drag of growing concerns about the need to save more, to deleverage, and to confront soaring medical costs will depress spending and living standards. Business investment growth will also be restrained for a considerable period. This reflects the three developments detailed earlier. The same applies to residential investment. It will certainly improve as time goes on and today's inventory of unsold homes is gradually drawn down. The deeper reality is that fewer and fewer people believe that buying a house is a good investment, as was already noted. To make matters worse, many cash-strapped baby boomers will be forced to unload their houses sooner rather than later.

The third component in equation (2.1) is Government Spending. Given growing demands of the global bond market for fiscal discipline, given growing fiscal hawkishness by average people who now read weekly about future national bankruptcy, and given the new power of the Republican Party in Washington, the fiscal deficit of 10 percent of GDP will have to shrink, largely by curtailed government spending. But by how much? IMF and World Bank officials insist that fiscal deficits exceeding 3 percent are unsustainable in the long run. To put it differently, deficits exceeding this level will excite the ire of the bond market and result in higher bond yields, which will depress growth, making matters worse. Reducing the deficit from 10 percent of GDP to 3 percent represents a *de facto* reduction in the growth of GDP itself by $10\% - 3\% = 7\%$, other things being equal.

Even though such fiscal contraction would be spread out over time, its cumulative effect would still be depressive. Moreover, the political pain triggered by such fiscal austerity makes it unlikely that politicians will actually make the required cuts, unless somehow forced to do so by currency and/or bond market vigilantes. The United States is not yet in that position, so Washington is now hoping to get away with longer-term deficit reduction of about 3.5 percent of GDP, not 7 percent. There is a heated debate as to whether the nation will even achieve this goal (which would leave the annual deficit at about $10\% - 3.5\% = 6.5\%$ of GDP), and whether the bond market might find such a deficit too high and ultimately go on strike anyway.

Whatever the case, the magnitude of deficit reduction that will be required one way or the other will be much greater than during any past recovery, and thus the Government Spending term in equation (2.1) will be a drag on GDP growth. Historically, a deficit of 2.5 percent of GDP in good times might have risen to 4.5 percent during a recession. This would have amounted to a stimulus of 2 percent of GDP during recession. The deficit would then fall back by 2 to 2.5 percent of GDP during the recovery as tax revenues rose and unemployment payments fell, representing a modest fiscal contraction.

Finally, there is Net Exports, always the great white hope for rekindled growth. The problem here is that *every* nation wants to boost domestic growth by boosting net exports. Yet since any one nation's gain from increased net exports will be offset by another's corresponding loss from lesser net exports, it is rare that a given country ends up restoring domestic growth from greater exports alone. (Recall here that the sum of all nations' individual trade balances must be zero.) Given U.S. addiction to imported oil, with higher long-run oil prices looming, it is hard to see a significant improvement in Net Exports, although the low level of the dollar on a trade-weighted basis may help exporters and tepid consumption growth may restrain imports.

A Tentative Forecast

When all these observations are quantified, the resulting GDP forecast for the remainder of the decade lies between 1.5 and 3 percent, with a mean of around 2.25 percent. This assumes, of course, that there is no adverse shock that might cause another recession during this period. On the surface, GDP growth of this magnitude may not seem so bad. Indeed, it is higher than we are likely to witness in Europe or Japan. However, appearances are deceiving. The "recovery growth rate" averaged over all business cycles of the twentieth century was 6.5 percent. This was the growth rate *required* to rehire idled workers of all kinds in a nation with a fast-growing workforce and a good growth rate of productivity.

With today's unemployment rate remaining very high, the 2.25 percent growth rate implied by the forecast based on equation (2.1) is woefully inadequate. The result could well be a "new normal" unemployment rate of 14.5 percent measured on a U6 basis, or 8 percent as measured by the more familiar headline statistic. This in turn would be sociologically unacceptable given the very modest safety net for those out of work in the United States, and given that American society is all about work. Indeed, the first question someone asks when meeting a new person in the States is "And what do you do?" Nowhere else is this true.

An Alternative Approach: National Income–Based Forecasting

Scientists and philosophers often speak of "duality" as one of the deepest and most counterintuitive aspects of reality. Thus, for every elementary particle in physics, there must exist its dual, an anti-particle; for every positive number there will be its negative; for a male there is a female; for light matter there is dark matter; for a coin there is a head and a tail; for market-clearing prices there must be market-clearing quantities in microeconomics; for good there is evil; and for fairness there is unfairness in ethics. The basic idea here is that there exists a hidden unity or "organicity" in almost every aspect of life, but that this can only be understood by appreciating the relationship of each entity to its dual.

What about in macroeconomics? Is there some equivalent fundamental duality? Yes. Gross Domestic Product (GDP), which we have just analyzed, is balanced by National Income (NI). Briefly, there are two sides to the GDP coin: the real side of the economy involving the *production* of goods and services (hence the *National Product*, as in equation [2.2]), and the financial side involving the *financing* of all economic transactions, including the payment of all wages and salaries *(National Income)*. In dollar terms, the value of each must be one and the same so that

$$\text{National Income} = \text{National Product} \qquad (2.2)$$

where, for simplicity, we are shortening Gross Domestic Product to National Product on the right-hand side. We can thus write NI = NP in shorthand. What this says, in effect, is that every dollar that is spent *for* something is spent *on* someone. We thus have a dual representation of economic transactions. Since the two quantities must be equal, it follows that the logic utilized to forecast NP will also generate an implicit forecast of NI as well, and vice versa. Yet the two forecasting logics involved are quite different, guaranteeing that two different sets of insights will result from applying each separately. If you do apply each and the resulting forecasts are *not* the same, then you will be forced to make suitable revisions in each, iterating until any underlying inconsistencies are resolved. Doing so helps keep an economist honest!

This important point can be restated in the form of a useful definition: A *valid* forecast of GNP is one in which an analyst's forecast of NI and NP are mutually consistent and equal.[3] We are now going to utilize the logic of NI-based forecasting to provide an independent set of reasons why GDP growth will almost certainly be subpar for at least the next seven years. This should enhance the persuasiveness of our previous GDP-based forecast of a disappointing decade of growth. *Note:* This less familiar approach to forecasting is more demanding than the previous one. If you found my previous conclusions persuasive, you can bypass this section. But I hope you persevere. I personally favor the more rigorous insights from NI-based forecasting.

What exactly is the logic of NI forecasting? This can best be seen by rewriting the normal definition of NI in the following manner, which may not *seem* to be about NI at all, but is:

Government Deficit = Net Private Savings
$$+ \text{Net Foreign Capital Inflows} \qquad (2.3)$$

This relationship is deceptively simple. For it can be expressed in several ways. The three variables can be written in dollar terms, or in percentage of NI terms. Also, the three terms can be transposed in insightful ways, for example, Net Foreign Capital Inflows must equal the Government Deficit minus Net Private Savings. The equation as written simply says that, if the fiscal balance of a country is a fiscal deficit of, say, 10 percent of GDP (as it was in 2009), then this must and will be funded by a combination of net private savings (household *and* business) and net foreign capital inflow, each expressed as a share of NI, or equivalently of GDP by equation (2.2).

For example, suppose net foreign capital inflow is 4 percent of GDP. Assuming that the fiscal deficit is 10 percent of GDP, this then implies that net private savings will be 6 percent of GDP. *The numbers must and do always add up.* Underlying prices and quantities change in such a way that the equation always holds true. Once again, equation (2.3) is simply saying that the money to finance the government deficit must come from somewhere, meaning either from the private sector or the foreign sector or both.

Now what exactly do we mean by "Net Private Savings" and by "Net Foreign Capital Inflows"? Net Private Savings represents National Income (equivalently total private income, that is, wages and profits) minus all private spending (consumption *and* investment in houses and factories and new equipment). We say "all" spending here to emphasize that we are lumping together business and household sector spending.[4] Net Foreign Capital Inflows is the amount of foreign savings that the nation must and does import each year to finance its trade deficit measured on a "current account" basis—the broadest measure of a trade deficit.

Most people are very confused by this reality. They understandably think that total net capital inflows (foreigners' investments in the United States minus U.S. investments abroad) represent the net amount of capital that foreigners *wish* to invest in the United States. Should they become disenchanted with U.S. assets, then net capital inflows will fall and U.S. interest rates would get driven higher. But the underlying story here is much more complex, and this conclusion is completely incorrect for counterintuitive reasons.[5]

A Half-Century of Data

Figure 2.2 offers a graphic depiction of our National Income equation (2.3) at work during the past half-century. Note critically that, for any given year, the value of the government deficit (the heavy black line) is indeed the sum of the values of the two other lines,

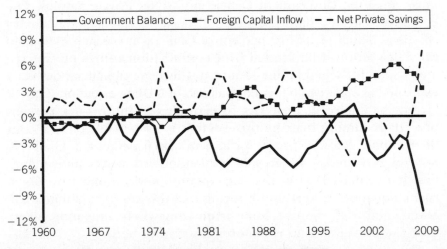

Figure 2.2   The Three Financial Balances (as a Percentage of Total GDP)

Note: For every year, the three data points must, and do, sum to zero.

Sources: U.S. Federal Reserve, Bureau of Economic Analysis.

just as equation (2.3) requires. They all add to zero. Amusingly, in 1969, you can see that all three had values of about 0, so you do not even need to know how to add in this one case! Now focus on the far right-hand side where the data for the recession years 2007–2009 are plotted. These data portray changes in the values of two of the three variables that are *astonishing* in magnitude. To begin with, note that Net Private Savings lurched from –2.4 percent of GDP to +7.7 percent, an unprecedented increase of 10.1 percent. This reflected the collapse of both household and business spending relative to total National Income that is a hallmark of the most recent recession. (Keep in mind that Net Private Savings is defined as the *difference* between National Income and Total Private Spending.)

In contrast, the value of the second variable (Net Foreign Capital Inflows) on the right-hand side of the equation fell slightly from 5.2 percent to 3.2 percent of GDP, reflecting an equivalent shrinkage of the U.S. trade deficit. (Remember that the net capital inflow is the mirror image of the trade deficit.) Our equation then *requires* that the government deficit appearing on the left must have risen by the sum of these two component changes (10.1% + (−2%)) = 8.1%. It did, of course, with the deficit soaring by an astonishing 8.1 percent, from 2.8 percent in 2007 to 10.9 percent in 2009. Once again, everything thus "adds up" in practice as it must in theory, according to the logic of equation (2.3).

Application of This Logic to Today's Crisis

To understand how helpful the logic of NI forecasting can be, let's apply it to today's recovery. Suppose that the Obama administration has the following two goals. First, it wishes to increase GDP growth by 2 percent above its current 2 percent growth rate to 5 percent per annum. This is the minimum growth needed to dent the U6 unemployment rate, for reasons we have already reviewed. Second, suppose the administration seeks to reduce the fiscal deficit by 7 percent of GDP from 10 percent of GDP today back to a long-run sustainable 3 percent. Are these twin goals compatible? No. Manipulation of the equations underlying (2.3) strongly suggests that it will be almost impossible for the nation to achieve these two worthy goals. *This is the problem we face.*

To see why, suppose that Foreign Net Capital Inflow (equivalently the trade deficit) does not change as a percent of GDP, or at least changes little, as is widely expected. Then in order to achieve the two policy goals cited earlier, Net Private Savings must shrink by 9 percent of GDP in order for equation (2.3) to be satisfied. This is not some random opinion, but is rather a logical necessity. But can Net Private Savings fall by this magnitude? Almost certainly not. To see why, recall the definition of Net Private Savings: National Income minus total Private Expenditures. Given this definition, then in order for NPS to fall by 9 percent, then either (1) private expenditure must rise by 9 percent of GDP, or (2) if this is unchanged, then National Income (which equals GDP) must fall by 9 percent, which of course signifies a major depression! (Or there could be some mix of these two adding to the required 9 percent.) But given our twin goals of reducing the fiscal deficit by 7 percent of GDP and increasing GDP growth by at least 2 percent over what it is today, then the only way Net Private Savings could fall by 9 percent of GDP is for private spending to explode by 9 percent. *Nothing else is logically possible given our goals.*

But Will This Happen?

How likely is it that private spending will soar? As the data in Figure 2.2 make clear, there has only been one time when the Net Private Savings term has fallen by this magnitude due to a boom in private expenditures. This was in the second half of the 1990s during the Clinton administration. It mainly resulted from an explosion of capital spending associated with rewiring the United States for the Internet revolution. As the data in the figure make clear, no other period in modern U.S. history witnessed any comparable rise in private spending, or equivalently, any comparable decline in Net Private Savings. There is virtually no likelihood that the period 2012–2020 will witness any such boom in capital spending. Of course, business investment spending is only one form of private expenditure that could increase significantly. Other forms include household spending and residential investment. But for reasons we have already reviewed, it is highly unlikely that either of these will fill the gap.

The longer-term trade-off we are left with is unappetizing. The nation can sustain a much-higher-than-usual fiscal deficit required to sustain GDP growth—exactly what the United States has done in the past three years when it ran deficits of 10 percent of GDP that were previously unthinkable. Or it can slash the deficit bringing the rate of economic growth back to zero, or worse. Or it can adopt a halfway-house solution and reduce the deficit very modestly, the strategy it seems to be pursuing. In either of the last two cases the unemployment rate will remain unacceptably high. Note how this conclusion reached via National Income analysis reinforces our earlier forecast arrived at via more standard GDP analysis.

The benefit of utilizing the national income logic in forecasting should by now be clear. It stems from the way it enables all-important flow-of-funds constraints (equation [2.3]) to discipline armchair GDP forecasting based upon the logic of equation (2.1). When such constraints are ignored, as they usually are, the result will be incomplete and misleading GDP forecasts. The higher-level forecasting logic embedded in the National Income constraints (2.3) is indispensable in helping us identify scenarios that *can* occur (because they are consistent with [2.3]) versus those that *cannot* occur because they are inconsistent with (2.3). Some two decades ago, I had the privilege of having lunch with the late economist James Tobin of Yale. In our discussion, he stressed this point to me. He commented that many faculty members of Harvard and Yale failed to understand the importance of exploiting the NI = NP duality when forecasting the economy.

Subsequently, the late Wynne Godley of Cambridge University came to specialize in this approach to forecasting. He wrote a primer on this topic for me nine years ago, and I now realize that his highly unconventional inferences about excessive private borrowing prefigured exactly what would happen during the global financial crisis of 2007–2010. This was long before various self-styled prophets claim to have foreseen the crisis. Moreover, the depth of his logic was as arresting as the dearth of logic has been on the part of many who claim to have called the U.S. housing market collapse. I am proud to join *Financial Times* columnist Martin Wolf and scholars at the Jerome Levy Institute as amongst the few who have recognized the importance of Godley's insistence on flow-of-funds analysis in valid forecasting. He deserves far more credit than he has had.

Exit from Gridlock: Mr. President, You *Can* Have Your Cake and Eat It, Too

Given the likelihood of subpar growth in the years ahead, of continuing high unemployment, and of increasingly vigilant bond markets, it is not surprising that a debate has been raging both in Congress and in the op-ed pages as to what government should do to prevent a Lost Decade. The two camps that have emerged consist of those who champion further stimulus spending (e.g., Paul Krugman and George Soros), even if it means larger deficits, as opposed to those who believe the deficit must be attacked right now regardless of the consequences for growth and employment (Harvard historian Niall Fergusson, British Prime Minister David Cameron, and former European Central Bank head Jean-Claude Trichet). The public is thus presented with an either/or choice between two highly problematic scenarios. Our earlier analysis is fully consistent with this depressing "either/or" conclusion.

Nonetheless, the positions staked out by both camps are wrong, as I now show. For it is possible to achieve higher growth rates of output and employment, to lower fiscal deficits placating the bond markets, as well as to achieve higher productivity growth and infrastructure improvement—all at the same time. If this Panglossian outcome seems at odds with the depressing analysis I carried out earlier, it is. Is this a paradox? No. For in my discussion above, I adopted the conventional view of what we mean by the size of the nation's "fiscal deficit," namely the difference between total government spending and total tax revenue. And I accepted the conventional wisdom that this must be reduced a lot. As it turns out, this concept of a deficit is highly problematic. A novel definition is needed, and will shortly be introduced. Once this is done, and a win-win policy is identified by utilizing it, then today's Dialogue of the Deaf on the Lost Decade can be replaced by an informed consensus as to what really needs to be done and *can* be done. The good news is that an exit from gridlock is possible, and is needed.

■ ■ ■

Socratic Dialogue: A Rethink of Fiscal Policy

President: I have read with interest what you have said, and am keen to discover what your exit from gridlock strategy amounts to. From where I stand, matters are quite discouraging. Just as you said, the supposed experts are divided into two distinct camps, namely deficit hawks versus deficit doves. And there is no middle ground in what you properly call a Dialogue of the

Deaf about deficit spending. The hawks have certainly gained the upper hand, not only in the States, but also in Europe and Australia, where deficit phobia is rampant. A dove minority, however, stresses that fiscal austerity as championed by the hawks will kill growth just as it is doing in several European economies. It argues that strong growth is the only legitimate way out of today's morass.

I myself am a short-term dove in this sense, but there is a serious weakness in our position. We doves have tended to ignore the likelihood that bond market vigilantes will no longer tolerate the growing burden of debt that ongoing fiscal deficits imply. Given the speed and the ferocity of recent vigilante attacks in Europe, this is too important a risk for us to ignore any longer. Finally, you are spot on in pointing out that we need GDP growth much higher than today's 2 percent rate if we are to bring total unemployment back down to normal. So what is your strategy that will permit Americans to have their cake and eat it too? And on what grounds can it be justified? No voodoo economics, I trust!

Economist: Thank you, Mr. President, for your interest. Before detailing my strategy, let me address your last point: On what grounds can it be justified? As you read earlier in Chapter 1, I champion a deductive approach to problem solving where Basic Assumptions or axioms are laid down up front, and a policy solution is then deduced from them by following the laws of logic. Assuming that parties of all stripes agree that the axioms are reasonable, then they *must* agree with the policy recommendation that results from the ensuing deductions.

President: Yes, I noted that point and found it both unusual and interesting. And as you said, it flies in the face of much current policy analysis where both sides stake out their positions, and then cherry-pick "facts" to back up their positions. Gridlock tends to result from the resulting shouting match. Can you deduce the solution to the Lost Decade problem in a deductive manner?

Economist: Yes. In fact I will do so in two ways. In the first instance, the deduction is quite simple, as it makes use of a redefinition of the concept of "deficit." Once introduced, this new definition leads quite rapidly to the win-win policy solution I believe in.

Importantly, I shall argue that this solution satisfies the four desiderata that everyone wants satisfied by *any* purported "solu-'tion" to today's crisis: much lower fiscal deficits to placate the bond market, much higher GDP growth, much lower unemployment rates, and a solution to our infrastructure problem.

In the second instance, the approach is more abstract. Based upon extremely important research by the economists Kenneth Arrow and Mordecai Kurz at Stanford University, it is shown that a single Basic Assumption can be utilized to deduce the same policy outcome at a much deeper and more persuasive level of analysis. At a more abstract level of analysis, this second approach clarifies when and why *very* large government deficits are sometimes fully justified. We are precisely at such a stage now. Given limitations of space, and the somewhat technical nature of the required deductions, I will simply sketch the argument graphically in the last part of the chapter, stressing its relevance and indeed its originality.

President: Good. Having two altogether different sources of support will be helpful if you really have deduced a solution that purportedly will satisfy most everyone. It will be that much easier to sell to Congress. Now let's cut to the chase. What is your policy solution, and how do you justify it via these two lines of argument?

Economist: The solution lies in redefining the very concept of a "deficit" in a manner that permits a new theory of "deficit spending," a theory that can be applied to the situation in the United States right now. When I say "new" here, let me be clear that the basic idea is not so much new as it is currently unrecognized. Out of some 500 op-ed columns on the subject of deficit spending that I have read in the past few years, I have seen perhaps four articles that set forth the basic thrust of this approach. Yet none of these four suggested that my approach to deficit spending could simultaneously satisfy all four desiderata that must be met to avoid a Lost Decade. Nor have I ever seen this approach justified by first principles stemming from the Arrow-Kurz theory that lies at the foundation of fiscal and macroeconomic theory. Given the urgency of the U.S. crisis, and given today's strong prejudices against ongoing large fiscal deficits, a *very* strong justification is needed for what I am going to propose. This will be provided.

President: Can you explain the main point here in the simplest possible terms?

"Good" versus "Bad" Deficits, and the Main Policy Proposal

Economist: Yes. Please consider Figure 2.3, which contrasts the fiscal status of two countries with ostensibly identical deficits. Assume that Country A's government spends $4 trillion on defense, administrative costs, interest expenses on its debt, and transfer payments such as Social Security and Medicare. Its tax revenues of $3 trillion fall $1 trillion short of this $4 trillion, so that the nation runs a deficit of $1 trillion. More specifically, its treasury department will have to issue $1 trillion in new government bonds. The expense of servicing this new debt (or repaying it) will fall on tomorrow's taxpayers, who just might renege on it if it gets too large.

As the magnitude of total national debt outstanding grows each year because of these marginal additions to total debt (i.e., each year's deficit), a point will be reached where the bond market fears future insolvency, or else a printing away of the debt. As a result, investors will demand higher yields, which crimp the growth rate of the economy, and cause the cost of

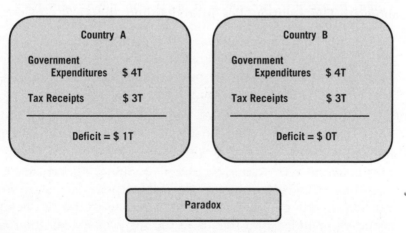

Figure 2.3   How to Fix the U.S. Economy and Labor Market While Not Upsetting the Bond Market Vigilantes

The Moral: It is the composition and quality of total government spending that matters, not the "size of the deficit."

refinancing the debt to explode. The infamous "debt trap" could soon be reached—a fiscal red hole from which few nations ever escape. Country A is modeled after the United States, of course, and during 2010–2011 investors worldwide began to question its long-term solvency, especially in light of the inability of both political parties to cope with runaway spending.

President: But what is different about Country B, whose revenues and outlays are identical to those of country A, but which you claim has no deficit? Is this a trick? Are you the Houdini of macroeconomics?

Economist: Thank you, but no. Country B differs in one regard: Of its total $4 trillion in spending, $1 trillion is spent on profitable investments (human capital and infrastructure investments) which are certified by an independent research organization to generate a *positive* expected return on capital, as calculated within the venerable field of public finance. The remaining $3 trillion are expenditures on defense, interest payments, administrative costs, and transfer payments like Social Security and Medicare. When bond market vigilantes understand this breakout, they see a nation whose necessary if unproductive spending of $3 trillion is fully matched by current tax revenue. So there is no deficit from *unproductive* spending.

On the other hand, the nation *is* borrowing an extra trillion dollars to invest in projects that are "certifiably productive," as it were, and that pay for themselves over time in the same way as any productive capital investments in the private sector pay off. So, overall, no new debt has been chalked up that future generations must service. That is why the figure shows a deficit of zero. The bond markets are placated, and interest rates are not driven up.

President: I am supposed to think of Country A as America today, and Country B as America the way it *could* be tomorrow, correct?

Economist: Yes. More specifically, think of Country B as the America that *would* be, were Congress able to redirect a good chunk of government spending (up to $1 trillion per year) away from existing spending toward productive spending. Historically, such spending included investments in the highway system, the space program, the Internet (known originally as the DARPANET), the interstate highway system, R&D, the energy grid, water resources, and so forth. Congress is not to *cut* $1 trillion as many deficit hawks would like. Rather, it is to *reconfigure* total spending so as to boost GDP, jobs, and productivity. There are no net layoffs, and no fiscal drag at all.

President: So your sleight of hand is to introduce two kinds of deficits, "good" and "bad" deficits as it were, that differ according to the type of spending that generated the deficit.

Economist: Yes. Emphasis accordingly must shift away from the overall size of the deficit to its composition of good versus bad spending. I am not claiming here that nonproductive spending is bad *per se*, as it is not. But it is spending that must be matched by tax revenues so as to no longer increase the burden on future Americans.

President: The principle here is straightforward, and come to think of it, in the private sector, no corporation would claim ongoing losses by "expensing" investment spending. Rather, the firm capitalizes the investment expense, and only deducts from income the amortized portion of the investment each year. In doing this, there is no "deficit" due to investment spending.

Economist: Yes, indeed, and it has long been recognized that governments should develop an accounting system that partitions its own expenditures analogously. Some governments have attempted to do so in the past, but this was neither expected nor required. Today, however, it would be wise for governments to develop a proper sets of books. For in coming years, transparency of this kind will be important for keeping the bond market at bay.

How the Proposed Policy Satisfies the Four Desiderata

President: As you doubtless suspect, I have a lot of questions about what you are proposing, although it is difficult to disagree with your basic logic. But before we pass from fantasy to reality, and I grill you on some of the details of your plan, please explain how this strategy would satisfy all four criteria that you cited previously: more rapid GDP growth, reduced unemployment, a contented bond market, and a solution to our infrastructure crisis. I do not understand this claim.

Economist: First consider GDP growth. Under the proposed strategy, GDP growth would be much greater than otherwise. To begin with, there would be no fiscal contraction of the kind we are already beginning to experience. The nature of the deficit would change, but not its size. Usually, when the IMF orders a debtor nation to slash its fiscal deficit from, say, 10 percent of GDP to 3 percent, the nation suffers a 10 percent – 3 percent = 7 percent loss of GDP, other things being equal. We saw why in equation (2.1), which defined GDP. Of course, this loss is often spread out over several years, lessening the pain.

President: Is GDP positively impacted in any other way by your plan?

Economist: Yes. The nature of the new spending—on investment rather than transfer payments—triggers all those "multiplier and accelerator" effects we learned about in Econ 101. These factors raise economic growth even more. Recall how, if funds are given to a master design firm to create a new airport, or whatever, this firm in turn will borrow against these funds and hire a large contractor who in turn will borrow and hire 15 subcontractors, and so forth. The jobs multiply, sometimes at an accelerating rate. This multiplier is estimated to be approximately 2.5 versus 1 when the money is spent on a transfer payment for keeping a given worker at his existing job.

There is yet another boost to GDP aside from the jobs multiplier story. When money is spent on profitable projects only—think bridges to somewhere rather than bridges to nowhere—productivity growth will rise with every dollar spent. And higher productivity growth implies higher GDP growth in the longer run.

President: Please elaborate.

Economist: When a nation lets its infrastructure run down, as the United States has, then the deterioration can reach a critical point. Bridges start collapsing much more frequently. The national electric grid is stressed out and falters. Blackouts become much more frequent. Old refineries experience safety and maintenance problems. Nuclear plants become much more hazardous. Traffic lines lengthen exponentially. As this happens, investment spending of the right kind can significantly boost productivity growth—much more than in normal circumstances—since it will both prevent systemic collapse and will permit an improvement over the status quo prior to collapse. This is very important since the United States may well be reaching a critical point of infrastructure collapse during the current decade. The nation simply must address its infrastructure crisis on a truly grand scale, and stop equating infrastructure investment with filling potholes.

President: So all of this propels GDP growth even higher. Growth benefits from a lack of fiscal drag, from the multiplier effect, and from higher productivity. What about job growth *per se?*

Economist: Job creation will accelerate much more rapidly under my plan than it otherwise would. First, faster GDP growth from the lack of any fiscal drag will itself create jobs. Remember, there will be no reduction of overall fiscal stimulus at all—just a *reconfiguration* of spending toward investment. Secondly, the shift of expenditures from transfer payment spending, which has zero job-creation effects, to investment spending with its knock-on accelerator/multiplier employment effects will cause a much greater rate of job creation than otherwise, as was just noted. Both of these points should be central to any strategy for accelerated job creation.

President: Shifting to another one of your four objectives, what will the bond market say about all this? Will it finally be satisfied that we have stopped mortgaging our future?

Economist: Most probably, provided you and the Congress make clear that you truly will rack up "good" deficits as needed, and bring to an end the buildup of bad debt that our children may one day default on, and that rattles the bond market. You will also have to persuade the bond market that your infrastructure program will restrict itself to investments that earn a *positive* expected rate of return on the funds borrowed to pay for them. I will discuss later exactly what that means in reality.

Incidentally, assuming that such investments will earn an expected profit, you have the option of funding them not merely by government borrowing (thus adding to the deficit), but also by raising private capital, possibly backed by a government guarantee. The ways in which governments can fund projects have proliferated in recent decades. By approaching bankers at the Macquarie Bank in Australia, which has specialized in such matters, you will be surprised by how many ways there are to skin this cat. You can also approach the governments of the States of Victoria in Australia, of Ontario in Canada, and the nations of Chile and Turkey to discover still other forms of creative government financing. Once a case can be made that the projects are needed and thus profitable in a sense which will be defined further on in this dialogue, then all kinds of financing opportunities will present themselves.

Finally, since the case for running a significant "good" deficit well into a business cycle recovery has not been made before, at least not in the political arena, it would help if you would direct the OMB to prepare a new set of government accounts that separate out capital investment spending from normal recurring expenditures. With these accounts in hand, you could demonstrate to an otherwise skeptical public and bond market how the "bad" U.S. fiscal deficit *properly computed* could drop to zero under the proposed policies over the next seven years or so. Once again, this deficit is the difference between unproductive (but necessary) government spending and total tax receipts. Showing this would help you win over deficit hawks and other naysayers in today's environment of deficit phobia and austerity.

President: Given today's mindset, this will be quite a challenge. But I like the way your proposal seems like Common Sense 101, to utilize one of your favorite phrases. You have put your case well, as far as it goes. Now, however, let me express some serious concerns. First, what you are proposing is quite radical, even if it is commonsensical. You are suggesting that those on the Left like Paul Krugman and George Soros are right in arguing that we should not significantly cut our fiscal deficit of 10 percent of GDP at all. They are dead set against any fiscal contraction that might further increase unemployment. But so are you. Where you seem to differ from them is your insistence that the *composition* of government spending must be changed, tilting it toward profitable investment spending on a veritable Marshall Plan scale, and away from unproductive transfer payments. Am I correct here?

Economist: Yes, and I find it extraordinary that in all their op-ed pieces, the two liberals you cite have not raised the all-important distinction between "good" and "bad" deficits as defined earlier. This should be *the* central point in any rethink of fiscal policy today.

President: Can the bold plan you are proposing be justified on any further grounds? A proposal this radical will need all the support it can get given today's deficit phobia.

A Further Justification of the Proposed Marshall Plan

Economist: Yes. To begin with, I have already given you the principal justification for the proposal: It satisfies the four national policy objectives stressed earlier. Had I gone a bit further, I could also have demonstrated that it is the *only* strategy that can do so given the very tight constraints that these objectives impose on U.S. policy makers. But let me now take a different tack and clarify why a wholly *new* strategy is called for at this juncture in U.S. history, due to a novel set of circumstances that have arisen and that will constrain your policy choices.

President: Is there in fact something really new about today's circumstances? Some dispute the claim that this time really is different.

Economist: Indeed there is. To begin with, policy makers must attempt to achieve much higher growth after failing to do so despite the largest monetary and fiscal stimulus in over five decades. This challenge truly is a post-war first! The level of distress in the labor and housing markets and in the public sector is also highly unusual. So is the extent of sluggish demand in the private sector. Finally, there is the growing likelihood that our aging infrastructure could go critical by the end of the decade. This is also new.

But what is completely new is that the United States for the first time in a century has outlived its welcome in the global bond market at the very time it will need ongoing fiscal stimulus to perform the heavy lifting of its recovery. Monetary policy can do little more than it has. Demand in the private sector is flat. Therefore only public sector borrowing and spending can do the job. Yet bond market vigilantes could soon be up in arms. At this writing, rating agencies have put the U.S. Treasury on their watch list. Higher interest rates and soaring debt refinancing costs could well be the result, just as occurred in several European countries during 2010–2011. The fact that U.S. yields recently have been so low should deceive no one about the future. The yields on many Euro-bonds were low too, until the firestorms of 2010 and 2011. Finally, the continuing fall of the dollar underscores how much confidence in the United States has already been lost overseas.

All in all, this set of new circumstances explains why a radically new strategy is called for, and the one I have sketched out is designed to accommodate *all* these realities. To state it differently, the proposed policy is consistent with all these constraints, unlike any other recovery strategy proposed to date. My strategy has the potential of transforming a Lost Decade into a Winning Decade in which the United States finally gets down to business, attacks the right problems in the right way, and satisfies all four of its principal policy goals in one fell swoop.

Three Potential Difficulties

President: I am with you thus far. We are indeed in a new situation, bound by new constraints, and a novel policy is in order. Nonetheless, I have some serious concerns about your own plan. First, does the nation really need the vast scale of public sector infrastructure you are calling for, up to $1 trillion per year over a decade, or a $10 trillion investment? This is a much larger figure than is usually cited. Second, is such a plan physically feasible? Do we have the nonfinancial resources to carry it out? Third, how can I convince investors that infrastructure projects once identified really are "profitable" and earn a positive rate of return on invested capital? As you know, the public is very cynical, and doubts that the government can do anything right. Boston's notorious "Big Dig" overrun is now seen as the rule, not the exception, of government projects.

Economist: Let me sketch answers to all three of your questions, each of which represents a legitimate concern. As to your first question regarding the scale of the investment plan that is needed, there are two considerations. First, how much infrastructure of various kinds would *ideally* be needed were the nation to decide to leave to its children and grandchildren top-notch infrastructure they can be proud of? As far as I know, this question has neither been asked nor answered. Rather, we hear piecemeal accounts of how much is needed to prevent bridges from falling down, or to fill potholes, or whatever. Second, how much public sector stimulus is needed to get the nation back on track with much faster growth and much lower unemployment, while placating the bond market? The answers to these two questions are critically interrelated in what I have proposed.

Ideally, the numerical answer to the first question would be the same as to the second! I will argue that this is precisely the case in the United States today. Up to an approximation, the nation needs $1 trillion of both government-initiated investment *and* of ongoing fiscal stimulus on an annual basis. This "fit" very much works in our favor, and this is fortuitous since there need be no such fit at all. For example, consider the case of Japan. On the one hand, Japan has little need of infrastructure spending due to excellent maintenance and ongoing investment over the decades. On the other hand, Japan needs ongoing fiscal stimulus because of its well-known stagnation.

Given these realities, my plan would not work in Japan: It already has the infrastructure it needs, so that further investment along the lines I have proposed would amount to building "roads to nowhere," so to speak. This is a code word for "roads that generate a *negative* expected return on capital invested." Any such projects would thus violate my plan's requirement that all investments be profitable, and not pose a burden on the grandchildren that upsets the bond market. Only "roads to somewhere" are allowed in my plan.

President: A combination of circumstances opposite to those of Japan would be those of a country that has a great need for deferred infrastructure investment spending, but whose economy is roaring along just fine so that no fiscal stimulus is needed at all. Is that correct?

Economist: Exactly. The question for the United States is thus whether we need both massive infrastructure spending *and* significant ongoing fiscal stimulus. Based upon the earlier analysis, my conclusion is that we do need both. I suspect you agree. As regards the need for infrastructure, the United States and the United Kingdom rank at the top of most lists as having the most dilapidated stock of public sector capital out of all the OECD nations. Neither nation has put a new roof on its house in half a century. Let me reemphasize that what is at stake is not merely the repair of deteriorating public sector capital stock, but the development of completely new capital stock of higher quality than that it replaces. For example, while we need to fix older roads and bridges and tunnels, we also need new high-speed trains, new energy grids, new oil refineries, and so on.

President: And don't forget the human capital investment that you mentioned earlier, if you really are shooting for the moon.

Economist: Yes, investment targeted toward jacking up productivity in both K–12 education and health-care infrastructure (see Chapter 3) will prove very important. To cut to the chase, when you compile a wish list of total public investment required to upgrade the entire infrastructure of the nation over the next decade—not just roads and bridges—then the sum lies between $10 trillion and possibly even $15 trillion according to many discussions I have had. For example, the National Academy of Engineers has estimated that over $4 trillion will be needed simply to repair and upgrade *all* of the nation's bridges and roads. That is before attending to any of the other kinds of infrastructure that are needed.

This is a very large country and it all adds up to a very large number when a decade-long perspective is adopted, or better a two-decade perspective were we truly serious. But what a moment: Is $10 trillion of new capital stock that large a number in a nation whose GDP is $15 trillion annually, and that has irresponsibly deferred infrastructure maintenance for five decades? The more I research and ask questions, the more this appears to be not a large amount at all. Perhaps $20 trillion would better approximate the *ideal* level of investment over, say, two or even three decades.

President: What you are calling for is a veritable Marshall Plan dedicated to infrastructure, in the broadest sense of this term. And if the figure really does amount to $10 or $15 trillion over a decade or so, then this would amount to at least $1 trillion of such spending a year.

Economist: Yes, and note that $1 trillion per year equals the size of the ongoing fiscal stimulus needed to prevent a Lost Decade from materializing. This is why I asserted that, in the case of the United States at present, there is a nearly perfect fit between the size of investment spending required and the size of fiscal stimulus needed throughout the decade, assuming that private sector spending continues to be inadequate for the level of growth needed to redress the unemployment crisis.

Going one step deeper, the payoff from the proposed strategy is even more compelling than all this suggests. As you know, the United States has been widely criticized for under-investing and overconsuming for several decades. We eclipse all other nations in spending a whopping 71 percent of GDP on consumption. The result of this imbalance has been exactly what the late Harvard economist John Kenneth Galbraith predicted long ago in his book *The Affluent Society:* private splendor, and public squalor. The proposed plan would reverse this situation, tilting the consumption share of GDP back to a more balanced 65 percent of GDP within a decade or so, while radically increasing the investment share.

Are the Needed Resources Available?

President: Good. My second question is whether we have the non-financial resources to undertake such a plan. For example, where would the manpower come from? I am taking your word that financial resources would be available provided there is good evidence that the spending will be productive.

Economist: Remarkably, we probably can garner the resources required. To begin with, the collapse of the housing industry saw 2,003,000 construction workers and engineers lose their jobs. As of mid-2011 there are still 1,137,000 construction workers looking for work. Additional slack in the system comes from today's relatively low level of corporate investment spending, and the resources this frees up. There is also the large army of unemployed workers outside of construction—many with skills—that have not yet been able to secure employment. Finally, there would and should be a reallocation of existing workers from sectors in trouble, including state and local governments, toward design, construction, engineering, and project management. As for new workforce entrants, talented students will pick up on this development and reorient their careers away from Facebook and finance and toward engineering and "making things." It is high time.

All in all, I do believe we have the resources needed to carry out the required investments. But look at matters in reverse. A belief that the required resources might *not* be available is probably mistaken. In a market economy governed by a price system, prices and quantities miraculously adjust so as to *make* resources available where they are *needed,* and they do so with an efficiency that has proven remarkable time after time. If opportunities to make a living shift toward infrastructure, you can be sure that the resources will follow.

President: Okay, you may be right that your policy is feasible. But is it *politically* feasible? For example, your plan requires a gradual shift of government spending out of sectors dependent upon transfer payments and into sectors supporting very large new infrastructure spending. That will be a hard sell, especially amongst Democrats.

Economist: Yes, some Democratic Party spokesmen will probably brand the idea as "heartless," but it should be easy for you to refute such claims, especially if you truly take charge and lead, which is what people want. You have two aces in your political deck. First, this plan will create more jobs than any other plan can, and politically, joblessness has become Issue Number 1 in this nation. Second, you must make clear this is not some zero-sum game where for every infrastructure job created, another job must be lost. Due to the job multiplier effect, there will be a significant net increase in jobs. Furthermore, to the extent that reduced transfer payments do adversely impact certain beneficiaries, it's time to remind such workers that the other shoe sometimes must fall in life. Your original stimulus program protected many state and local workers' jobs, whereas no protection was afforded to those in construction. It may well be time for a flip-flop here in the name of net job creation, as well as in the name of fairness.

Legal System Difficulties—NIMBYism in Particular

President: There is one final aspect of feasibility that worries me and that you have failed to mention. This concerns the role of the U.S. legal system in implementing your plan. Assuming you are correct that we have the labor and capital required for the proposed investments, will our legal system permit the plan to be realized? Or will it be stymied by NIMBYism—that "not-in-my-back-yard" form of project paralysis? Will well-intended projects languish in courts during years of lawsuits, thereby discrediting the entire program and driving returns negative?

Economist: You are now putting your finger on the obstacle that bothers me the most. This really is a sink-or-swim issue. I have discussed this matter with lawyers and public policy analysts. The root question seems to be whether the federal government on its own has the authority and the power to push through this kind of an investment agenda. No one has given me a convincing answer. However, there is solace in the example of the construction of the vast Interstate Highway System over the decades following World War II. President Eisenhower utilized national security arguments to insist upon construction. I myself can recall those large ICBM missiles being shipped around the country to widely separated missile silos. Of course, this was during the height of the Cold War, and the U.S. landscape was much less developed than it is now.

President: All this is true, but the reality is that today's legal system is much more complex, and specialized interest groups are much more embedded than they used to be. For example, there was no firmly entrenched environmental lobby to prevent the construction of Route 80 across the country lest the habitat of some rare brown-spotted squirrel be disturbed.

Economist: This is true. Nonetheless, you should make it a priority to gather the best legal information you can on this issue. The role of the Supreme Court will be very important. They recently voted for a significant expansion of the right of eminent domain whereby private property can be seized on behalf of private sector commercial interests, provided that the larger community will benefit from job creation and other "externalities" resulting from development.

President: Yes, and this was a very controversial verdict. Nonetheless, it hints at ways your program could succeed. Perhaps the twin needs for job creation today and better infrastructure for future generations would provide a legal basis for a much broader federal mandate than has hitherto existed. This is well worth thinking about.

Economist: There is a further argument that bolsters expanded eminent domain in the public sector. It is easy to think of infrastructure improvement as a luxury—one to which the nation can perfectly well say "No." We have done so for decades. But it is not, in fact, a luxury. It is fast becoming a necessity for the simple reason that infrastructure deterioration will begin to go critical, thereby threatening the public's safety and welfare. On these grounds, I can foresee a day when the Supreme Court steps in and mandates infrastructure spending for reasons of public safety. This might happen after hundreds of people are hurled to their death after 20 more bridges collapse, or after a series of severe brownouts drive up unemployment and cause hundreds of deaths in hospitals.

President: You are being a bit sloppy here. Do not forget that the Supreme Court does not mandate anything. It merely arrives at verdicts. What would happen is that Congress in Washington would pass a law ceding vast new powers to the federal government in the interest of "timely, necessary infrastructure investment and maintenance." States' rights lawyers would presumably challenge such a law in the Supreme Court, and the court in turn could rule on behalf of the federal government. This is perhaps the best hope.

Economist: You are correct. One other improvement needs to be made in the battle against NIMBYism. Game theory teaches us the importance of awarding generous side-payments to losers in breaching bargaining impasses. Such payments are often the best way to transform a zero-sum game into a positive sum or win-win game. I have always thought that we are not creative in designing them, and do not utilize them enough. This is especially true in the case of contending with NIMBYism.

The Identification and Ranking of Public Investment Projects by Their Return

President: I have one final concern about your plan. How will we identify those profitable investment projects that should be undertaken? How do we assure ourselves that we will end up with high return bridges to somewhere as opposed to boondoggles to nowhere? As I already said, almost everyone is cynical about the government's ability to do anything right anymore.

Economist: I am glad you are pressing me on this issue, as it lies at the heart of my proposals. I have argued for a truly large-scale investment, a domestic Marshall Plan as you put it. We need this not only because ongoing fiscal stimulus is required to solve the four problems the nation must solve, but also because we owe future generations a capital stock superior to what we have now.

To support this effort, there must be a large, new public/ private Infrastructure Bank with significant foreign support. Just as the Old World helped finance the New World when English and German banks helped finance the U.S. canal systems and railroads of the nineteenth century, the New World now can help the Old World rebuild itself with their surplus savings— providing of course that returns from doing so are attractive.

President: Several people have proposed infrastructure banks since I took office. Executives at the Fluor Corporation are very keen on this, I believe, and they are not alone. So are many politicians, including myself. In a related direction, the eminent New York financier Felix Rohatyn wrote an excellent book a few years ago about the proper role of government in financing infrastructure, *Bold Endeavors*.[6] He revealed the indispensable role of government in creating the infrastructure of the nation during the past two centuries. But what you are proposing sounds somewhat different.

Incidentally, does the United States actually need foreign investment? I thought your proposal would be financed domestically.

Economist: We do and we do not need their capital. This is tricky. To begin with, since we run a large trade deficit of about $500 billion, we *automatically* receive large net foreign capital inflows of a corresponding magnitude. You will recall from the flow of funds discussion earlier that net foreign capital inflow equals and finances the trade deficit (equation [2.3]). What matters is whether these funds flow into purchases of more T-bills by foreigners, or into more productive investments. I think we would benefit politically by having investors like the sovereign wealth funds of Singapore, Norway, and China represented on the board of the proposed infrastructure bank. Their presence and possibly their capital would reduce the temptation of politicians in Washington to meddle in the selection of investment projects. But in reality, foreigners can perfectly well go on investing in T-bills, and we would then finance the program domestically.

When you ask whether my proposal is different from Rohatyn's, the answer is yes. It is different partly because the scope of what I propose is so large, and partly because of the need to focus on the incentive structure and politics of the new bank and its activities. Three main questions arise here. First, how do you identify at an analytical level which projects should be funded in which order? Second, what incentive structure will prevent "politics" from undermining the program's integrity? And third, what kinds of mixed public/private investment structures should be utilized?

As I am not going to expand further upon this last point, it is simply worth noting that modern finance and investment banking have developed a remarkable tool kit for helping governments optimally finance worthy projects. As mentioned earlier, the contributions of Macquarie Bank and others have shown that there will be some blending and sequencing of private and public financing that will be optimal for any given project. The United States is a complete laggard here, and we could learn a lot from the experiences of many foreign countries and their investment bankers.

President: What about my final concern, identifying and ranking potential projects? Can this be made nonpolitical?

Economist: The new infrastructure bank would hire several hundred very well-trained and very well-paid analysts skilled in both private sector and public sector investment evaluation. Their job would be to evaluate *all* potential projects from a master list, and to then quantify and rank their risk-adjusted expected returns in order from highest to lowest. There could be 22 candidate high-speed rail systems. Some would end up with returns of 14 percent, others with –9 percent. With such a ranking in hand, investments would then be made in the order of the highest return to the lowest return—where the cutoff point would be the appropriate benchmark market rate of return. Precisely how to make such assessments is discussed next.

President: But how can this process avoid being politicized? Is there any objective way to estimate expected returns on capital invested in a new bullet train or highway system?

An Objective Assessment of Returns

Economist: The good news on this front is that, during the past 50 years, we really have learned how to assess the expected risk-adjusted returns from both private and public investments. And these two kinds of returns must be calculated very differently. As for ranking public-sector investments, recent analytical discoveries have in effect breathed new life into the time-honored field known as Public Finance. Many of these issues were addressed in a fully unified manner in one of the landmark books in the history of macroeconomics, a 1970 book entitled *Public Investment, The Rate of Return, and Optimal Fiscal Policy.* As is noted later, this treatise unified four different branches of economics into a whole, and addressed many of the concerns you have cited. It was coauthored by the economists Kenneth Arrow and Mordecai Kurz of Stanford University, and will be discussed at length further on.

President: What exactly is it that makes public investments much harder to evaluate than private investments?

Economist: It is the issue of "externalities," otherwise known as "nonmarket effects" or "spillover effects" that make public sector investment analysis more difficult. If you and I invest in an ice cream parlor, our goal is to maximize returns from the production and sale of ice cream. Returns are easily measured. An observer just counts the dollars in versus the dollars out to arrive at net profit. The discounted stream of future profits divided by the capital needed to create and open the shop is the rate of return on investment.

President: Whereas the decision to create the Interstate Highway System had spillover effects that were very difficult to forecast and calculate. Is that it?

Economist: Basically, yes. The difficulty does not center on projecting total costs, but rather on projecting total *benefits*—and note that I do not say revenues. To be sure, if you build tollbooths every 50 miles of highway, there will be unambiguous benefits in the form of revenues. But above and beyond these, there will be the government tax revenues earned on the huge increase in GDP generated over the decades as new cities and suburbs grow up around the highway system. An Interstate is merely an artery, but commerce gets carried out in the capillaries and veins that end up surrounding it. Computations have shown that this enormous infrastructure project during the decades after World War II served to create a New America, with large investment returns to boot. The same was true of the creation of the Internet, a very low-cost spinoff of ARPA research in the 1960s, and originally known as the DARPANET. The Rohatyn book cited earlier sketches the large payoffs historically reaped from mega-investments, and does so in a very accessible manner.

President: Are you saying that somewhat intangible benefits like these can be now be modeled and quantified like return on investment (ROI) in the private sector?

Economist: Absolutely. Let me give you another example. The GDP of India would increase considerably should India gain the infrastructure needed to reduce commuting time in half. Remember that GDP is a pie that is baked in offices and in factories, not on overcrowded and delay-plagued train platforms. Government will receive a large ongoing tax dividend from the new income made possible by better Indian rail service, a figure estimated to be for larger than the cost of the required infrastructure. And this measure of return does not include revenues from selling tickets.

President: What about Amtrak rail service in the northeast U.S. corridor? People always complain that it loses money.

Economist: Their complaints are largely misplaced. Ticket sale revenues were never intended to measure the total profit or return on a public service like Amtrak between Washington, DC, and Boston. These trains permit millions of people a year to get where they are going fast, and to work more, regardless of weather conditions. The government receives tax revenues on the extra GDP realized.

President: You will agree that the risk in estimating both the costs and benefits of public projects will be very large. Doesn't this risk have to be significantly discounted, thereby lowering the expected risk-adjusted returns of the project?

Economist: No. The economist Kenneth Arrow showed long ago that, because of the government's ability to widely diversify risks across its huge portfolio of investments, the correct "social" risk premium in this context is in fact zero. This boosts returns on public investment above returns on comparable private investment (other things being equal) since significant risk premiums *are* appropriate in the private sector.

President: But you agree that there will be large risks?

Economist: Yes, as there are whenever Johnson & Johnson decide to introduce a new product line. Just ask their R&D directors how risky this can be! There is always large risk in any project. The problem is that public sector officials to date have had less of an incentive to *assess and manage* their risks than have their counterparts in the private sector. But there is a much more important point lurking here. Since when should America turn its back on risk? The answer is, never.

Keeping Analysts Honest in the New Bank

President: The second question I have concerns the politicization of the ranking of projects that you expect your highly qualified analysts to generate. What will keep them and the system honest?

Economist: To begin with, the analysts hired by the new bank are to be *very* highly paid, with their performance fully dependent upon transparency and objectivity of their analyses. Their high pay reflects the "Singapore Model" wherein government officials of importance are paid extremely well so as to avoid the temptation of corruption. Second, the results of their analyses will be public, transparent, and available online, with outside parties available to contribute their concerns and suggestions. Third, foreigners should and probably will be involved both as investors and board members. Powerful Congressional representatives hoping to get "their" negative return projects approved on the basis of their political clout will have trouble explaining their reasoning to those Norwegian, Singaporean, and Chinese investors sitting on the infrastructure bank's board!

President: It is said that the advent of cost/benefit analysis in the 1960s created more honest politicians in Washington than ever before. Officials finally had to justify the costs of projects they favored. Are you extending this logic?

Economist: Yes, and to a much higher degree. Historically, the same thing happened with the invention of double-entry bookkeeping in Genoa in the fifteenth century: For the first time investors could actually learn where their money was going! It became harder to steal it from them. All in all, I would like to see the large management consultancies and investment banks incentivized to support this new infrastructure bank. As for young people interested in finance, as so many now are, this could become a "cool" place to work, a high-profile career opportunity, much as the Peace Corps became under Presidents Kennedy and Johnson.

Need for Powerful Leadership

Economist: There is one final area where the ball lies in your court, Mr. President. This concerns *leadership*. You will have to endorse and sell this proposal to the people—not just to Congress—assuming you believe in it. In doing so, you must talk up to the people. Do not just offer "hope," your campaign theme, but concrete hope showing that there really is a pot of gold at the end of the rainbow, that is, that concrete problems can be solved, and the American dream restored. Many Americans now believe that today's problems cannot be solved given today's contentious gridlock. You might attempt to restore optimism in the following two-step manner:

> **Step 1:** Explain that the nation must solve all four challenging problems identified earlier if this is not to be a Lost Decade, and if we are to bequeath to our children a better future. Spell out all four challenges at every opportunity: the need to create jobs, to raise the rate of GDP growth, to redress the infrastructure scandal, and to avoid increasing the nation's stock of "bad" debt so as to keep global bond markets at bay.
>
> **Step 2:** Demonstrate that there is one and only one solution that solves all four problems at once. Don't just state this. Demonstrate it aggressively, with the use of arresting visual aids of the kind presidential candidate Ross Perot once successfully used. And having won the people over, embarrass the members of Congress if they try to play partisan politics and derail your plan. The Senators of ancient Rome were supposedly more frightened by the mob that the emperor could stir up than by the emperor himself. So stir up the beast to demand action. Do not leave it to Congress. With all due respect, doing so has been your biggest mistake to date.

To win over sufficient votes in Congress, you should exploit two political opportunities that bolster your case. First, the proposed strategy is win-win in nature and should be able to be supported by both sides of the aisle. The Left can claim that this is Big Government coming to the rescue of the nation as in the 1930s. The Right for the first time can claim that resources will be allocated nonwastefully by a new independent bank, in strict accord with capitalism's insistence upon a proper return to capital. Second, you should remind members of Congress that, in forthcoming elections, their refusal to support the legislation is equivalent to opposing the electoral mantra of "jobs, jobs, and jobs." By the time of the election dates of 2012 and 2016, opposing large-scale job creation will not go over well with voters.

President: Good observations. And yes, there really is a lot of common ground to unite both sides of the aisle behind your proposal. And as you keep stressing, there really is nothing either Left wing or Right wing about it.

In concluding this discussion, I want to go back to an intriguing claim you made early on. You said there are *two* very different ways in which you can deduce your proposed strategy from first principles. What is the second?

Economist: The second is altogether different. But first, be sure you understand how the earlier discussion proceeded from a set of Basic Assumptions. The type of deductive logic used was to list four principal policy goals, and then to determine whether a policy exists that satisfies all four. I have done that, and shown that such a policy exists. With a more formal macroeconomic model at hand, this result could be strengthened to show that the proposed solution is the only solution that can satisfy these particular criteria.

A Deeper Approach to Justifying the Proposal

President: What then is the second approach?

Economist: To understand the second way in which the proposed policy uniquely satisfies a few very basic axioms, advanced macroeconomic theory is needed, in particular the deductive logic utilized in the Arrow-Kurz book cited earlier. All I am going to do is to sketch the nature of the argument here, and to do so at a qualitative, not a quantitative level of analysis. This will suffice to express the main ideas, ideas that are very interesting indeed.

President: Can you please express these core ideas *very* simply?

Economist: Yes. Suppose you want to fly yourself and a friend to the moon and back in the shortest time possible. You have a good rocket to get you there. What do you do? First, you have to determine the best trajectory to get you there and back, where by "best" I mean "most fuel-efficient" trajectory. This is not easy, or course, since there are an infinite number of trajectories, each requiring a different amount of time and fuel. Second, you must figure out how to adjust the rocket's thrusters along the way so that the rocket sticks to the optimal trajectory once it has been identified.

President: What does this have to do with anything?

Economist: Hang on, please. Now consider an economic Philosopher King who views running his economy in a similar fashion. His goal is to target the maximal well-being of the citizenry (suitably defined), and to figure out how to use fiscal and monetary thrusters to help achieve maximal well-being. In particular, he must determine the size of deficits and surpluses in both the private and public sector, as well as the mix of private sector and public sector investments that maximizes well-being. What should the Philosopher King do? What policies will be optimal, given his goal?[7]

President: So optimally controlling a rocket ship to minimize fuel consumption is somehow analogous to my efforts to set economic policy on a course that avoids a Lost Decade and maximizes happiness? And you will now tell me that your main policy proposal is the only one that maximizes the well-being of the citizenry. Is that correct?

Economist: Yes. The principle basic assumption this time, as you suggest, is the maximization of well-being—a much more abstract axiom than concrete policy goals like reducing unemployment, raising growth, shrinking the deficit, and so forth. Moreover, you might be surprised to know that the analytical model required to solve the Philosopher King's problem is almost identical to that required by the captain of the rocket ship to determine a least-fuel trajectory.[8]

President: Is the concept of "maximizing the well-being of the people" well-defined, or is it a bit fuzzy?

Economist: One of the great successes in economics and philosophy during the past seven decades has been the clarification of exactly what this means, and even of how to measure it. The concept originated amongst the early British utilitarians such as Jeremy

Bentham, who proposed that government policies should be chosen so as to "maximize the greatest good of the greatest number." In more modern guise, this policy objective becomes, "maximize the aggregate satisfaction of all the people," where each person's "satisfaction" is measured by that person's *own* intensity of preferences for the alternative outcomes at stake.[9]

President: So what exactly is the link between this highly abstract objective and the policy proposals you have set forth? Does maximizing the greatest good truly imply your jobs-creating infrastructure investment plan, thereby justifying it from first principles, as you put it?

Economist: Yes it does, assuming a host of subsidiary assumptions are introduced to flesh out the model. And not only does it justify my program, but it also sheds new light upon why deficit spending on a very large scale will *sometimes* be socially optimal, for reasons far transcending Keynes' concept of boosting aggregate demand during recessions.

There are two steps in implementing the logic required of the Philosopher King. Just as the captain of the rocket ship must identify the least-time trajectory *and* determine the right setting of the control instruments (e.g., the thrusters) at each point in time, to remain on course, so must the Philosopher King.

Step 1: Determine the right trajectory of economic outcomes that are optimal (the satisfaction-maximizing time paths of consumption and of private and public sector investment).

Step 2: Identify the right setting of the government control knobs (choice of public investments, of tax rates, and of fiscal deficit levels) that is required to maximize public satisfaction. As in the example of the rocket ship, there will be a unique set of values for the control knobs at each point of time that will maximize public satisfaction.

President: That is quite a mouthful. Is there a graphic way of portraying all this?

Economist: Yes. Figures 2.4(a) and 2.4(b) should make all this quite clear. Please understand that any data appearing here are hypothetical. The analysis is purely illustrative.

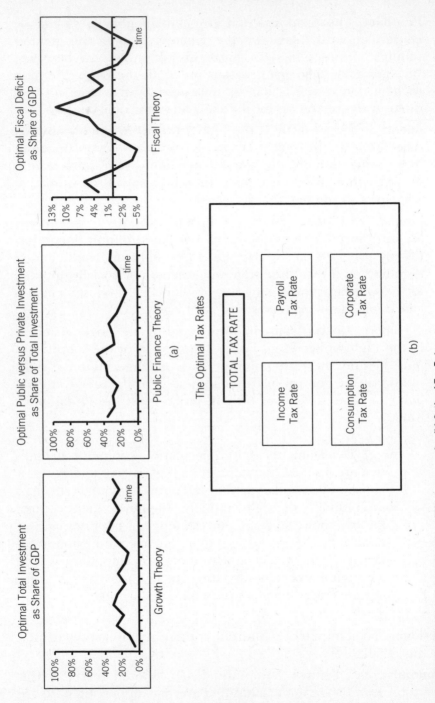

Figure 2.4 (a) Arrow-Kurz Unification of Macroeconomics (b) Optimal Tax Rates

Source: Strategic Economic Decisions, Inc.

To maximize welfare first requires solving simultaneously for the three optimal trajectories-over-time seen in Figure 2.4(a), as well as for the optimal tax rates shown in Figure 2.4(b). Arrow and Kurz showed why this is necessary, and how to do so. The first graph represents the optimal GDP-share of total investment spending (private and public). In solving for this, you also solve for the optimal share of consumption and savings. But this is not shown.

President: Does this first trajectory offer a way of showing that a nation may be saving and investing too much of GDP (like China), or too little of GDP (like the United States)—familiar criticisms of both nations?

Economist: Yes. There is an optimal in-between level of investment, one for each country. Traditional growth theory focused on determining this path. But prior to the Arrow-Kurz theory, no distinction was made between private sector investment and public sector investment. But such a distinction must be made: Both are crucial for public welfare (the right number of houses *and* the right amount of public transport). Yet the logic for determining the optimal mix of both is highly complex since the meaning of "high return private investment" is so different from "a high-return public investment."

President: Isn't that what the second trajectory in the middle graph is all about?

Economist: Yes. Here you must solve for the optimal share of private versus public investment, given the optimal GDP-share of total investment. Arrow and Kurz provided the logic to do so. This optimal share will differ across time as shown, since during some eras, returns are greatest to private sector investing, but during other eras, returns are greatest to public sector investing.

President: Aren't the two problems indicated in the first two graphs interdependent with each other? That is, wouldn't the determination of the optimal *total* share of investment spending (as opposed to consumption) depend on the *mix* of returns available in both the private and public arenas?

Economist: Yes, indeed. This is why you must solve for both trajectories simultaneously. Arrow and Kurz demonstrated how to do so. Note that you are not solving here for two optimal numbers, but rather for two optimal *trajectories* over time. Moreover, these trajectories are not "fixed," but rather are contingent upon how external "state" variables evolve over time. This complicates matters still further.[10]

President: Well, all this does seem to make sense, given how you explain it. There will be times when private investment seems most "needed," for example, young GIs returning from World War II all needing houses in which to rear their baby-boomer children. And there are times like today when there seems to be a surfeit of houses, and a dearth of good public transportation to move people around.

Economist: This is exactly the point, and you have given a good example that I will come back to.

President: And you will argue that we are right now at a juncture where higher returns (properly measured!) will accrue from massive public sector investment rather than from private sector investment, correct?

Economist: Yes, indeed, and this is true because of our deferred infrastructure maintenance over the past half-century, and because of our overinvestment in housing. Regrettably, the nation has acted in a way that fulfilled John Kenneth Galbraith's prediction of a nature showcasing "private splendor and public squalor."

Rethinking the Role of Deficit Spending from Scratch

President: How does a decision to run large government deficits fit into all this? The third and last graph of Figure 2.4(a) seems to focus on deficits.

Economist: Yes. This graph shows the optimal size of the government deficit over time as a share of GDP. The reason that fiscal deficits are part of the analysis is that public borrowing is sometimes *required* if social welfare is to be maximized. What is not shown (for the sake of simplicity) is that there is an analogous trajectory of private sector borrowing indicating the times when the private sector should run deficits versus surpluses. Moreover, the two different deficits/surpluses are interrelated at a deeper level. There will be times when the private sector *should* run a surplus that can fund a public sector deficit, and vice versa. Remember, the money to fund *any* deficit must come from somewhere as we noted in the context of equation (2.3). But let's avoid this complication here.

President: What does all this say to people who instinctively disapprove of *government* deficits?

Economist: It says: "Discard your prejudices against government deficits. To begin with, if you are philosophically prejudiced against public sector borrowing, no matter how high the rate of return might be, than you will logically be compelled to reject private sector deficits as well, since the roles of the two deficits are symmetrical in maximizing welfare, when properly understood." Equivalently, you could say: "To claim that government deficits are intrinsically bad is tantamount to telling families in the private sector that they should never take out a mortgage, since debt is bad. If they do not have enough saved up to buy a house entirely with cash when the children are growing up, then they should lump it and rent." A final way of expressing this is: "If you are the Philosopher King and you are attempting to maximize societal welfare, then you can do so only if the private and the public sectors borrow and save optimally over time. Their situations are symmetrical."

To be sure, excessive borrowing can be bad, and should be limited. This is achieved within the Arrow-Kurz framework by imposing constraints on the accumulation of debt over time (whether household or government debt). Thus, when the optimization required by the Arrow-Kurz logic is carried out, while there may be short periods when huge deficits are required, the overall accumulation of debt over time will *not* be allowed to exceed appropriate levels in either the private or public sector. Such constraints are needed because, as we are reminded over and over, excessive borrowing either by government or by households amounts to an externality, or public bad. You will read more on this in Chapter 4 when I examine the lessons of the global financial crisis of 2007–2009. I demonstrate that excessive leverage was the primary culprit, not "greed" or regulatory incompetence.

President: So all in all, what Professors Arrow and Kurz showed is that it is both necessary and possible to determine all three of the optimal paths sketched in your graph: the optimal level of investment spending over time, the optimal mix of private and public investment over time, and the optimal level of the fiscal deficit or surplus over time. And all three must be determined simultaneously because all three are interdependent. And everything here follows from the appealing principle of "maximizing the greatest good for the greatest number," so to speak. Is that it?

Economist: Yes, and that principle could also be dubbed "maximize efficiency" or "minimize waste." They are all one and the same.

President: But what's in your Figure 2.4(b)? How do taxes fit in here?

Economist: Oh, I forgot to mention this. It turns out that Arrow and Kurz accomplished even more. Remember, there are *two* steps involved in our overall problem, as I mentioned up front. The first is to determine the rocket's optimal trajectory to the moon and back, the three trajectories of Figure 2.4(a) in the case of economics. The second task is to determine the precise settings of the control instruments (the "thrusters") that make it possible to adhere to the optimal trajectories at each point along the way. The authors showed how to determine within economics the right setting of the control instruments needed to achieve this goal, that is, the right level of total taxation *and* the right mix of the different tax revenues available. This is indicated in Figure 2.4(b). Once again, these optimal tax rates must be determined simultaneously with the three trajectories of Figure 2.4(a).

The optimal total tax and the optimal composition of taxes will be dynamic, of course. These variables will be trajectories that change along the journey, and must be monitored and altered en route. Breaking further new ground, the authors determined the exact conditions under which a dynamical economic system *can* be optimally controlled, that is, if and when a suitable setting of the various tax rates exists.

The issue here is known as "macro-controllability," a branch of economics separate from public finance, fiscal policy, and growth theory. Arrow and Kurz extended the theory of controllability to incorporate these other three fields within it, and in doing so achieved perhaps the greatest synthesis or "unification" within macroeconomic theory that has ever been achieved. Yet because their book was necessarily mathematical, it remains largely unknown outside the hallowed halls of academia.

President: All this is mind-boggling to a noneconomist like myself, and is completely new. It gives new meaning to the concept that "everything depends upon everything else." You stated earlier that their work paves the way for a much deeper understanding of when and why very large deficits can sometimes be needed. Is there a deeper message lurking here about the appropriateness of deficit spending? After all, you are proposing to keep the U.S. fiscal deficit at today's record high level of 10 percent of GDP, at least as conventionally measured. Are Arrow and Kurz on the same track as Lord Keynes was in proposing deficit spending as a remedy for recessions? It is odd that you have not mentioned Keynes in all this.

When Very Large Deficits Are Justified: A Unification of the Arrow-Kurz and Keynesian Theories

Economist: There is a very good reason why Keynesian theory has not been mentioned. The Arrow-Kurz theory was set forth within a "classical" economic framework of full employment and no business cycles. Thus there is no need for anything Keynesian within it. The reason why there are deficit cycles that *look* Keynesian (as shown in the third graph) is because the optimal mix of private versus public sector investment returns fluctuates across time. This mix will sometimes call for greater investment spending (and hence borrowing up front) in the public sector and less in the private sector, and at other times it will call for the reverse. For example, there will be times when the private sector should borrow a lot for the mortgages of those returning home from war to build houses for their young families. There will be other times when higher returns are reaped by investing in deteriorating public infrastructure as opposed to more McMansions. This important "cycle of investment opportunities" can perfectly well coexist with a full employment economy free of business cycles.

President: So running deficits to pump up demand in business cycle downturns was not part of the Arrow-Kurz fiscal story at all?

Economist: No, it was not. But because of much more recent work by Kurz and others that extend "classical" economics to include fluctuating animal spirits and business cycles, their original theory can in principle be extended to include Keynesian concerns.

In this case, the optimal government deficit sketched in the third graph in Figure 2.4(a) will be large when animal spirits and hence private investment are low in a recession. Conversely, the fiscal deficit will be small or even negative when animal spirits and private investment are high. That would be purely Keynesian.

President: So can the two different rationales of Keynes and of Arrow-Kurz for running government deficits be combined?

Economist: Yes, and this is the main and final point to be raised. If someone asks: "Under what sets of circumstances will the public welfare be maximized by running *very* large fiscal deficits?" The answer is: "To maximize social welfare, the fiscal deficit should be very large if the returns to public investment are much higher than in private investment, *and also* if animal spirits in the private sector are flagging so that Keynesian cyclical stimulus is needed to increase aggregate demand." And *vice versa* for when there should be a significant fiscal surplus. All these relationships are symmetrical in that they work in reverse.

President: So you claim that this pair of circumstances justifying large deficits accurately describes the situation in the United States at the moment: The potential returns from infrastructure spending are large because of past neglect and because of new opportunities, *and* because animal spirits are poor throughout the private sector due to the global financial crisis, to 30 years of excessive binge-borrowing by households, to growing retirement worries, and to soaring medical costs.

Economist: Correct, but do not forget we are talking about large "good" deficits that arise from productive spending—not from bad spending that further burdens our children with more debt. Remember, one of the four main objectives in preventing a Lost Decade must be to calm the bond markets. At present, this is not being done. And this is something that neither Keynes nor Arrow and Kurz discussed. It is a new constraint.

For any economists who advise you and who might be interested, the argument I just made as to when very large deficits are needed is sketched more formally in the Appendix that follows. I included this since my arguments here will be unfamiliar to most economists.

Thank you, Mr. President, for listening to my proposal. I hope I have fulfilled my principal goal: to demonstrate the existence of win-win policies to prevent a Lost Decade, policies that are consistent with all four desiderata laid out at the start, and that are justified more fundamentally by the single axiom of "maximizing human welfare." Ultimately, my message is one of optimism: There exists a policy solution sufficiently win-win in nature to break partisan gridlock on the entire deficit spending issue that has now has paralyzed debate in the country. It really is possible for you to have your cake and eat it too, Mr. President.

Appendix: The Case for Very Large Deficits and/or Surpluses

Consider an economy with public goods and externalities of the A-K (Arrow-Kurz) variety. Suppose private consumers and investors have the objective of selecting state-dependent policies that maximize their expected utility. And suppose their government watchdogs select policies that maximize societal felicity, that is, the sum of utilities across people.

Next let us introduce two cycles into this optimization model. The first cycle is a Markov process consisting of two dominating states, A and B. Let state A denote a world in which all consumers possess a McMansion, yet public transportation is so dilapidated that citizens living in these dream houses cannot get to work without an undue waste of time and energy. In state B, the situation is reversed and recalls Japan in 1970: There were bullet trains that were the wonder of the world, but the Japanese lived in small houses lacking basic amenities. Then the solution to the Arrow-Kurz optimization problem will be to shift resources from the private to the public sector when the system is in state A where transportation is needed, and private housing is not. And this transfer will be reversed when the system is in state B where private housing is needed, and public transportation is not.

Now let us add a simple two-state Keynesian business cycle to the Markov model. There are now two new states C and D. State C denotes flagging animal spirits and recession (e.g., slack private demand), whereas state D represents robust animal spirits and a private-sector boom. Recall that there are no business cycles in the neoclassical A-K model. We can then construct an nth order Markov process consisting jointly of the investment-cycle state *and* the animal-spirits state. In this model, the system will migrate at any point in time to one of the four possible joint states: AC, AD, BC, or BD.

When this A-K model is suitably constrained and optimized over the relevant space of policy functions, utilizing a generalization of the Pontryagin maximum principle from optimal control theory, then social welfare will be maximized by running very large public sector deficits when joint state AC is visited (high returns from public transport investment and a low level of animal spirits in the private sector), whereas a very large fiscal surplus will be optimal when joint state BD is at hand (high returns from private-sector housing investment and a high level of animal spirits).

This model provides completely new support to the concept that large fiscal deficits are indeed optimal in certain environments, and are required for investment-cycle reasons far transcending Keynesian animal-spirits reasons. Importantly, there is a duality whereby, in some states of the system, the household will be a net borrower (as when everyone after a war needs a mortgage to buy a house in which to raise a family), and in other states the household will be a net lender. But the same is true of the public sector, which itself will run deficits in states where it is utility-maximizing to do so, and surpluses in other states of the system. There seems to be little or no awareness of this private/public sector symmetry.

In this regard, the great achievement of the A-K contribution in my eyes was to dissolve the putative difference between "macro" (fiscal) and "micro" economics, and to show how there is one and only one fundamental problem in all of economics: to identify and implement an optimal allocation of *all* resources (private and public) across time so as to maximize public well-being.

Resolving the Entitlements Spending Crisis

How to Drive Health-Care Spending Down while Increasing Access

A century from now, historians and sociologists analyzing the likely decline of the West between 2000 and 2050 will understand what really took place, and why. At present, we do not, as we focus merely on symptoms of decline such as rising debt loads, cutbacks in basic services, and policy gridlock. Our descendants will understand the deeper story that played out, a story of those internal contradictions that undermined liberal democratic capitalism, just as internal contradictions of a different kind discredited communism between 1960 and 1990.

In the case of communism, the contradictions stemmed from system-wide incentives that made it rational for individuals to act in a way that promoted economic decline rather than growth. In the case of liberal democracies, the contradictions stem from incentives for politicians facing reelection to forever mortgage the long-run future. They do so by promising constituents ever-higher levels of benefits that can never be paid for. The true fault in this case lies neither with "craven politicians" nor with "greedy voters." Rather it stems from the overall incentive structure of the political system, a structure that will lead to the demise of the welfare state as we know it unless current policies are changed.

This chapter does not focus on this deep political philosophical story, a story that Chapter 6 will touch upon. But it squarely confronts the entitlements spending crisis which lies at the heart of it, and which will dwarf all other economic challenges facing most western democracies between 2020 and 2050. I restrict myself to the case study of the United States, and address what can be done to salvage its long-run fiscal integrity during a period when some 79 million baby boomers cease contributing to the kitty and start drawing it down.

Almost all my emphasis is on health-care spending, since this by far is the dominant challenge as compared to Social Security. But Social Security is reviewed as well. The good news is that it is possible to solve the entitlements spending problem, just as we saw in the preceding chapter that a Lost Decade can be prevented in the shorter run. Moreover, the policy solutions that I propose are once again win-win in nature and, since they can appeal to both the Right and the Left, they should dampen today's Dialogue of the Deaf and break today's policy gridlock.

The Broader Picture

Whereas Chapter 2 focused on resolving the Lost Decade prospect of the period 2011–2020, the present chapter focuses on the much longer-run period of 2020–2050 when a far greater crisis will engulf the United States. If spending on Medicare and Social Security is not reined in, the cumulative unfunded liabilities in the range of $40–$55 trillion will sink the United States financially before the middle of the century. The actual size of these liabilities will depend upon unknowns such as future interest and inflation rates, economic growth, and life expectancy. This crisis is perhaps the only truly systemic risk acknowledged by both sides in today's Dialogue of the Deaf. The data in Figure 3.1 present an optimistic forecast in which entitlements double only as a share of GDP. Other forecasts show the total rising to over 25 percent of GDP if health-care expenditures are not reined in. In looking at these data, do not confuse the government health-care costs shown with *overall* health-care spending, private and public. The latter figure is now in excess of 18 percent of GDP and could well rise to 35 percent by mid-century.

This crisis is even worse than most concede because of the collateral damage it implies for U.S. military capability. Promises of social benefits win votes, whereas promises of increased military preparedness do not. The Obama administration has already begun canceling a number of leading-edge military programs, such as the F-22 fighter, for budgetary reasons. In the space program, things have even reached the point where the United States must now ask

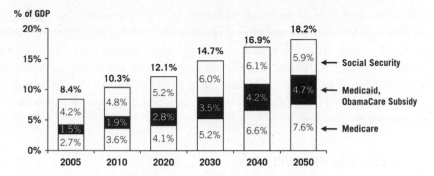

Figure 3.1   Entitlement Spending Will Almost Double as a Share of GDP by 2050

Spending on Medicare, Medicaid, and Social Security will soar as 79 million baby boomers retire and health-care costs climb. Total spending on federal health-care programs will triple.
Source: Congressional Budget Office, 2011 Long-Term Budget Outlook.

permission from the Russians to ferry our astronauts into space, since we have now terminated the space shuttle.

Yet these cuts to date are nothing compared to what will occur when the entitlements deficit begins to hit hard after 2018. Worse, China has recently made its long-run military and economic ambitions abundantly clear. Its officially acknowledged growth rate of defense spending is 12.6 percent. The unofficial rate is apparently 14 percent. U.S. disarmament will almost certainly embolden China further. Should we pare U.S. defense spending and disarm as most European nations did in order to fund their cradle-to-grave welfare states, will we not behold Chinese warships patrolling the coastlines of Brazil, India, Africa, and even the United States? Unlike many other nations, China will have a putative reason to do so, namely to "protect" its massive infrastructure and resource investments already underway in most corners of the earth.

In the first part of the chapter, I propose an unconventional solution to the runaway health-care spending crisis. This is the only possible solution that leads to much greater access to health care *and* to an overall reduction in health-care spending as a percentage of GDP. This very strong claim does not merely represent my opinion, but rather is a deduction proven formally in Appendix A. In the second and final part of the chapter, I discuss Social Security. However, most of the attention in this chapter is placed upon health-care spending for three reasons. First, the projected red ink from such spending dwarfs that of Social Security. The numbers really are shocking. Second, solving the problem of health-care spending is inherently much more difficult, both economically and politically, and thus requires more insight. In health care, a product is being produced, distributed, and consumed, while in the case of Social Security, nothing is produced or consumed; all that is at stake is how to resolve the cash flow difficulties arising from the payment of a national annuity.

Inherent Complexity of Health Care

The third reason for the focus on health care is that the nature of the product is highly complex and different from any other product, for reasons first pointed out by the Stanford University economist Kenneth Arrow in a landmark 1963 paper on the economics of health care.[1] Illnesses arrive randomly and usually entail big expenses. Thus, to transfer the risks involved, costs must be paid by some form of third-party payer, whether private insurance companies or government. Worse, there are "externalities," "public goods," and "moral hazard" aspects of health care that imply that the private sector cannot produce the required products and services efficiently on its own.

The government thus must be involved in the production and distribution of health care, as much as many wish this were not the case. These complexities along with the huge financial stakes involved have transformed health-care reform into the Spaghetti Bolognese of public policy problems. It is so complex that virtually no one has figured out how to disentangle the contentious issues involved in order to arrive at a convincing set of reforms.

Policy advocates of different persuasions have taken advantage of this confusion to press their own particular agendas. Predictably, they cherry-pick data to support their own biased objectives. Hence, on Monday we read a convincing essay about how the "efficiency" of the Cleveland model of health-care provision provides the right template for a national solution. Then on Tuesday we read that tort reform is what is truly needed. On Wednesday we read again about the need to abandon the traditional fee-for-service approach. On Thursday, we read about the inevitability of health-care rationing, and how poor people served by Medicaid will face long waits for third-rate services. The same article will deal with the "inevitability" of death squads of one kind or another limiting our right to life. On Friday, we read about the potential role of nurse-aides to alleviate the problem of the looming shortage of doctors that is increasingly being acknowledged.

Distinguishing the Forest from the Trees

What is missing is any articulation of the distinction between the forest and the trees of health-care reform. Think of the trees here as those myriad micro-issues just cited (e.g., the desirability of the Cleveland model), and the forest as those twin macro-issues of overall access to health care and total expenditure. How does each micro-issue impact overall access and cost? Even if a given micro-proposal sounds good, shouldn't it be required to pass a test as to whether it increases access and reduces total expenditure? After all, these *are* the two societal objectives that matter. Yet we rarely see an article in which micro reforms are persuasively linked to macro objectives. There is no micro–macro consistency. Worse, the complexity of the system ensures that, whereas untold numbers of lobbying groups press for micro reforms of many stripes, almost no one represents the interests of the whole—the citizenry keen on improved access and reduced expenditures. After all, it is *their* standard of living that will collapse if costs continue to soar.

This is a good example of the point that the late Mancur Olson stresses in his *Rise and Decline of Nations*. As empires get rich, special interest groups become so entrenched that there is no one left representing the collective interest of the people as a whole. So has it become in health care. So politicized are the claims and counterclaims of the individual interest groups, and so lost are the people as a whole that paralysis and confusion set in. Consider those polls showing that about half the American people support ObamaCare, and half do not, while almost all admit that they do not understand it at all.

This recalls a theorem in statistics showing that "complete ignorance" about a matter is best represented by assigning equal odds (in this case 50/50 odds) to all possible outcomes.[2] This says it all: The greatest debate on any major policy reform in many decades was so poorly communicated by the rival interest groups involved that the American people ended up in a state of complete ignorance. What an indictment of today's Dialogue of the Deaf!

The approach adopted in this chapter is altogether different, and shoots for complete clarity, not confusion. We deliberately ascend to that level of abstraction required to address *the* fundamental question about health care that lies at the heart of today's debate: How can the increased quantity of health-care services that will be needed by an aging population be provided without the nation going broke in the process? Or, equivalently, can we enjoy both increased "access" to health care in a meaningful sense of that word, along with control of total expenditures far more ambitious than anything else proposed to date? Or is this simply not possible? Is there an inescapable trade-off between these two objectives?

The Solution

The answer I deduce is that both goals are achievable provided that we adhere to a *single* overall policy requirement as we attack the myriad of policies required in reforming the overall health-care system. The requirement is that the overall (aggregate) supply of health-care services must increase at a rate faster than the growth of demand. At the micro level, this requires that each particular reform (e.g., medical tort reform) must conform to this supply-greater-than-demand goal in its own market. I am being a bit sloppy here because, as will be seen, the words supply and demand are famously ambiguous. The correct statement is that the "supply curve" must shift outward faster than the "demand curve" in the sense of elementary Econ 101. Don't panic! The idea here is really very simple, and it will be explained later with the help of some very simple graphs.

Remarkably, this one requirement is necessary and sufficient for the delivery of far more services to more people, and for a significant *decrease* in total health-care expenditures rise a share of GDP. This will be seen to be a theorem, not mere speculation. Conversely, if this supply-greater-than-demand requirement is violated over the long run, total expenditures go to infinity. In this case either the nation will veer toward bankruptcy, or else health care will become very severely rationed as it already is in many other nations. It will be shown that ObamaCare violates this supply/demand requirement due to the primacy it places on demand as opposed to supply. I will derive these surprising results from three Basic Assumptions further on, using a simple supply/ demand model drawn from Econ 101. An elementary geometric proof will be given in the main text, which any reader will understand. A formal proof will be found in Appendix B at the back of the book.

The awesome power of deductive logic will thus play an important role in delivering excellent news on the health-care front, just as it did in Chapter 2, where I deduced in two different ways that the United States need not suffer a Lost Decade. Remember yet again that a principal rationale for this book is to demonstrate the true power of precisely this kind of reasoning—reasoning so clear and compelling as to turn down the volume of today's Dialogue of the Deaf, and to arrive at consensus, not gridlock.

Anyone doubting the logical possibility that we can have our cake and eat it, too, in health-care reform should reflect upon what happens in sectors of the economy other than health care. We produce more food of comparable quality at a cost representing a lower share of GDP than in the past, far more phone calls for a lower share of GDP, more computers, more consumer electronic products, and so forth. The reason why in all these cases is that the supply curve shifted outward faster than the demand curve over time, when these concepts are properly understood. *Why should health care be any different?* It need not be, for reasons to be seen, and it is astonishing to me that this possibility was never discussed during the entire health-care debate. All parties involved incorrectly assumed that, with rising demand for health-care services, total national expenditure would have to continue to rise, just as it has in the past. This assumption was incorrect.

What is also incorrect is the assumption that one goal of health-care reform should be "cost control," or "bending the cost curve," as many put it. This is misleading. It is total expenditure control that matters, not cost control. Success in the former guarantees success in the latter. But the converse is *not* true, and many proposed cost controls (e.g., reducing what Medicare pays surgeons for a given procedure) will be seen to *increase* total expenditure due to the law of unintended consequences. Surgeons unhappy with reduced reimbursements will switch fields, causing supply to contract and total expenditure to rise. This too will be demonstrated graphically.

The Ideal: More Health-Care Services, Lower Total Expenditures

I start off with a brief overview of the U.S. health-care debate. This overview is quite different from most others in that it analyzes the debate in terms of its implications for the future supply and demand of health-care services. Particular emphasis is placed on ObamaCare in this regard, and the specific provisions of the 2010 legislation are summarized, because there is widespread ignorance of the true content of the new law. Next, our main result is established on how to reform health care. Three Basic Assumptions (axioms) are introduced that "almost anybody" would wish a good system to satisfy. A simple supply/demand model is then fleshed out.

This model demonstrates graphically how any health-care system consistent with the fundamental supply-greater-than-demand policy requirement cited previously will satisfy all three Basic Assumptions. ObamaCare as currently formulated is then shown to violate either one or two of the three Basic Assumptions. The irony here is that President Obama himself implicitly endorsed all three assumptions in stating his own health-care reform goals. What went wrong? Poor economic logic won the day.

A Supply/Demand Assessment of ObamaCare

President Obama's health-care initiatives have focused on controlling exploding health-care costs and improving insurance access for low- and middle-income individuals and families who either do not have insurance or struggle to pay for it. Few would argue with the merit of either goal. Currently, an estimated 50 million Americans are without health insurance—a number that is expected to balloon to 60 million by 2015 without reform.[3] At the same time, the United States spends 50 percent more on health care per capita than the next highest-spending country, yet ranks 50th in total life expectancy. Furthermore, the growth rate of such medical expenditures is out of control. While the overall price level increased 17 percent from 2000 to 2006, health-care premiums increased 87 percent over the same period.[4] Such escalating health-care costs have thus made health-care reform essential to future national solvency.

On March 23, 2010, President Obama signed the Patient Protection and Affordable Care Act into law. The new law, and changes that have been made to the law by subsequent legislation, clearly focuses on provisions to expand coverage *and* control health-care costs. First, via new health insurance exchanges, 48 million Americans will be able to purchase affordable health coverage at lower rates. Second, an estimated 5.6 million Americans with pre-existing conditions will no longer be denied insurance—banning such discrimination completely by 2014. Third, tax credits for small businesses and for individuals will help Americans pay for insurance. Specifically, by 2014, nearly 60 percent of small businesses will be eligible for tax cuts of up to 50 percent of their insurance premiums. Additionally, middle-class individuals who do not receive insurance through employment may receive significant tax credits toward the new health insurance exchanges. Finally, health-care reform will prevent personal bankruptcies by capping annual out-of-pocket costs for families who receive insurance through the exchanges or a small business.

On a second front, the Act introduces a number of measures to control medical expenditures. But a tension always existed between these two goals of increasing coverage and controlling costs. First, expanded insurance coverage will result in a sudden surge of demand by millions of previously uninsured Americans and thus *raise* the total cost of health care in America, other things being equal. Second, while measures to control costs were included, such as reduced reimbursements to physicians for Medicare services rendered, the provisions to do so were problematic from the start. For example, the legislation's concept of cost control is self-contradictory because most cost-control measures end up restricting supply, which in turn not only raises prices but also generates rationing of care. Third, the new Act provided little of what was actually needed, namely a radical increase in the supply of services that both lowers costs and meets increased demand without rationing.

Since almost all public discussion has centered on the demand side of health-care reform (greater access to insurance), as does ObamaCare itself, and since there is little appreciation of the critical role of supply, what is needed up front is a *supply-side assessment* of health care, pre- and post-ObamaCare. In this section, I start off by reviewing several supply-side challenges to the health-care market prior to the new Act. While much of the blame in Washington for escalating health-care costs in the past has centered on rapacious private insurance companies and greedy doctors, supply-side developments played a role as well: a grouping physician shortage, an inefficient distribution of medical services, and a complete failure to automate services that should have been automated long ago.

Next, I offer a summary of how the new Act impacts both the demand and supply-side challenges. The Act's unfortunate bias toward boosting demand much more than supply is identified. Finally, I introduce three Basic Assumptions that a good health-care system must satisfy, and from these deduce a general solution to the entire problem.

Pre-Act Supply-Side Challenges

Before assessing how the new Act addresses health-care supply shortages, it is important to understand the supply-side challenges that already existed before the bill was passed. Two recent research reports on U.S. health-care supply discuss this issue in depth. First, in November of 2008, Michael J. Dill and Edward S. Salsberg of the Association of American Medical Colleges (AAMC) wrote an extensive report outlining the ongoing and escalating physician supply shortage in the United States. In their report, "The Complexities of Physician Supply and Demand: Projections Through 2025," Dill and Salsberg recommended a 30 percent increase in U.S. medical school enrollment and an expansion of graduate medical education (GME) positions to accommodate faster growth in the demand for medical services.[5]

Such recommendations were based on "recognition of factors likely to influence future physician supply and demand, such as the aging of the U.S. population and the physician workforce." Indeed, according to their research, which assumed a continuation of current supply and demand patterns (i.e., their analysis did not factor in Obama's health-care reform and its impact on demand), the United States would, at best, have a shortage of 124,000 physicians by 2025.

Dill and Salsberg then predicted the impact of these shortages on the health-care system. In particular, they cited the prospect of much longer patient wait times, shorter visit times with physicians, and, in some cases, loss of access altogether. Additionally, given the mounting evidence of health-care quality variation based on geography and socioeconomics, they suggest that more rural and poorer areas of the country, especially in the South and West, would suffer the most under existing supply and demand patterns. Again, their research took place prior to 2009 and thus did not consider the impact of increased demand for health services from the new Act.

A second research report, prepared on behalf of the Physician Foundation and directed to President Obama in September 2009, "Physicians and Their Practices under Health-Care Reform," reinforces several of the AAMC's earlier findings on supply shortages while overlaying the impact of increased demand from the forthcoming health-care act. In this report, the Physician Foundation calls upon the President and Congress to assist with the expansion of medical schools, to lift the Medicare graduate medical education cap, and to consider shortening the length of medical training required.[6] The report also discusses the issue of the lack of primary care and rural physicians. Their shorter-term recommendations include the need for increased investments in technology and information services to improve the productivity of medical services of all kinds.

Summary of the New Act

I now want to discuss how ObamaCare has impacted the supply/demand imbalance cited earlier. Did it improve matters, or exacerbate the preexisting imbalance? But before reading on, you have a choice. You can either continue straight on, or else you can first consult Appendix A at the back of the book. Appendix A will permit you to review many specific provisions of the new Act in bulletized form. Surprisingly few people who discuss health care seem to understand these provisions. I have made this summary different from other summaries I have seen by factoring it into two complementary parts: first, ObamaCare's impact on demand, and second, its impact on supply. The material in Appendix A will deepen and reinforce what now follows.

Ineffectiveness of the New Act's Provisions for Supply

Given the detailed supply-versus-demand provisions of the new Act summarized in Appendix A, and given the pre-Act supply-side challenges cited earlier, where do matters now stand post-Act? Three serious issues arise in this regard.

Supply/Demand Imbalance To begin with, the new legislation is very much biased toward policies that increase demand for health-care services, at the expense of initiatives to increase future supply. More specifically, in contrast to the Act's provision for increased demand ("access") reinforced by concrete requirements and penalties for both individuals and companies regarding insurance mandates, the provisions for increasing supply of health-care services are surprisingly vague and long-term oriented. Indeed, when Edward Salsberg of the AAMC, coauthor of the 2008 study cited earlier, was recently asked about this matter, he replied:

> The bill does not do a lot to *directly* raise the supply of health-care professionals. It has a number of provisions that might lead to a change in specialty and geographical distribution, such as the incentives for primary care and the changes in the National Health Services Corp. program. The Health Resources and Services Administration has also been creative in providing additional funding to increase primary care and support for education. In the longer term, it may be the strengthening of the workforce data collection and the establishment of the new National Workforce Commission that will help raise awareness of the need to increase the education and training pipeline.[7]

Salsberg's key insight lies in the recognition that the new bill does not do much to "directly" raise the supply of health-care professionals. While the demand provisions have teeth (laws, penalties, and fines), the supply provisions at best constitute a wish list. The difference is stark and disturbing.

Reimbursement Incentive Effects The new Act is silent on the disincentive effects that physician reimbursement policies have on the supply of health-care services. Professor Tyler Cowen of George Mason University, who specializes on the supply side of the health-care issue, is convinced that the new Act will necessarily result in extensive rationing of services. As he wrote in the *New York Times* on December 11, 2010:

> The underlying problem is that doctors are reimbursed at different rates, depending upon whether they see a patient with private insurance, Medicare, or Medicaid. As demand increases

relative to supply, many doctors are likely to turn away patients whose coverage would pay the lower rates. Let's see how this works. Medicare is the major federal health program for the elderly, who vote at high rates and are politically influential, and so it is relatively well financed. Medicaid, which serves poorer people, is paid for partly by state governments, and the poor have less political clout than the elderly, so it is less well financed.

Depending on the state and on the malady, it is common for Medicaid to reimburse doctors at only 40 percent versus 80 percent the rate of Medicare. Private insurance pays more than either. A result is that physicians often make Medicaid patients wait, or refuse to see them altogether. Medicare patients are also beginning to face lines, as doctors increasingly prefer patients with private insurance. Access to health care will become problematic, and not only because the population is aging and demand is rising.

Unfortunately, the new health-care legislation is likely to speed this process. Under the new law, tens of millions of additional Americans will receive coverage, through Medicaid or private insurance. The new recipients of private insurance will gain the most, but people previously covered through Medicaid will lose. . . . If you hear of a new solution to the health care puzzle, put aside the politics and instead think through the endgame. *Ask not about the rhetoric, but rather about the reimbursement rates.*

The Shortage of Physicians Crisis A topic that is rarely discussed by those proposing reforms to health care is the looming shortage of doctors. This is extremely important for the coming explosion of health-care spending since nearly 60 percent of worldwide health-care spending is accounted for by the clinical workforce. Looking forward, a mass exodus of currently practicing physicians will occur at the very time when demand explodes due to baby boomer retirement. More specifically, more than one-third of doctors practicing today are over 55 and plan to retire within 20 years. Additionally, the shortage of doctors will be particularly acute in cardiology, oncology, and geriatrics, all of which serve the swelling numbers of the elderly. You might think that the sharp increase in demand that is predicted would trigger a corresponding increase in supply. But this standard economic assumption does not hold true in the health-care sector. The supply of doctors is highly regulated as are so many other aspects of health care.

The AAMC estimates that the United States could face a shortage of between 124,000 and 159,000 doctors by 2025. Yet this estimate does not take into account the disincentive effects on the supply of physician services due to the reimbursement rate problem just discussed. For the nonrich on Medicare and Medicaid, the heightened rationing of services this shortage portends could reach crisis proportions. But the situation is even worse. Compounding the wave of retirements that are coming is the fact that the number of medical school graduates choosing to pursue a career in family medicine has already fallen by 27 percent since 2002, and this decline could well accelerate. The number of general surgeons in the United States has decreased by 26 percent since 1981. Emergency rooms are already bursting to capacity, and there is a shortage of on-call specialists. The statistics are frightening indeed.[8]

Inexplicably, the new health-care Act gives little heed to this shortage of doctors, and fails to propose policies to redress it. In fact, the new Act exacerbates the physician-supply crisis by cutting funding for training new doctors. In a January 19, 2011 *Wall Street Journal* article, Dr. Herbert Pardes, CEO of New York-Presbyterian Hospital, explained how. To begin with, the government began to foster a future doctor shortage in 1996 when Congress capped the number of new doctors Medicare would pay to train, a practice that continues to this day.

> Training new doctors has substantial costs because of all they must learn and how carefully they must be supervised. Without Medicare reimbursements, many hospitals could not afford to maintain these critical training programs. . . . Recently, the President's National Commission on Fiscal Responsibility and Reform proposed cutting Medicare funding to train doctors even further, by $60 billion through 2020. If this cut is enacted, the doctor shortage would get far worse. . . . We cannot insure 32 million more people and cut funding to train doctors when one-third of all doctors are over age 55 and plan to retire.

But there are solutions, as Professor Cowen also pointed out in his *New York Times* column: "We could go further by giving greater scope to nurse practitioners, admitting more immigrant doctors, reforming malpractice law, and allowing cheap, retail Wal-Mart medical care, all to increase access and affordability. Yet these changes do not seem to be in the offing, so access is likely to decline." Note that all these policies are supply-side by nature.

Many other approaches exist for redressing the coming supply-side crisis, notably health care delivered by expert systems, and these will be discussed later in this chapter. For the moment, what we have seen is that the new Act has virtually no supply-side teeth. At best, the Act implicitly encourages increased supply via the elimination of "inefficiencies" over time. Haven't you heard that promise before coming from Washington? Overall, what is striking about ObamaCare is its asymmetrical focus on expanded demand at the expense of expanded supply. What can be done to remedy matters?

A Supply-Side Solution to the Health-Care Crisis

It will now become clear why I have analyzed today's status quo through the lens of supply and demand. It turns out that, unless the proper dynamics of future demand and supply growth are given primacy of place in health-care reform, no solution to the crisis is possible. But when a proper supply/demand perspective is adopted, a lasting and workable solution to the health-care challenge can be identified. But what exactly *is* a "proper perspective" in this context?

The concept is somewhat abstract, and will require a quick review of some *very* basic Econ 101. With this review in hand, our main result follows: a derivation of the overarching supply-greater-than-demand policy requirement that a health-care system must satisfy if it is to be consistent with our three Basic Assumptions. We will utilize this policy requirement to arrive at some concrete proposals that can resolve today's health-care crisis in a truly win-win manner. Incidentally, it is in this last section that concrete *micro*-policy proposals such as tort reform and enhanced automation of services can be properly appraised for their macro value.

Review of the Law of Supply and Demand

While most of us assume that we understand the simple concepts of supply and demand, we really do not, as they are actually quite subtle. The late Paul Samuelson of MIT (America's first Nobel laureate in economics) always stressed this point.

To appreciate this, suppose that you want to predict the future price of widgets. Suppose you believe that, because of new consumer trends, demand will rise from 200 million units this year to 300 million next year. Given this development, you intuitively conclude that the price of widgets will rise dramatically. But wait: Didn't I learn in Econ 101 that *supply must always equal demand* at any market equilibrium? But if this is true, then won't supply also have to increase to 300 million units to equal the demand forecast? But if both supply and demand rise in tandem, why would the price need to rise at all? Confused? You are in good company!

What the true law of supply and demand predicts will happen is that both supply and demand will increase to some output level lying between 200 and 300 million units, say 250 million. Price for its part will also rise, but less than you originally suspected. Why will it rise? Because on the one hand, a higher price is required in order to encourage higher supply (up to 250 million from the initial production level of 200 million). On the other hand, a higher price is needed to encourage reduced demand (down from 300 to 250 million). This is how the new market equilibrium output of 250 million is achieved. You now understand supply/demand/ price somewhat better, but you are still somewhat confused. In particular, you don't know how to predict which of an infinity of market outcomes will occur because you do not know how to unscramble supply from demand, analyze each separately, and then put them back together. How would you predict an output of 250 million as opposed to 230 or 280 million in our example?

To fully understand what is happening, you must make *the giant leap* required to make sense of all markets, and of much basic economics. More specifically, you must abandon the intuitive urge to think of changes in price or quantity in terms of numbers, and the tendency to forecast these numbers. For this will get you nowhere, as you have just seen. Rather, you must think more abstractly about what economists call supply and demand functions, or "curves," and try to forecast how each *curve* will change for the particular product and time horizon you are analyzing. The matter is summarized in Figures 3.2(a) and 3.2(b), which appear in the first chapter of any Econ 101 textbook.

Figure 3.2(a) simply defines "market equilibrium" price and quantity as the point E where the supply curve and the demand curve intersect. Of course, the very concept of a supply and demand curve is itself quite subtle, since such curves do not in fact exist

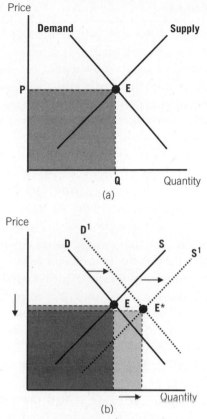

Figure 3.2   (a) Supply and Demand Curves—Depicting a Market Equilibrium E (b) Supply and
Demand Curves—Depicting a Change in Equilibrium from E to E*

except as hypothetical constructs! To understand why recall that a
given supply curve specifies how the quantity supplied will change
as prices change. The same holds true for a given demand curve. The
construct is hypothetical since, at any given point in time, there will
be only *one* price and *one* quantity that you can observe. Thus, all other
points on a supply (or demand) curve will represent what you think
the quantity supplied (demanded) *would* be for each different possible price. Each curve is hypothetical in this sense. One last point:
Recall that the supply curve usually slopes upward, indicating that
higher prices encourage greater output. Conversely, the demand
curve slopes downward, indicating that higher prices discourage
consumption.

How to Forecast Price Changes

Figure 3.2(b) sketches how you might ideally forecast a change in market equilibrium from E to E*. It is deceptively simple: just make your best forecast as to how each of the two curves will shift (and the reasons behind both shifts are usually unrelated), and then take note of the new point of intersection E*. This will be your best forecast of future price and quantity, generated by a prediction of how two hypothetical constructs will shift. *This is the true meaning of the law of supply and demand.* It rubs in that you cannot forecast future changes in price or quantity without taking both supply and demand properly into account. This is done by representing each in terms of curves (functions), not numbers.

Samuelson's point was that, while most students may learn all this in their studies, they soon forget it. Hence in the real world, you regularly encounter misleading predictions as to how "prices will rise because of soaring demand," as if supply plays no role, or "prices will fall because of a glut of supply," as if demand plays no role, or "health-care cost controls will reduce health-care expenditures," as if most cost controls do not possess incentive effects that reduce supply and hence raise prices and expenditures. No wonder most future price forecasts are so poor! The failure to consider the mutually intersecting roles of supply and demand is absent from almost all discussions about health-care reform, dominated by their populist emphasis on "more access for everyone."

Why Most Supply/Demand Analysis Is so Poorly Implemented in Practice

Even those who do understand the basic points just raised do a poor job in applying the law of supply and demand in real-world forecasting applications. Why is this true? I think there are two basic reasons. First, in most real-world applications, people are frightened off by the statistical challenge of "estimating" the location of a given market's supply and demand curves, and then of predicting how and why each curve will shift over the forecast period. Doing so is difficult, whether at an intuitive or at a more formal level of analysis.[9] Most policy analysts do not know how to do so, and thus bypass such analysis in practice. Nonetheless, in an issue of great national importance like health care, it *must* be carried out lest erroneous forecasts result, and bad policies be adopted.

A second reason that we rarely see supply/demand curve analysis in policy papers—and never in newspapers or magazines—stems from the fact that the very concept of a supply or demand "curve" is abstract and counterintuitive. As stated previously, this is because any such curve is in effect a hypothetical construct specifying what quantity *would* be supplied/demanded at any and every price. This reality intimidates many analysts.

Interestingly enough, I have looked for years to find a college economics curriculum with a course on price forecasting. But I have never seen one! Now what does that tell you about the extent of economic literacy when the behavior of price changes, from oil to wheat to health care, is front-page news all over the world? We all talk about and speculate on prices, but know little about how they will change, and why. This offers yet another example of the price paid for the absence of deductive logic in public policy dialogue.[10]

Using Supply/Demand Analysis to Forecast Total Expenditure

Most supply/demand models are used to predict what will happen to price. If we believe the demand curve will shift out to the right in a market, while the supply curve will remain where it is, we can learn from the model how much price will rise, which is what we want to know. We also learn that the quantity produced at equilibrium will increase, but that is usually of no interest. Now in our health-care analysis, we wish to focus on a third variable that is rarely discussed, namely changes in the *total expenditure* implied by the market equilibrium. Total expenditure is just the arithmetic *product* of the two coordinates P and Q at the equilibrium point where supply equals demand, as we see in Figure 3.3. That is, total expenditure will be $P \times Q$. In a soft-drink market, if Q is 40 million bottles, and P is $2 per bottle, then total expenditure is $40 \times \$2 = \$80$ million.

Geometrically, this product is simply the *area* (length times width) of the rectangle defined by the dotted lines stemming from the equilibrium point. And as we see in Figure 3.3, it is possible to compare the change of total expenditure by simply comparing the areas of the two rectangles corresponding to the "before" and "after" equilibrium points E and E*. We will exploit this fact in depth in what follows. This completes the review of those simple supply-and-demand concepts that we will utilize.

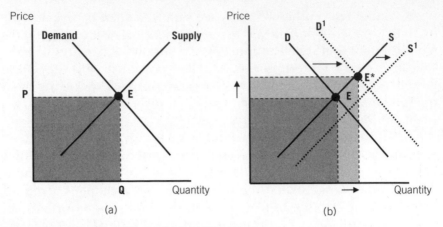

Figure 3.3   Computing and Comparing Total Expenditure

Three Basic Assumptions for an Optimal Health-Care System

The three Basic Assumptions are assumptions that almost anyone on any side of the health-care debate would find reasonable. Once these axioms are introduced and justified, I demonstrate in Proposition 1 the fundamental policy requirement needed to satisfy all three of them, namely that the supply curve must shift outward more rapidly than the demand curve. Proposition 2 establishes that bankruptcy results if demand shifts outward faster than supply does. Proposition 3 demonstrates how ObamaCare satisfies at most two of these assumptions, and possibly only one, with dire consequences for health care and indeed for the nation's fiscal future.

What is particularly interesting is that our Basic Assumptions closely parallel President Obama's stated goals for health-care reform. What the three propositions reveal is that the *reasoning process* connecting the Obama administration's original goals to its policy conclusions was very problematic. Otherwise, how could ObamaCare be inconsistent with these goals? With distinguished economists like Lawrence Summers and Christina Romer on board at the time, one wonders how we ever could have witnessed such economic illogic, especially given the extremely high stakes involved.

Increased Access to Health Care

This first Basic Assumption is that health-care coverage should be significantly expanded. This is sometimes referred to as the desirability of greater "access" to health care, or greater "demand" for it. Both increased coverage and increased demand are modeled geometrically by an outward (rightward) shift of the aggregate demand curve for health-care services. "Aggregate" means we have lumped all such services into a whole. More specifically, we assume that at *any* given price for health-care services, there is greater demand than before. This is what it means for the entire demand *curve* to shift outward.

This increase in demand will be fueled in practice by an increase in health insurance coverage, and by the aging of the population as well. Note that we are limiting ourselves in Assumption 1 to increased demand alone, represented by the outward-shifting demand curve, and *not* to an increased quantity of services that actually get delivered at the new equilibrium. Increased demand need not guarantee an increase in quantity, as we shall soon see.

There are both moral and economic justifications for the assumption that more people should have access to health care and to insurance coverage. On economic grounds, it is widely believed that civilized modern societies should provide universal health insurance of one form or another. There are two reasons for this. First, it is believed that a healthy workforce improves economic output and efficiency. Second, as regards insurance, the opportunity to pool and socialize risk has long been recognized. Yet modern economic theory goes one step further and demonstrates that the economic norm of efficiency ("No waste!") *requires* such pooling of risk. The main point in a health-care context is that we no longer need a *moral* justification for risk-pooling, since economic efficiency requires it.[11]

This is not to say that moral considerations are irrelevant to the health-care access debate, for they are not. Yet the situation has always been murkier from a moral stance than from an economic stance. Among the principal moral issues that arise are: Does a citizen have some kind of an absolute right to health-care coverage? And if so, does "society" have an obligation to fund such coverage, if the citizen cannot? On the first point, some theorists claim that the right to health care is a "primary good" in the sense introduced by the late Harvard philosopher John Rawls, namely a good that is absolutely necessary for everyone, such as food and shelter. This is of course the liberal position.

Conservatives, however, often argue that there is no absolute right to health care, and that "socialized medicine" may bankrupt the country. Their champion would be the late Harvard philosopher Robert Nozick. The core issue here is one of the deepest in all of moral theory, namely that of distributive justice: How should the economic pie be allocated, and why? Who owes what to whom? This is discussed in the last chapter of this book.

For the moment, the main point is that the norm of economic efficiency *alone* implies the need for greater risk-sharing and for some version of universal coverage, to use a term that has become politically charged and should not be. There is no need to rely upon subjective "fairness" arguments for the reasons Kenneth Arrow established in his 1953 and 1963 papers that we have cited. His arguments also exposed the ineligibility of "free market solutions" to many health-care problems. These various arguments should help to bridge the Left-versus-Right divide in health-care policy since everyone espouses efficiency as a societal norm—liberals and conservatives alike. After all, who wants the opposite, namely waste? This concludes our justification for the first Basic Assumption, namely the need for greater access to health care.

Increased Supply of Health-Care Services

This second Basic Assumption requires that, whatever the nature of the health-care reform plan to be adopted, a greater *quantity* of health-care services must be delivered in the future. This is because of the growing need for them, largely due to demographic reasons, and because of the increased insurance coverage that is likely under ObamaCare.

This assumption complements Assumption 1 in a natural manner. To begin with, note that the president's goals (and my own) of "more access" to health care via new insurance will be vacuous without a guarantee of an increased supply of services. In economic terms, the supply curve of health-care services must shift outwards (rightwards) to complement the outward shift in the demand curve specified by Basic Assumption 1. If it fails to do so, or for some reason shifts backwards, then a big problem arises: The price of services (where the new supply and demand curves intersect) plotted on the vertical axis will have risen sharply, unless this is "prevented" by price regulation that inevitably gives rise to rationing. Rationing almost always implies that the rich will have access to services, but the poor will not.

To sum up, "more access" provided by extended insurance will prove a Pyrrhic victory without more supply. Those possessing expanded insurance will discover that, despite their newfound ability to pay, their phone calls to doctors will go unanswered. In just this vein, Dr. Herbert Pardes, CEO of the New York-Presbyterian Hospital, has publicly warned of a coming shortage of doctors and of unanswered phone calls as a result of ObamaCare.[12]

Longer-Run Reduction in Health-Care Spending

The third Basic Assumption reflects the necessity for a longer-run *reduction* of total health-care spending from today's level of 18.6 percent of GDP. Note that this specifies a long-run reduction in total cost as a share of GDP, not merely a decrease in the growth rate of total cost of Medicare as President Obama sought. This is a very significant difference.

The forecast explosion of U.S. health-care spending from today's 18.6 percent of GDP to upwards of 30 percent by mid-century imperils the fiscal health of the country, and will place every other worthy goal of government spending out of reach. The solvency of the U.S. government itself will be at risk, its creditworthiness will continue to be downgraded, interest rates will rise, and debt-servicing costs will explode nonlinearly.[13] A flattening out or, better yet, an outright reduction of health care's share of GDP is required to spare us these indignities, assuming that the United States wishes to be able to afford infrastructure investment, education funding, Social Security, and a strong defense system. This is why I have introduced this third Basic Assumption.

President Obama's second main goal in health-care reform (the first was expanded access) was a reduction in the growth rate of total expenditures on health care. This is similar in spirit to our Basic Assumption 3, but much weaker. The cost of health care as a share of GDP would still rise, but at a lower rate. My assumption is far more extreme. The prospect that total health-care spending could actually *decrease* as a share of GDP was never once discussed as a possibility during the entire health-care reform debate of 2007–2010. Nonetheless, I believe my stronger assumption to be absolutely necessary in the long run, given the overall goals of our nation. Health care may be important, but it is hardly the altar on which all other goals should be sacrificed.

Are These Three Basic Assumptions Incompatible?

How could significantly increased demand matched by increased supply (Assumptions 1 and 2) possibly be compatible with outright reductions in the total cost of health-care spending (our Assumption 3)? This is surely too good to be true! After all, many critics of the president viewed his own more modest goals of increased access and a reduced *growth rate* in total health-care spending as incompatible. The resulting politics were predictable. Proponents of ObamaCare celebrated the first goal (increased access), whereas opponents focused on a future explosion of costs, which they claimed would increase the growth rate of health-care spending. They made political hay of such Democratic legislative tactics as attempting to pay for the new system by stealthily reducing future payments to doctors by over $400 billion in future years, one form of "cost control." The debate about health care on the op-ed pages degenerated into a *reductio ad absurdum*. Recall this *Wall Street Journal* editorial from December 3, 2009:

> We have now reached the stage of the American health-care debate when all that matters is getting a bill passed, so all news becomes good news, more subsidies mean lower deficits, and more expensive insurance is really cheaper insurance. The nonpolitical mind reels!

The Three Main Results

The good news is that all three Basic Assumptions we have proposed *are* in fact mutually compatible, as I will now show.

> **Proposition 1:** Consider a national health-care market whose aggregate supply and demand curves possess normal upward and downward slopes respectively. Suppose the government implements a reformed health-care system such that the aggregate health-care supply curve shifts out to the right faster than the aggregate demand curve does, no matter how large or how small this "shift gap" may be, and no matter how rapidly the demand curve itself may be shifting outward.
>
> Then any health-care plan consistent with this fundamental policy requirement will satisfy all three of our Basic Assumptions in the longer run. More specifically, whereas total health-care spending may increase in the shorter term,

it will always peak and then decrease continually toward zero in the long run. Our policy requirement is both necessary and sufficient for this happy outcome to occur.

Note: The time required before total expenditure peaks, and the subsequent rate of decline will depend upon specifics such as the slopes of the supply and demand curve, the rates at which the two curves shift outward, and the health-care price/quantity coordinate values at the outset. In particular, the greater the rate at which the supply curve shifts out relative to the demand curve, the more rapid will be the decrease in total expenditure after it has peaked. Additionally, the more the outward shift of the demand curve is slowed down via the elimination of demand for wasteful and reduplicative services, the faster total expenditure will fall.

Proof: An intuitive, geometric proof is sketched below, and a formal proof can be found in Appendix B at the back of the book.

The Macro–Micro Link in Health Care

Proposition 1 is a macro-requirement about the entire health-care system. Suppose we model the "product" being supplied/demanded in an abstract manner as some index of "aggregate well-being" of the population as a whole. "Price" will be the dollar cost to the nation per unit of well-being, and "quantity" will be the number of units of well-being delivered. Total expenditure, as always, will be Price × Quantity. An increase in price increases supply and reduces demand for units of well-being. Since "aggregate" or macro health care is some weighted sum of the individual micro components of health care (MRI scanners, diagnostic tests, surgeons, and so on), Proposition 1 carries clear implications for what must happen at the micro level if the macro conditions of the Proposition are to be met.

In the simplest case, suppose that there are n sectors, each with its own supply and demand curve. Suppose, moreover, that the supply curve shifts out faster than the demand curve in every sector. This would guarantee that the conditions of Proposition 1 will be fulfilled since the aggregate supply curve would shift out faster than the aggregate demand curve would. A weaker requirement would be that curve shifts of this kind take place in "enough" sectors such that, in aggregate, supply shifts out more rapidly than demand. Very technical problems of market "aggregation" arise here and are outside the scope of this book. The most intuitive way to think about all this is to understand that the law that applies to the forest must be consistent with the law that applies to the trees.

In the discussion that follows, concrete policy proposals will make clear how important this consistency between the forest and the trees really is. I shall also discuss exactly *how* any supply curve can be shifted outward much more rapidly, as is required by Proposition 1. Particular emphasis will be placed upon the need to decartelize, deregulate, and automate the provision of health-care services. For the increased competition and productivity that these reforms give rise to is what outward-shifting supply curves are all about. They lie at the heart of what is needed for successful health-care reform.

Overall, Proposition 1 offers very good tidings. The United States need not go broke in providing a far greater quantity of health-care services to far more people than ever before—because it can do so with total expenditure *falling* as a percentage of GDP. As in the case of our Lost Decade analysis, we really can have our cake and eat it, too. But now for the bad news—two final Propositions that are sobering:

> **Proposition 2:** If health-care reform does not meet the preceding policy requirement, and in particular if the aggregate demand curve for health-care services shifts outward more rapidly than the supply curve, then total expenditures will rise without limit to the point of bankruptcy and a systemic collapse.
>
> **Proof:** Please refer to Appendix B at the end of the book.

The final piece of bad news concerns ObamaCare:

> **Proposition 3:** The Obama administration plan satisfies the first of our three Basic Assumptions (more demand for services via expanded insurance), and possibly the second (more supply of services). But it does not satisfy the third Basic Assumption (a longer-run reduction in total health-care expenditures as a share of GDP).
>
> **Proof:** A simple geometric proof appears after the geometric proof of Proposition 1 that follows.

Two Simple Geometric Proofs

> **Geometric Proof of Proposition 1:** I now present an intuitive geometric proof of our first result.

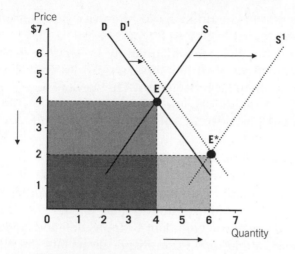

Figure 3.4   Have Your Cake and Eat It, Too!
Total Expenditure *Drops* from $16 to $12, but Quantity Supplied Rises by 50 Percent.

Think of the two market equilibria E and E* shown in Figure 3.4 as representing the health-care market "before" and "after" new policies are put in place that satisfy our fundamental policy requirement. The numbers shown for each axis are hypothetical and illustrative. The period shown could represent, say, 15 years. Note in the figure that the supply curve shifts outward far more than the demand curve does over the period in question, as required by Proposition 1. Since the outward supply shift must be greater than the outward demand shift each and every year, by assumption, the cumulative gap between the location of the supply and demand curve grows larger and larger over time.

It is this *cumulative* gap that is shown in the graph over the hypothetical period of 15 years. Now note that the total expenditure on health care (to be interpreted as a share of GDP) decreases by 25 percent. This is proved by the fact that the area defined by the price/quantity rectangle associated with the new equilibrium is smaller than the area of the initial rectangle. More specifically, the area $4 \times 4 = \$16$ defined by the first market equilibrium drops to $\$2 \times 6 = \$12$ in the new equilibrium, a 25 percent reduction. Note that this is true even though demand has increased, and even though the quantity of services delivered has increased significantly, as desired, rising 50 percent from four to six units as seen on the horizontal axis. On the other hand, the price per unit of aggregate service has decreased from P to P* on the vertical axis.

In short, a much-increased quantity of services gets delivered, unit costs to patients and their insurers are lowered, and the total expenditure to the nation decreases. The "proof" here is purely geometric, and only applies to the example appearing in our graphs. But the underlying logic is fully general, as is shown in proof in Appendix B.

In cases (not shown here) where the slopes of the supply and demand curves are different from those shown in the figures, or where the curves are nonlinear, or where the initial coordinate values are different, total expenditure may initially rise. But a point is always reached where the cumulative supply/demand curve gap is big enough to ensure that total expenditure always falls thereafter. In the special case where the supply and demand curves are linear, total expenditure is a downward-open parabola with a unique maximum expenditure peak.

Proof of Proposition 3: We now see how ObamaCare fails to satisfy our Basic Assumptions. Figure 3.5 geometrically represents what could well happen under ObamaCare in the worst case. Note first that the supply curve is shifting backwards. This reflects (1) the adverse implications of statutory reimbursement-rate policies discussed previously, (2) the looming shortages of physicians, discussed previously, and (3) other manifestations of the supply/demand imbalance resulting from ObamaCare discussed previously. Conversely, the demand curve shifts out to the right as in the previous figure, reflecting (1) ever more elderly people, and (2) expanded insurance coverage provided by the new Act.

We have made the magnitude of these two shifts equal and offsetting, partly for illustrative purposes, and partly to reveal the true risks of ObamaCare. Please study the result carefully. First, the unit price of services increases sharply from P to P* as can be seen on the vertical axis. Second, the quantity of services Q offered at equilibrium does not change at all. Tens of millions of people will receive no care. And third, the total expenditure on health care explodes, as is seen by comparing the total areas of the two rectangles defined by the before-and-after equilibrium points E and E*.

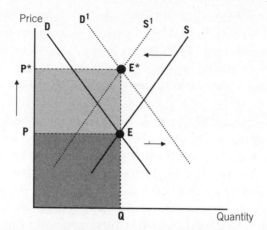

Figure 3.5   Fate of Health-Care Spending under ObamaCare: Worst Case

Note that the area of the "after" rectangle is nearly twice that of the former, *even though not one new unit of output is generated* on the quantity axis! In short, ObamaCare in this worst-case model will only satisfy the first of our three Basic Assumptions: There is greater "access" in the sense that the demand curve has shifted outward. But it satisfies neither of the other two assumptions, namely increased quantity and reduced total expenditure. The result is health-care rationing, and possible national bankruptcy as total expenditure explodes.

An Analogy from Agricultural Reform

Figure 3.5 makes clear the true cost of ignoring supply: a systemic disaster. Catastrophic outcomes of just this kind have been witnessed many times before. One example that sticks in my own mind was that of agricultural reform in Tanzania in the 1960s under Prime Minister Julius Nyere, a good and farsighted liberal who simply did not understand economics. To placate consumers in the cities, particularly the then–capital city of Dar-es-Salaam, Nyere mandated price reductions (and other controls) for crops. He did so, claiming that greedy farmers were being unfairly rewarded by high prices, and that consumers would benefit from lower prices.

The result, of course, was exactly what Figure 3.5 shows: Farmers pulled out of agriculture (the supply curve shifted backward). There was a shortage of food and rationing since prices were not allowed to soar to their true new supply/demand level. Living standards declined, and all this happened in the name of "helping the poor and punishing rich farmers." I happened to visit Tanzania in 1968 on a gap year from college, and having just studied microeconomics, I learned firsthand how not to better the lives of "the people" by price controls.

To be sure, ObamaCare may not generate an actual backward shift in the supply function, so that the outcome need not be as alarming as in the figure. However, given our earlier discussion about disturbing supply-side deficiencies that existed even before ObamaCare, and given the increasing alarm over supply by experts throughout the country, then the supply curve *could* in fact shift backward. More probably it will shift outward, but much more gradually than the demand curve will. If so, then as Proposition 2 implies, the long-run result will be bankruptcy or else rationing and black marketeering.

One anecdote is interesting in this context. Shortly before Christmas 2010, I was in New York City and visited four different doctors, an annual Christmas ritual for me. Three of the four offices had posted signs that Medicare patients were not accepted, signs I had not noticed in past years. Signs for the poor to stay away? Signs portending rationing? Signs of the future?

Can the Supply Curve Shift Way Out? If So, How?

In this final section on health care, I wish to integrate the real-world critique of the current health-care system presented at the start of this chapter with the more abstract analysis of our three Propositions and Proofs. The goal is to identify some broad-gauged policies for achieving a better health-care system. In this regard, the fundamental question for policy makers is: Can concrete policy reforms drive the nation's supply curve out faster than the demand curve? And if so, how? My answer to this question may well surprise you, but it is based upon both economic theory and an impressive amount of supporting data: Not only can policy reforms do so, but the American public has the right to *demand* that they do so, given the all-important stakes involved in health care. After all, if supply has trumped demand for markets in TVs, computers, telephones, food, clothing, and most other goods and services, then why should it not do so in health care where the stakes are overwhelming?

In order to make the case that the supply curve of medical services can shift outwards much faster than it has, let's review exactly what causes supply curves to shift outward in the first place.

What Exactly Shifts a Supply Curve Outward?

There are three basic ways in which the supply curve for a given good or service can be shifted outward. First, this can be achieved by expanding the existing stock of workers and capital (machines) producing the good. This creates a bigger "factory," and the level of output at any given price will increase—the very definition of an outward shift in the supply curve.

Second, an increase in productivity will shift the curve outward. This occurs when, due to technological progress, existing workers learn how to work "smarter" and as a result can produce more output per hour at any given price than before. The supply curve again shifts outward even though, this time, there are no new workers or factories. For examples of the power of productivity growth, just think of how the invention of double-entry bookkeeping and of the limited liability corporation caused an explosion in the formation of businesses, how the original Green Revolution dramatically increased crop output and defeated Malthusian predictions of mass starvation, how the invention of the microchip revolutionized the speed and capacity of the computer in accord with Moore's Law, and how the invention of the steam engine, electricity, and nuclear power gave the modern world the energy required for history's three industrial revolutions to occur. I recently came across a fascinating statistic: Energy expended by human beings amounted to about 95 percent of total energy expended in economic activity three centuries ago. This share has now fallen to about 5 percent.

Third, the more deregulated and competitive a market becomes, then the more rapidly the supply curve shifts outward. Nothing impedes the growth of productivity more than anti-competitive cartels, as Adam Smith recognized as early as 1776. To restate this point in modern economic terms, true economic efficiency ("the biggest pie possible given the resources available") requires *perfect* competition, that is, a competitive structure free of cartels, oligopolies, monopolies, and so forth. The more competitive a sector is, the greater its productivity growth will be, and thus the more rapidly its supply curve will shift out over time.

Supply Curves and Rising Living Standards

In a very fundamental sense, the concept of economic progress (equivalently rising living standards) implies that households spend a smaller share of their income on "old" goods every year so that they can afford either "new" goods (an iPod, or a trip overseas), or else at least as many old goods of superior quality.[14] But this can only occur if supply curves shift out faster than demand curves, as we saw in the discussion of Proposition 1.[15] In this regard, Proposition 1 was as much about the requirement for economic progress in general as it was about the control of total expenditures on health care.

This is a very important point. Simply consider the course of economic progress during the twentieth century. The share of our incomes we spend on most any product of comparable quality declined dramatically. Of course, we may spend more as a share of our income on certain goods if they are higher quality. But when quality improves, you are really introducing a new good.

But then there is health care! The share of all of our incomes spent on health care (for a constant level of health) rises endlessly because of rising prices for services, ever-rising insurance copayments, and ever-rising insurance premiums—at least for those of us "lucky" enough to have ever-worse insurance! The expenditure impact is even worse when doctors refuse to accept the insurance we have already paid for, as keeps happening to me. Indeed, to have my throat looked at cost me $5 when I was five years old, versus $350 in the same Upper East Side building in New York last Christmas. I was not paying more for an increase in quality of service delivered. Moreover, I had to write a check on the spot for my treatment. Nondeductible, of course.

Sound familiar? In this case the supply curve had not shifted outwards at all over many decades. This price inflation was partly due to a lack in productivity growth in the scheduling and delivery of the services rendered. Nothing had changed, including my treatment. It was like a time warp. Now this is *not* an indictment of the entire health-care industry. After all, myriad forms of technological progress have improved the diagnosis and treatment of many, many illnesses over the last several decades. It is simply an indictment of the way in which an individual consumer visiting a doctor for a routine illness pays much more than he used to, spends as much time as before, and receives care that is not notably better in many cases. Where was that medical care ATM that would have made going to the doctor as easy as cashing a check had become?

Where Health Care Went Wrong

What exactly has prevented a suitable outward shift in the health-care supply curve? Was cartelization and lack of competition a cause? Absolutely. Was lack of productivity growth due to cartelization and other developments a cause? Absolutely. Was a lack of sufficient expansion in the quantity of factor inputs (more medical school graduates) a cause? Absolutely. Can such constraints be relaxed, resulting in the required large outward shift in the supply curve that is needed? Absolutely, and it is high time that this be recognized as a national priority, and that it occur. A portion of the infrastructure investment Marshall Plan proposed in Chapter 2 should be dedicated to increasing productivity in health care.

In concluding this discussion of health-care reform, let me sketch a rough blueprint of what must be achieved in *practice* so that our three Basic Assumptions can be fulfilled. I shall sketch a sample of reforms needed not only on the supply side but also on the demand side of this bedeviling market. My main goal is to demonstrate how specific policy proposals can and should be factored into their supply and demand *curve* implications. Only if this is done—and it never has been done to the best of my knowledge—will we be able to arrive at an entire collection of policies that, when aggregated, satisfy the fundamental policy requirement: The aggregate supply curve must shift outward faster than the aggregate demand curve. And only if this requirement is satisfied can we be spared national insolvency due to runaway health-care spending, as Propositions 1 and 2 make clear.

As I am not a health-care expert, please view the following proposals as a sample of what true experts might propose. What matters is the logic involved, and this is what I will emphasize. I start off with demand-side reforms. In this case, the more that new policies slow down the outward shift of the demand curve for legitimate reasons—or even reverse it—the better.

Some Valid Demand-Side Reforms

First, suppose tort reform would cause doctors to order fewer reduplicative tests and thus reduce today's artificially inflated demand for tests and services. Such a reform would shift back the demand curve for legitimate reasons, and accordingly should be enacted.

Second, suppose that traditional fee-for-service physician payment schemes could be replaced by more holistic schemes that would incentivize physicians to see a given patient less often, for comparable care. Then this reform should be embraced since it shifts the demand curve backward, again for legitimate reasons.

Third, suppose that "first dollar insurance coverage" encourages an excess demand for medical services. Then such coverage should be eliminated so as to shift back the demand curve. Consumers would allocate their dollars much more carefully if they have to pay up front for their treatment, until of course a reasonable cap is reached where insurance kicks in. The cap could depend upon a persons' income, with higher caps for richer people.

Fourth, suppose that penalizing patients with demonstrably bad lifestyles would cause them to adopt better lifestyles and have fewer health problems due to smoking, lack of exercise, obesity, alcohol, drugs, and so forth. Then penalties should be imposed on such patients to shift the demand curve backward.

Fifth, suppose that a growing number of allegedly medical "needs" are not really needs, but mere desires as in the case of much plastic surgery, and of certain life-extension procedures. Then patients should pay the freight for such services. The penalties imposed would shift the demand curve backward for valid reasons.

Many other demand-reduction policies exist, and several of these were cited in the discussion that appeared earlier in the chapter.

Some Valid Supply-Side Reforms

I have already touched upon such supply-side reforms earlier. Let's review some specific examples.

First, let us agree that the number of health-care professionals who graduate from medical schools has been artificially constrained during past decades. It is often alleged that the AMA and other groups represent *de facto* cartels whose interests favor a restricted supply of professionals. Then the interest groups involved should be encouraged to increase supply. With the large number of physicians approaching retirement age, resistance to increased supply might be much less than expected. If physicians and their lobbies do not play ball, they should aggressively be fought, as well as circumvented by new arrangements to the extent possible. If it proved possible for government successfully to take on the American Tobacco Trust, the Standard Oil Trust, AT&T, and any number of labor unions, why should it be held hostage to self-serving medical cartels when national solvency is at stake?

The government has plenty of leverage in this regard. Consider the restrictions upon medical school enrollments. Everyone knows how difficult it is for able undergraduates to get into medical schools. Several publications have recently run articles on the number of Americans students forced to obtain training in the Bahamas. The government should order all qualifying U.S. medical schools significantly to increase their class sizes or else face a cutoff of all federal grants to their host universities. I suspect expansion would occur lickety-split.

Second, recall that the new health care Act has provisions that attempt to achieve "cost reductions" of the wrong kind and in the wrong way. Lowering reimbursement rates to Medicare professionals is a notable example and was discussed earlier. All such provisions should be scrapped. Telling professionals that "we will pay you less" is a sure way to shift the supply curve backwards, just as Julius Nyere learned from his misguided agricultural reforms. Once again, the proper way to control costs is via a reduction in total expenditure which in turn is achieved by reining in demand and optimally increasing supply as in Figures 3.3, 3.4, and 3.5. A failure to understand this is why most discussions of "bending the cost curve" are either misleading or wrong. They fail to capture the feedback effects between supply and demand so crucial for forecasting total expenditure.

Third, suppose that tort reform will encourage more doctors to enter a given medical field, and will also deter more doctors from exiting it due to fewer malpractice lawsuits and to reduced insurance premiums. As a result, tort reform shifts the supply curve outward and should thus be implemented. Additionally, to the extent that tort reform reduces doctors' incentives to order redundant and unnecessary tests, the demand curve for such tests and services shifts backwards. This is an example of a policy that is ideal in that it shifts the supply curve outward and the demand curve backward.

Fourth, suppose that productivity growth in health care has been suppressed—either deliberately or unwittingly. A deliberate suppression would occur should the medical profession fight efforts to automate record retrieval, and other services. Or else it might oppose an augmented role for nurse practitioners, just as many lawyers fought the advent of paralegals several decades ago. An unwitting form of productivity growth suppression would stem from the cozy atmosphere fostered by groups shielded from competition, for whatever reasons.

For example, it is well known that state-owned companies have much lower productivity growth than their private sector counterparts. By analogy, consider the poor productivity of teachers belonging to public school teachers unions versus their private school counterparts. After all, necessity *is* the mother of invention, and there is not much necessity to innovate within cozy, protected environments. The policy implication here is that any suppression of productivity growth should be targeted and dislodged on a sector-by-sector basis throughout the health-care profession.

Fifth, suppose that the medical profession opposes the substitution of capital for labor as job-threatening, as in the prospective development of expert-system-based automated medical care. Then both government and citizens' groups alike must vigilantly oppose such Luddism, and automated care should be vigorously pursued. But once again, given the looming shortage of physicians, resistance here may prove less than expected.

To the best of my understanding, the greatest promise for a dramatic outward shift in the health-care supply curve lies in precisely this area of "intelligent automation." But this is a sleeper topic that few health-care professionals seem to discuss, much less champion. It is also an area in which there is widespread misunderstanding of the opportunities at hand. Because I have some personal experience in the construction of expert systems, let me briefly digress on this particular source of greater productivity.

Expert Systems and Automation

In researching this book, I was struck by how people in the medical profession seem oblivious to—or even hostile to—the promising new technologies of expert systems. These are not simply systems that replicate low level jobs, for example, automated operators who replace telephone operators and ask you for the name and address of the person you are calling. Rather they are platforms in which the expertise of true professionals (e.g., the *best* doctors in any field) is encoded and then utilized in an interactive manner. The result is that an automated expert is "there" to diagnose you 24/7, to have a discussion with you, to ask you highly sophisticated questions, to consult with other professionals, to test you, and then to tell you exactly what to do next.

As the author of reputedly the first expert system in the field of finance 25 years ago, *Interest Rate Insight*, I learned first hand about the extraordinary potential of this field.[16] I first interviewed the late James Tobin at Yale University to ascertain the most problematic misunderstandings and biases of people who forecast the economy and interest rates. I interviewed many others as well including Benjamin Friedman at Harvard, and Vance Roley at the University of Washington, both distinguished macroeconomists. Their "wisdom" ended up encoded in a simple-to-use interactive system that helped many people make sense of interest rates back when they were very high, volatile, and important. A user would specify his assumptions about the future of the economy, in hopes of learning from the system what would happen to interest rates. An automated "expert" would then identify any logical inconsistencies in his assumptions, and explain why they mattered. The user would then reformulate his scenarios, and arrive at an improved forecast of interest rates. All this was done back in 1987 when computers lacked computing power, and when expert system technology was in its infancy.

Given today's vastly improved technology, there is no reason why I should not be able to consult an expert medical system of the following kind. Whenever I have a routine medical problem, I should be able to go to any CVS pharmacy open 24/7, enter a small fully automated booth, call up my fully automated medical record with my Social Security number, have my pulse, my blood pressure, and my blood tested, and finally have an interactive discussion with a group of eminent doctors whose expertise has been suitably encoded. A prescription for what ails me will be printed out and given to me, assuming my ailment is routine. If tests show that it is not routine, and my automated doctor will know this, then he will instruct me where to go for further analysis. Indeed, the names and addresses of the right doctors for this specific purpose will be printed out for me on the spot. To do this, my expert only needs my zip code.

The total cost will be $15, not the $350 I recently paid for exactly this treatment with a real-life doctor who was not as good an expert as the expert system could be. This fee should be split between participating pharmacies, the technologists who created the system, and the doctors whose wisdom was encoded. The doctors receive an ongoing royalty. The most important point here is that over 90 percent of all visits to doctors are routine in nature, and therefore "replicable" in expert-system lingo. Furthermore, payments for visits to doctors constitute a very significant share of total health-care expenditures, as was noted earlier.

The government should create a task force and fund a program to develop such systems at many qualifying universities. This program should be spearheaded by computer experts from MIT, and by doctors at Harvard Medical School and Johns Hopkins. Students should compete with one another to create a large number of such systems utilizing the best medical intelligence available. They should be motivated by large cash prizes for developing "winning" platforms. Venture capitalists should then be approached to transform these fledgling enterprises into large, scalable, well-capitalized businesses. Such a program has been needed for decades, but it is now possible. My belief is that automation of this kind will eventually play the most important role of all in shifting the supply curve *way* out. Why must we wait any longer?

Importance of Health-Care Reform—A Postscript

Were the market whose irrationalities I have analyzed the market for white truffles, no one need care. But the market at hand is the U.S. health-care system, the largest sector of the largest economy in the world. Just as I called for a new Marshall Plan to rekindle growth and redress the U.S. infrastructure deficit in Chapter 2, I am now calling for an analogous plan to remedy the supply/demand imbalance of the entire U.S. medical system. In achieving this end, ObamaCare is not as much of a problem as many critics claim. After all, it contains some very good provisions, especially on the demand side. And since it focused almost exclusively on demand, it can be extended to include supply in a natural manner. Fortunately, the supply and demand sides of this market are largely "separable," and this should facilitate reform.

Thus we do not need to repeal the new health-care Act, but rather to extend and amend it.

Redressing the Social Security Deficit

By comparison with health-care spending, Social Security is a modest problem both in cost and in complexity. The critical difference is that, in contrast to health care, no product is being produced and consumed. The product is simply a national annuity of sorts whereby workers pay into a social insurance fund during their working years, and then secure an annuity when they retire. The three issues that make Social Security a problem are (1) the front-loaded structure favoring those that retired earliest, (2) the demographic bulge of the baby boomers causing a declining "dependency ratio" (number of workers per retiree), and (3) an increase in biological longevity. In and of themselves, these problems pose no great difficulty. In principle, all that is needed is to postpone the retirement age, reduce the indexation of or even the level of benefits, and slightly raise taxes on workers. The problem lies in the politics surrounding which mix of these "fixes" is best. So touchy are sentiments surrounding Social Security that the subject has been deemed "the third rail of U.S. politics." Touch it and you are dead.

Whereas I had a lot to say about health-care reform that was unorthodox, if commonsensical, this is not the case with Social Security. In concluding this chapter on entitlements, I only want to identify some solutions that already exist and are well known in the field. Before I summarize these potential solutions, however, a caveat is in order. The analysis that follows is quite conventional in that it retains Social Security in its current form, namely as a non–market-based public pension whose benefits are paid by the federal government. There are those who believe that the entire program should be privatized in one way or another, and proposals to do so have proliferated in recent years. President George W. Bush included partial privatization on his policy wish list.

My own view is that the system should not be privatized. To begin with, the usual reasons given for privatization are flawed because free market solutions will fail to achieve the optimal amount of risk-spreading required by economic theory. Additionally, the prevailing politics will make privatization impossible. Finally, the volatile stock markets of the past 15 years along with the inability of most people "to take responsibility for their old age" militate against a private sector approach. Just note the small fraction of those who could have fully funded their IRAs that actually did so.

The Problem

Social Security is a social insurance program officially called Old-Age, Survivors, and Disability Insurance (OASDI), in reference to its three component parts. Starting in 2015, program expenses will continuously exceed cash revenues. Four reasons account for this. First, baby boomers are aging, resulting in a lower ratio of workers contributing to the pot to retirees. The number of workers paying into the fund was 5.1 per retiree in 1960, 3.3 in 2007, and is projected to fall to 2.1 by 2035. Second, the birth rate will continue to be low, at least compared to that of the baby-boom period. Third, life expectancy will continue to rise. And fourth, the government has borrowed and spent the accumulated surplus funds known as the Social Security Trust Fund, while counting the funds as revenue, rather than as debt, as it should have.

Until 2037, the government has the legal authority to draw on general government funds above and beyond the Social Security payroll tax revenues. Thereafter, however, the government must rely solely upon the pay-as-you-go payroll tax revenues. The problem is that payroll taxes will cover only 78 percent of the scheduled payouts after 2037. This declines to 75 percent by 2084. Unless current law is changed permitting government to draw upon nonpayroll sources of revenue, benefits would have to be severely cut or else payroll tax rates would have to rise sharply.

One way of quantifying how much of a challenge this is to the nation is to discount all unfunded annual shortfalls to a current present value. The most common estimate of this "unfunded liability" is $5.4 trillion as of August 2010 data. This is the amount of money that would have to be salted away today such that its interest and principal would cover the annual shortfalls in future years. If current assumptions about future longevity, interest rates, and growth rates prove too optimistic, the unfunded liability could easily reach $15 trillion. Note, however, that this is only a fraction of the size of the unfunded Medicare/Medicaid liability, which is estimated to lie between $25 and $40 trillion.

Another way of quantifying all this is to note that, looking forward 70 years, the average annual shortfall is 1.92 percent of the payroll tax base, or 1.0 percent of forecast GDP. Additionally, the annual cost of Social Security benefits represents about 5 percent of GDP at present. This is projected to increase to 6.1 percent by 2035, and then decline to about 5.9 percent by 2050 and then to remain at that level. Once again, while this deficit is large, it is not daunting and there are many ways to eliminate it. Before turning to a summary of some proposed solutions, let me cite a useful caustic comment by Professor Paul Krugman of Princeton University that accurately puts the Social Security shortfall into broader perspective:

> The Congressional Budget Office report finds that extending the life of the trust fund into the 22nd century with no change in benefits would require additional revenues equal to only 0.54 percent of GDP. That is less than 3 percent of federal spending—less than we're currently spending in Iraq. And it's only about one-quarter of the revenues lost each year because of President Bush's tax cuts. Given these numbers, it's not at all hard to come up with fiscal packages that would secure the retirement program, with no major changes, for generations to come.[17]

Despite his admittedly liberal bias, Krugman on this occasion is right that remedies requiring small changes are at hand. Let's investigate some of these.

Proposed Solutions

Before detailing some solutions that have been proposed, it is important to reiterate a point Federal Reserve Bank Chairman Bernanke has stressed: Reform is much less painful now, up front, than it will be later on. For example, raising the payroll tax rate to 14.4 percent from the current rate of 12.4 percent during 2009, or else cutting benefits by 13.3 percent during 2009 would have largely resolved the system's problems indefinitely. But if no changes in tax rates or benefits are made until 2035, these amounts must increase to 16 percent and 24 percent respectively.

We conclude with a brief summary of several solutions that have been proposed for shoring up Social Security.

1. **The Congressional Budget Office Study of July 2010:** This reported the effects of a series of policy options designed to eliminate the "actuarial balance" shortfall, which over the 75 year horizon is 0.6 percent of U.S. GDP. On today's GDP of $14.5 trillion, this amounts to about $90 billion per year. The amount would grow in proportion to GDP growth. One policy option that eliminates the 0.6 percent shortfall would be to raise the payroll tax rate from 12.4 percent to 14.4 percent over the next 20 years. An alternative solution was recently proposed by Stanford University Professor Michael Boskin. He recommends adopting a new and more conservative inflation index to be used in "indexing" benefit payments over time.

2. **The AARP Study of February 2010:** The American Association of Retired Persons (AARP) has identified six ways of increasing Social Security revenue, and three ways to reduce costs. To raise revenues: (1) raise the cap on taxable earnings to 90 percent—this would reduce the predicted shortfall by 39 percent; (2) increase the payroll tax rate—each 0.5 percent tax hike eliminates 23 percent of the shortfall; (3) raise taxes on benefits paid—this could reduce the shortfall by 10 percent; (4) preserve the estate tax on estates over $3.5 million—this should reduce the shortfall by 27 percent; (5) extend program coverage to newly hired state and local government employees—this would generate a 10 percent shortfall reduction; and (6) invest 15 percent of the Trust Funds into stock and bond index funds—this results in a 10 percent reduction.

   On the cost side, the AARP proposes (1) adjusting the cost-of-living-adjustment (COLA) provision so as to reduce outlays by 18 percent of the shortfall; (2) increasing the normal retirement age to 70 so as to reduce the shortfall by 36 percent; and (3) adopting progressive indexing of benefits to prices, not wages, resulting in a further decrease in the shortfall. This last measure is similar to the Boskin proposal. Clearly, a mix of some or all of these nine proposed changes in the system would render Social Security solvent for the long run, assuming that the actuarial and economic assumptions made come true.

3. **The 2010 Urban Institute Study:** This study recommends the five options of (1) reducing the COLA by one percentage point thereby reducing the shortfall by 75 percent; (2) increasing the full retirement age to 68 thereby reducing the shortfall by 30 percent; (3) indexing the COLA to prices rather than wages, except for the bottom third of workers, thereby reducing the shortfall by 65 percent; (4) raising the payroll income tax cap (currently at $106,800) to cover 90 percent instead of 84 percent of earnings thereby reducing the shortfall by 35 percent; and (5) raising the payroll tax rate by one percentage point thereby reducing the shortfall by 50 percent.

These findings reinforce the understanding that the Social Security funding crisis can be resolved by a combination of relatively painless policy changes aimed at reducing benefits and raising revenues. All that is missing to implement these is leadership.

Conclusion

This concludes our overview of the entitlements crisis. Health-care spending is by far the most serious issue in this debate. I have tried to demonstrate that we can achieve the goals both of expanded coverage and reduced total expenditure (as a share of GDP) provided that an all-out attack is made on the supply-curve of the market. In this context, we have seen that more conventional remedies like "bending the cost curve" and outright "cost control" either have no meaning, or else do not amount to solutions at all.

What matters is *total expenditure control*, and this is best achieved by shifting out the supply function more rapidly than the demand function. During all the debates about health care over the past five years, I have never once seen this point raised. To be sure, there are those who preach the need for more supply given the looming shortage of physicians that we confront. But it is not enough to propose increasing supply. It is the supply *curve* that must be the object of discussion. This is not simply an opinion, but rather a deduction from elementary economic principles, as I stressed earlier.

In the case of Social Security, the problem is both lesser in size and much easier to fix. There are several sets of reforms, any one of which would make the program solvent throughout the current century. But one thing is for sure: We are living longer, and we are all going to have to work longer too.

Finally, in keeping with the spirit of this book, I hope most readers will agree that there is nothing Right wing or Left wing in the health care and pension policies that I have proposed. Rather, it is glorified Common Sense 101 and is thus consistent with the fundamental thesis of this book.

4

Preventing Perfect Financial Storms

When Everyone Was Too Clever by Half

What is happening in the credit markets today is a huge blow to the Anglo-Saxon model of transactions-oriented financial capitalism. A mixture of crony capitalism and gross incompetence has been on display in the core financial markets of New York and London. From "NINJA" subprime lending, to the placing and favorable rating of assets that turn out to be almost impossible to understand, value, or sell, these activities have been riddled with conflicts of interest and incompetence.

These events have called into question the workability of securitized lending, at least in its current form. The argument for this change—one that I admit I once accepted—was that it would shift the risk of term-transformation (borrowing short to lend long) out of the fragile banking system and onto the shoulders of those best able to bear it. What happened, instead, was the shifting of the risk on to the shoulders of those least able to understand it.

—Martin Wolf, "Why the Credit Squeeze Is a Turning
Point for the World," *Financial Times,*
December 11, 2007

Widely acknowledged as the dean of world financial commentators, Martin Wolf outdid himself in these prescient comments made during the early days of the global financial crisis of 2007–2010. Going deeper, Gretchen Morgenson's *Reckless Endangerment* argues that a self-dealing network of politicians/lobbyists/regulators/bankers enriched themselves at the expense of the broader public. Greed on stilts! While Wolf and Morgenson and many others are right in what they say, they fail to point out that much deeper forces were at work here—forces that would transform the credit collapse into a genuine Perfect Storm. These deeper forces were identified only 15 years ago in a completely new concept of market risk developed by Mordecai Kurz at Stanford University. This, incidentally, is the same Kurz who coauthored the book on fiscal policy with Kenneth Arrow that was central to our Lost Decade story in Chapter 2. Kurz's new theory of endogenous risk (risk that bubbles up from *inside* an economic system) shows that the greed, incompetence, and conflict of interest stressed by Wolf certainly exacerbate Perfect Storms, but are not in fact necessary for their occurrence.

The primary purpose of this chapter is to explain how such storms arise, and to do so from first principles utilizing the paradigm introduced by Professor Kurz. His theory represents the "higher order of deductive logic" I utilize in this chapter to help clarify an otherwise intractable problem, just as I drew upon the Arrow-Kurz logic in Chapter 2. Because this new theory permits an identification of the true causes of market risk, and does so at a deeper level than ever before, it makes possible two other important advances. First, it can help policy makers identify valid policies for preventing or at least mitigating future financial market storms. That is, the field of risk management receives a boost. Without understanding exactly what *causes* Perfect Storms to arise, meaningful storm-prevention policies cannot be identified.

Second, the field of risk assessment receives a boost. There are of course many perspectives on market risk, including the popular "fat tail" theories celebrated by Nassim Taleb in his delightful book *Black Swan*. But these theories usually describe risk rather than explain it at a fundamental level. Once again, without an understanding of the factors that give rise to risk in the first place, how can risk be properly assessed? For reasons stressed by Taleb and others, it is simply not enough for quants to massage historical data in an effort to determine the true probabilities of future events. For the probabilities of future events such as market meltdowns that define future risk cannot be assessed without first assessing the probabilities of the underlying causes of such events.

One caveat is in order here at the outset. The global financial crisis of 2007–2010 consisted of two main stages. In the first stage, the mortgage banking crisis in the United States and the United Kingdom held center stage. In the second stage, the crises in these two nations spread across the globe like wildfire immediately after Lehman Brothers was allowed to go under in September 2008. I shall focus on the first stage because this is where the greatest confusion and misunderstanding lies. I ignore the second stage because the causality here is well understood: The collapse of Lehman Brothers and AIG precipitated a panic-driven cessation of interbank lending among all major financial institutions. No bank could trust any other bank to repay a loan of any maturity, and global lending came to a standstill. This in turn caused the crisis to go global, and to impact Main Street as well as Wall Street.

The discussion in this chapter divides into two halves. The first half identifies the four principal sources of the Perfect Storm, viewed at a suitable level of abstraction. In order to do this, I introduce the new logic of endogenous risk, and explain it from scratch. Building on this analysis, I deduce in the second half of the chapter what should be done to prevent future Perfect Storms. There are two main policy proposals. The first requires a scaling down of leverage in financial institutions far greater than today's "financial reforms" can achieve. This is because excess leverage is far more dangerous than is generally perceived. The second proposal requires too-big-to-fail institutions to isolate their risky proprietary trading activities from their banking activities. Fortunately, progress has already been made in this second policy arena.

Neither of these proposals is novel, on the surface. But I want to justify both policies at a much deeper level than has been attempted to date. In particular, I want to demonstrate why excess leverage of the kind still plaguing the banking system is a nonmarket "externality" or "public bad" that government *should* rein in for fundamental reasons of public welfare. The reasons why this is true have not been clearly articulated during the recriminations of the past four years. Without an understanding of exactly *why* excess leverage is so dangerous, and without greater public outrage over the issue, champions of true financial reform will find it very difficult to oppose the all-powerful financial lobby that is resisting meaningful reform. Additionally, a failure to introduce these two reforms will increase the probability of future Perfect Storms, making them more likely than is already feared. In addition to stressing these two primary reforms, I identify a host of secondary proposals that are already generally recognized as necessary to strengthen the financial system. These will be reviewed briefly.

The Four Origins of Today's Financial Crisis

There were four principal sources of the global financial crisis (GFC). These appear in the schematization of Figure 4.1, a schematization that outlines the flow of this chapter. I will stress the role of the upper box on the left the most. Rarely has bad economic theory ("modern finance") exacted such a large price from society as it did during the GFC. It led to the creation of financial weapons of mass destruction, to irresponsibly high levels of leverage, to an arresting underestimation of risk, and to a cozy markets-know-best philosophy of deregulation that culminated in the GFC. These corollaries of bad thinking go a long way to explaining what caused the crisis *without* invoking the more familiar Wolf-Morgenson explanation based upon self-dealing and greed.

The new theory of market volatility of Mordecai Kurz was specifically developed as an antidote to many of these difficulties of classical financial theory. It has been able to explain some 90 percent of observed volatility as opposed to the 20 percent

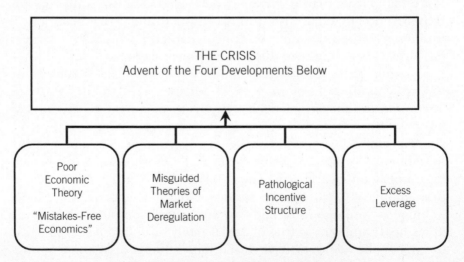

Figure 4.1   What Caused the GFC? The Interplay between Four Developments

Source: Strategic Economic Decisions, Inc

explained by classical theory, and in doing so to better model the real world. Accordingly, I shall devote considerable time to explaining this new theory, showing how it can explain and help to predict Perfect Storms, and in doing so highlight the shortcomings of classical finance. This in turn leads to a discussion of policies for preventing future GFCs. The contents of the other three boxes in Figure 4.1 are also discussed, with a particular emphasis on the precise meaning of "excess leverage" and why it must be reined in by much more stringent legislation than has been proposed to date.

Bad Economic Theory—Debunking the Conceits of Modern Financial Economics

We will start off with a discussion of the first of the four smaller "boxes" appearing in Figure 4.1, namely the domination of financial economics by highly unsatisfactory economic theory developed between 1960 and 1990. This theory is usually referred to as Efficient Market Theory. More technically, economists refer to it as the theory of "rational expectations." What I mean by poor economic theory will become clearer in what follows. But here at the outset, a summary definition will be helpful: A theory (whether in physics or economics) is "poor" if it neither explains nor predicts real-world data and if, at a deeper level, its Basic Assumptions are indefensible. In the case of good theories, the reverse is true: the Basic Assumptions from which the theory is deduced are judged "eminently reasonable," and the resulting theory has the power both to explain and predict real-world data. Additionally, a good theory must be "falsifiable" in Karl Popper's sense. In what follows, Kurz's new theory becomes a foil against which the deficiencies of classical financial theory will become crystal clear.

In the case of finance, the efficient market theory is a poor theory insofar as: (1) It posits as a basic (if implicit) assumption that participants in markets do not make mistakes (properly defined); (2) it assumes that all risks can be hedged which, when combined with the no-mistakes axiom, implies that leverage is not a significant problem; (3) it assumes that everyone in a market knows how to correctly "price" the news—there are no disagreements as to how to interpret news; (4) it predicts a level of volatility that is about one-fifth of what is observed in reality—with no Perfect Storm being possible; (5) it gave rise to the creation of new financial securities that did not perform as they were supposed to, and in fact became weapons of massive financial destruction; and (6) it implies that markets left to themselves always function quite well, and will not break down.

As this case study will show, poor *theories*—not just poor policies—can be very deleterious to the public welfare. They affect how we think, and thus how we regulate, or deregulate for that matter. The GFC was an important reminder that bad thinking can lead to bad policies, and that bad policies matter.

I believe that the new theory of endogenous risk developed at Stanford University is the appropriate antidote to the problems caused by the Efficient Market Theory. Like most good theories, it does not reject the predecessor theory—Efficient Market Theory—but rather generalizes it. It thus includes classical finance as a special case that will only work under conditions that will rarely if ever be encountered in the real world. This was the case with Einstein's general theory of relativity, which incorporated Newton's theory of gravity as a limiting special case. Specifically, if and when space-time can be approximated as "flat," not curved, then Newton's laws work just fine.

An endnote discusses how the new theory of endogenous risk can incorporate not only Efficient Market Theory as a special case, but also many of the insights of Behavioral Finance—the first effort to create a theory superior to that of Efficient Markets. As a bonus, the new theory makes falsifiable predictions of future prices and quantities, as did classical Efficient Market Theory, whereas most behavioral finance theories fail to do so.[1]

My job is now to explain the new theory, and convince you of its power. I shall demonstrate how it can explain the emergence of Perfect Storms. Moreover, once the new theory is understood, the true deficiencies of classical Efficient Market Theory will become crystal clear. In particular, I will demonstrate how traditional financial theories have blinded many policy makers, bankers, quants, and investors as to the true nature of risk, and hence the true likelihood of Perfect Storms.

Preconditions for a Perfect Storm in a World of "Good" People

Consider an idealized world of people devoid of incompetence, stupidity, greed, irrationality, and corruption. In such a world, can there be a Perfect Storm? In other words, *need* we lay the blame for what happened on the kind of factors cited by Martin Wolf earlier?

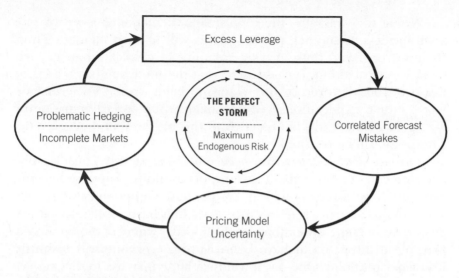

Figure 4.2   The Deeper Origins of Perfect Storms

The answer is no, as we now see. Of course, the existence of greed, incompetence, and self-dealing certainly exacerbated the magnitude of the storm, but that is all. The true sources of distress lay deeper.

Please consider Figure 4.2, which will be central to this discussion. It exhibits the four preconditions for a Perfect Storm to occur in a hypothetical world of people who are competent, rational, and good. In the middle of the figure there is "The Perfect Storm—Maximal Endogenous Risk." While I do not like jargon, this word "endogenous" lies at the heart of the new theory and is what gives rise to Perfect Storms. The kinds of risk it incorporates are intuitively appealing, so bear with me.

Precondition 1: The Right-Hand Oval—Correlated Mistakes   Suppose that the world is sufficiently complex and confusing that most of us have different forecasts about future events, whether these be prices (the value of the stock market in a year), or macro events (the probability of war, recession, global warming, or whatever). By a "forecast," I mean a person's own, subjective betting odds (probabilities) on future events given his or her current information. When people have differing forecasts, as is usually the case, at most one person will end up having been "correct," although usually no one is completely correct. People who discover that their forecasts were incorrect react by shifting their financial portfolios and revising their then-future forecasts.

When they change their portfolios, demanding more of one asset and less of another, market prices will in turn change. Thus, "being wrong" can cause market volatility. In classical finance, such behavior is ruled out. It is assumed that no one ever changes his or her probabilistic forecast due to having been wrong. For everyone has "rational expectations," which means their forecasts are never wrong. Readers of this book may find this off the wall, but it is true. This point will be revisited later.

But how much volatility can arise from being wrong? Consider two extreme cases to understand this important point. Suppose half the investors have forecasts that are X percent higher than what they will learn to be true, whereas the other half have forecasts that are exactly X percent lower than reality. Thus, when reality emerges, proving all investors to have been wrong, everyone will reshuffle his or her portfolio. One result will be a large increase in the *quantity* of trades that results. *Price* however will not change, since for every investor that was X percent below reality, there was an offsetting investor that was X percent higher. In short, the "mistake structure" in this particular market is self annihilating, and hence price volatility (risk) will be minimal. This elementary observation makes clear that market volatility (risk) will be greatest when most all investors are wrong in the *same* direction. In this case, price and quantity both will change dramatically.

This is the case of what Kurz calls "correlated mistakes" or "correlated forecast errors" and it is a very important source of volatility that has been overlooked in earlier theories since mistakes were axiomatically ruled out by these theories. Now if a correlated mistake occurs in an unimportant market (e.g., a bet on the future price of cognac), then society at large will not be affected. Yet if the correlated mistake is a bet on house prices nationwide—a bet placed by millions of average investors on their most important asset—then the consequences for society can be very large indeed. During the recent Perfect Financial Storm, this first precondition for a Perfect Storm was met in spades.[2]

Precondition 2: The Left-Hand Oval—Problematic Hedging   Life would be a lot less risky for almost all of us if we could perfectly hedge *all* the risks in our lives, another stringent assumption of classical theory. But as Professor Robert Shiller of Yale and others have shown, many of the most important risks in our lives cannot be hedged. These include the probability of unfairly being fired, the probability of having to sell a house when house prices are low rather than high, the probability of a good marriage remaining a good marriage and not ending in divorce, the probability of stock prices being high versus low during the month we retire and seek to annuitize our wealth for a guaranteed lifetime income.

You might suppose that nonhedgability of this kind will become less of a problem as instruments for improved risk-hedging become more available (e.g., many types of "derivative" securities). While there has been great progress along these lines in recent decades, it is well known in the economics community that many of the most important risks will never be able to be hedged due to problems of "moral hazard" and related issues in economic theory.[3]

On top of the nonavailability of hedges to smooth out some of the bumpiest moments in our lives, there is the fact that hedges can break down and malfunction just when they are most needed, as in times of crisis. Recall the terrifying U.S. market crash of 1987, "Black Monday." Also recall the collapse of the hedge fund Long-Term Capital in 1997. In both cases, distress was compounded and hence "risk" was greater when numerous hedges ceased to function. The problem here is quite simple. A hedge is constructed on the assumption that, whenever the price of asset A drops, the price of some other asset B will rise. Statistical analysis reveals such patterns, which are then utilized to construct hedges.

But in times of crisis, the prices of assets A and B may both fall in tandem. Poof goes that hedge! Billions upon billions of dollars have been lost by people including PhD quants who never allowed for this source of risk and market pandemonium.[4] In the case of the recent Global Financial Crisis, not only did hedges melt away, but huge quantities of securities (not merely mortgage-backed assets) proved unhedgable and indeed unsalable, as Martin Wolf correctly pointed out earlier.

Precondition 3: The Lower Oval—Pricing Model Uncertainty Have you ever been in a car with other impatient passengers, vainly trying to locate a destination on a roadmap when you cannot read the map? Confusion and mistakes result. The same idea arises in finance due to investors' inability to read another kind of map. Do you recall from school the idea of a "function" F? For example, consider $Y = F(X)$, expressing the concept that variable Y is a function

F of some other variable X. Suppose X denotes "the news" in some market, and Y denotes market price. Then the function F transforms or "maps" this news X into price Y. In traditional finance and indeed economics as a whole, it was always assumed that, *if investors knew the news,* then they would know the price, or more correctly, the true probability of price that would result. Everyone knows and agrees on the function F. This is called Pricing Model Certainty.

Now let's consider a different function Z = G(Y) where Z denotes the price of mortgage-backed securities—that class of weird, new-fangled assets that melted down during the GFC. Let Y in this case represent the mortgage default rate on single-family houses. So this time, the function G specifies mortgage-backed security prices as a function of mortgage default rates Y.

Suppose, finally, that investors neither understand nor agree on the nature of the function G. More specifically, assume that everyone knows that everyone else is uncertain about the true nature of G. Then, even if everyone knows the news about the default rate, they will not know the price of the associated securities. In my own research, I have called this Pricing Model Uncertainty. Then it can be proven that, the greater this type of uncertainty is, the greater the volatility of the market will be. In the case of a bubble, the greater the magnitude and duration of the bubble will be. When the bubble bursts, the greater the resulting crash will be. Price "overshoot" thus occurs in both directions. Classical financial theory assumes that Pricing Model Uncertainty does not exist. This is one reason why classical theory has trouble explaining market booms and busts, and why it underestimates risk.

The existence of Pricing Model Uncertainty in the recent Perfect Storm was implicitly acknowledged by Federal Reserve Chairman Ben Bernanke in a speech he gave at the Plaza Hotel in New York some four years ago, early in the financial crisis. He apparently asked a large audience: "We know the news, but can anyone in this room stand up and tell me what this stuff (mortgage-backed securities) is worth?" I cannot remember the exact details of this speech that I did not attend, but I read about it with great interest as I was writing a paper on Pricing Model Uncertainty at that very time. Martin Wolf expresses a similar view in his comment cited at the beginning of this chapter when he points out that these assets were "almost impossible to understand, value, or to sell."

The reason why this particular type of uncertainty generates price overshoot can be intuitively summarized as follows: The more a group of investors know that the pricing model is unknown, for example that "no one knows how high is high or how low is low," then the more each trader will have an incentive to stay with the trend (thus prolonging overshoot on the way up and down) rather than exit early and be penalized for relative underperformance.

So this is our third precondition for a Perfect Financial Storm: maximal Pricing Model Uncertainty. It is important to note that the kind of risk being generated here encompasses short-term volatility as well as longer-term trends, including what traders call momentum-driven overshoot.[5]

Precondition 4: The Topmost Box—Excess Leverage The last requirement for a Perfect Storm is that the various parties involved be maximally leveraged, just as both banks and homeowners were in the years preceding the GFC. The intuitive reason for precondition 4 is pretty obvious. Just think of yourself having made a significant investment without any leverage. From the start, there is the risk that this investment will either increase your wealth or reduce it. Now, suppose that you make the same investment, but you leverage your position 1:1, that is, you borrow half and put the other half down in cash. While you can now gain much more wealth if the investment pays off, you also face the prospect of losing much more of your net worth if the investment sours. Since most all humans attach much more importance to losing what they have than to gaining more, there is an innate tension between having too little leverage (not being willing to assume a mortgage to buy a house for a growing family), and having too much leverage (not being able to sleep well at night).

Interestingly, it is possible to utilize the economics of uncertainty to calculate the optimal amount of leverage for any investor, as long as we know the individual's "taste for risk" (and this can easily be measured), and the risk/return investment opportunities he or she confronts. This result can then be extended from the case of an individual to groups of individuals and indeed to all members of society. This is very important: For once we can define the *optimal* amount of leverage for an individual or for society as a whole, we can then determine whether or not there is *excess* leverage for either. This point will be stressed further on when we discuss policy solutions to financial crises. As will be shown, it turns out that excess societal leverage is a true "public bad" that must be regulated. For the moment, what matters is the role of excess leverage in *amplifying* the endogenous risk that the other three preconditions would give rise to on their own. This amplification process is highly nonlinear, and can explode into fat-tailed events.

The Importance of the Four Preconditions: Six Propositions

It is now possible to summarize the importance of the four preconditions of Figure 4.2 in the form of six summary propositions.

Proposition 1—Perfect Financial Storms Can Arise *without* Malfeasance   In a world of "good" people (e.g., a world without malfeasance, incompetence, or conflicts of interest), then the higher the values of each or all of the four precondition variables (e.g., the greater the leverage), the greater will be the resulting market turbulence. When all four variables assume "high" levels, a true "perfect storm" results with very fat-tailed outcomes. In the earlier discussion, I have attempted to make intuitively clear how each variable on its own increases risk. Without a much more formal analysis, however, it is impossible to demonstrate how pernicious the nonlinear *interactions* between high levels of each can be.[6] Happily, the recent global financial crisis offers a real-world example of the magnitude of distress that can result from precisely such interactions. Remember that during this recent crisis, all four variables assumed values of "high," as I have taken pains to demonstrate.

All in all, the best way to think about Figure 4.2 is to understand that market volatility and societal distress increase explosively with increases in the values of the four preconditions. We can now extend this finding in an obvious manner.

Proposition 2—The Magnitude of Perfect Storms is Increased *with* Malfeasance   Suppose we relax the "good people" assumption made previously. We now incorporate stupidity, greed, malfeasance, conflicts of interest, and the general incompetence that Martin Wolf cited. Suppose, moreover, that the net effect of such real-world deficiencies is to *increase* the excesses that result without these influences. For example, suppose that (1) house prices are driven even higher because of false promises of price appreciation by sellers and brokers, and/or because regulators failed to impose higher down payments as prices soared; that (2) bogus theories of risk assessment by bank supervisors and others end up discredited because they failed to incorporate considerations of endogenous risk; and that (3) incentives are skewed so as to transform the concepts of "due diligence" into a bad joke (NINJA [no income, no job, no assets] loans), and so forth. Then the amount of market risk and price overshoot predicted in Proposition 1 will be even greater. In sum, these human foibles that commentators stress, and that are frequently cited as the "causes" of the crisis, emerge as add-ons to the deeper story told in Figure 4.2. Thus little more will be said about them below, which is not to deny their importance.

Proposition 3—Why Perfect Storms Cannot Arise in Classical Financial Theories What kinds of assumptions did efficient market theories introduce that ruled out as *impossible* every one of the four preconditions cited earlier—and by extension, Perfect Storms? Briefly, classical finance was predicated on four main assumptions that produced this result.

1. Mistakes-Free Economics There can be no "correlated mistakes" as a source of volatility. This is because the so-called assumption of rational expectations incorporated within these theories assumes that, while the future is uncertain, all investors possess the same probabilistic forecast of the future, *and* that this forecast is correct. That is, while no one is assumed to know the future because of uncertainty, all investors know and agree upon the true probabilities of future outcomes. Thus they do not know if it will rain or shine next August 23, but they are assumed to know that it is 20 percent likely that there will be rain rather than sun. This is the "relative frequency" probability than can be computed from historical data (e.g., it has rained 20 percent of the time on all August 23 dates during the past century). Since everyone has access to the same data, and has an equal ability to crunch the data, all agents end up with the same probability forecast. It is correct and it remains correct across time. There are no structural changes. This assumption goes by the term "stationarity" in statistical theory.

The result is "mistakes-free economics" in the sense that no one will look back and say: "Gosh. Things have changed. My forecast based upon historical data was wrong. Structural changes like the advent of global warming have changed the odds of rain and shine. There is no longer an objective truth that I can mine from the historical data. Thus any forecast I arrive at will be subjective, and others will have forecasts different from mine." More often than not, it is the advent of difficult-to-predict structural changes (e.g., the rise of China, the invention of derivatives, or the advent of global warming) that make our forecasts wrong, *ex post*. Moreover, given the irrelevance of much historical data about such new developments, different investors will inevitably hold diverse beliefs (forecasts) about the future. Sometimes these will be both correlated *and* wrong.

At other times, forecasts can be wrong because of psychological "biases" of the kind stressed in modern behavioral finance. No structural changes *per se* are needed for such biases to exist. Finally, at still other times, forecasts are wrong because the phenomena being forecast are inherently counterintuitive. Thus, the ancients were wrong in supposing that the sun rotated around the earth, despite lots of data suggesting that it did. They did not understand that it only *appeared* that the sun orbited the earth, but that in fact the earth was spinning on its own axis. Note that in this case, people's mistakes did not reflect "irrationality" at all, but rather outright ignorance. There are many analogous situations in economics, some of which are reviewed further on.

To sum up, the classical theory's assumption of "stationarity" (a structural-change-free environment) rules out Precondition 1 of our Perfect Storm story. It guarantees that everyone will learn the truth by crunching historical data, and that there will be no panic selling (or buying) as investors discover they have been wrong. Structural changes do not occur. Mistakes do not occur. Check any finance textbook you wish, and you will never find the word "mistakes" in its index. In contrast to all this, within the new theory of endogenous risk, the advent of structural changes is all-important in explaining not only why mistakes occur, but why forecasts are both diverse and subjective, and why market risk is thus much greater than in classical theory.[7]

2. Perfect Hedging   Classical theory also traditionally assumed that *all* uncertainties not only can be hedged, but must be hedged in order that all goods and services be efficiently allocated. This was one of the principal findings of the seminal 1953 paper by

Stanford's Kenneth Arrow, which I cited in Chapter 3. This paper extended the concept of "market equilibrium" from a world of certainty about the future to a world of subjective uncertainty.[8] But as Robert Shiller at Yale and many others have documented, many of the most important risks we face neither are nor ever will be able to be hedged. This is the famous "missing markets" problem in economic theory. It is one, but only one, reason why markets *cannot* know best and hence will not know best in many cases, and hence often allocate resources inefficiently.[9]

It is also assumed in classical theory that hedges do not melt down and malfunction as they usually do in periods of extreme market turmoil. More specifically, the assumed "stationarity" (non-changeability) of the environment guarantees that the correlation of asset prices within a hedge never changes: There are no periods when the prices of all assets within the hedge start moving in the same direction, thus undermining the hedge.

3. Pricing-Model Certainty

All classical theory stipulates that, given the news X about any asset market, then everyone will know the correct new price Y of the asset. Everyone knows all the road maps linking news to price, or to use my earlier notation, they know the function F mapping news into price. Moreover, what they believe they know about F is assumed to be correct.

4. Optimal Yet Irrelevant Leverage

Classical theory assumes that investors will optimally leverage their positions in accord with their own risk tolerances. "Excess leverage" *per se* is rarely discussed. Intuitively, why would leverage be an important source of market risk when it is assumed that all investors know the correct probability of all future events (and prices), and can hedge away any undesired uncertainty via the perfect hedge assumption cited previously. The result is a theory predicting much less volatility and risk than Kurz's theory.

Classical theory also predicts a very different kind of risk: "exogenous" as opposed to "endogenous" risk. The distinction here is all-important. These two adjectives derive from the Greek *exo* and *endo,* referring loosely speaking to external and internal. In classical theories, the only source of risk concerns variables exogenous to the system, for example a change in Fed policy, or a change in tax rates. Endogenous risk refers to all other sources of risk, sources bubbling up from *within* the system, such as the volatility spike that occurs when investors experience correlated mistakes and a high degree of leverage. Scholars such as Robert Shiller have found that external news can only explain about 20 percent of observable market risk. When endogenous risk is added in, some 90 percent can be explained as Kurz has shown in his research. Thus endogenous risk is all-important.

The main point here, to conclude, is that in a classical setting of no mistakes, no endogenous risk, and of complete hedging markets, leverage is not an interesting source of risk. In the real world, where the converse of these assumptions holds true, leverage becomes all-important. Taken together, these four assumptions of classical theories ensure that such theories will predict a far lower level of volatility and risk than a successor theory that rejects all these assumptions as unrealistic. In short, classical theories cannot in any way predict the occurrence of Perfect Storms in financial markets.

Proposition 4—The Fundamental Conceit of Classical Financial Theory Gets Exposed The comments and behavior of bankers, economists, and policy makers during the past 30 years make abundantly clear the power that efficient-markets financial theory has had. The paradigm led to the development and production of an array of dazzling new financial products. The increasingly dominant "markets knows best" view adopted feverishly by then–Fed Chairman Alan Greenspan and others led to reduced regulation in many aspects of financial market activity. The conceit that risk could be optimally "sliced and diced" and indeed nearly eliminated on a *decentralized* basis (i.e., via the market alone) pervaded both Wall Street and the City of London. But none of it was true. Instead, it was a bad joke, one debunked theoretically by Kurz's new theory, and empirically by the experience of the world financial crisis, and of many related crises in the past.

Proposition 5—Excess Leverage Is the Most Important Policy Variable in Explaining the Perfect Storm What can be said about the policy implications of our analysis in Figure 4.2? To understand this, a very important distinction must be made between what engineers call "state variables" and "control variables." A state variable is a variable that is "taken as given." It cannot be significantly changed via human policy. Examples of state variables include the greediness of people, the inability of people to make correct forecasts, and human incompetence. A control variable on the other hand is a variable that can be changed by policy choices. Control variables are often referred to as *policy variables* in economics.

The only control variable and hence the only policy-relevant variable in our four preconditions is excess leverage. This is indicated in Figure 4.2 by the fact that the top-most variable "excess leverage" is in a rectangle rather than an oval. The other three variables are state variables about which we might complain, but can do little. The all-important point here is that we are largely whistling Dixie when we wail on about missing hedging markets, hedging meltdowns, forecast mistakes, pricing-model confusion, and the incomprehensibility of complex financial products.

Quite simply, you are not going to change these aspects of reality. They are state variables. The same can be said about greed, yet another state variable. In proposing to regulate greed, we might as well go further and propose exorcising sexual aggression in teenagers. Greed is a fact of life, and any suggestion that bankers today are intrinsically greedier than they used to be will be hard to defend. To be sure, there has been a proliferation of *opportunities* to be greedier, and to appear to be greedier (e.g., a hedge fund manager getting mega-rich via 400-to-1 leverage made possible by financial engineering). But basic human instincts have not changed.

This is not the case with leverage: It *can* be regulated, it has been regulated, and it must be reregulated given its all-important role in hatching Perfect Storms. This is the main message of Figure 4.2, which I ask you to revisit one last time. When we consider a host of concrete policy reforms introduced later in the chapter, controlling leverage will emerge as the most important challenge for the reasons previously given. It *can* be dealt with. It is a policy variable.

Proposition 6—The New Theory Could Revolutionize Risk Assessment   Much is now being said about the burgeoning field of "risk assessment." It is a truth universally acknowledged that the world needs superior risk assessment. Experts assume that with ever more data, better crunched than ever before by ever more risk management consultants, we may soon be able to assess the true risks of future

Black Swans. Is this true? The new theory of endogenous risk cuts both ways in helping us answer this question. On the one hand, it promises hugely improved *qualitative* risk assessment. For now that we have discovered four new determinants of market risk (the four Perfect Storm preconditions of Figure 4.2), we can monitor them and determine whether they are pointing towards another Perfect Storm, or not. Thus, dramatically improved qualitative forecasting may be at hand.

On the other hand, it can be proven as a theorem that endogenous risk cannot be quantified with the precision that traditional exogenous risk can be (e.g., the objective probability of rainfall being the percentage of rainy days every August over a long sample period). For example, a simple change in beliefs about the future by a group of investors can change the "true" probabilities of the future in a way that cannot be objectively assessed. The situation recalls the Heisenberg uncertainty principle in quantum physics: the mere act of observing a particle's position changes its momentum, and vice versa.[10] Despite this particular limitation to the ambitions of risk quantifiers, Kurz's new theory has profoundly deepened our understanding of when and why fat tails and Black Swans will occur. We finally know what variables to look for before we start "assessing" the wrong risks as we so often have in the past.[11]

This completes our discussion of the role of "bad economic theory" in Figure 4.1, the first of four different causes of what went wrong in the global financial crisis. The second development to which we now turn can be viewed as an extension of this first cause, although the emphasis here is on poor *political* theory as opposed to poor economic theory.

Misguided Theories of Market Deregulation—"Markets Always Know Best"

The advent of laissez-faire regimes associated with President Reagan and Prime Minister Thatcher transformed the dominant philosophy of government regulation of the economy. In the case of financial markets, the advent of a new "hands-off" philosophy was reinforced by the rise of the Efficient Market Theory in financial economics. After all, if markets really do know best, who needs government interference? We once again witnessed how important ideas can be in impacting policy, just as John Maynard Keynes observed in pointing out that we are all slaves of the ideas of defunct economists.

To understand how dramatic an impact this philosophical revolution had in financial regulation, just consider the two graphs of Figure 4.3. We see here that government largely abandoned the use of two of its most important regulatory tools for regulating financial leverage: (1) the margin requirement for purchasing

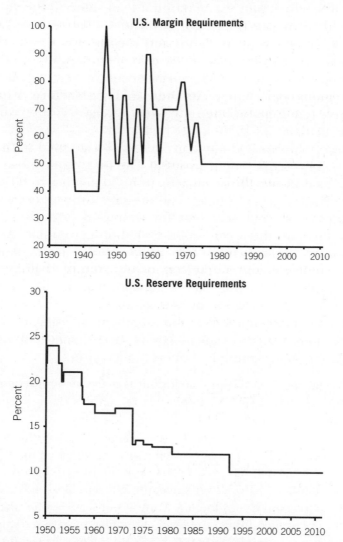

Figure 4.3   Deregulation Gone Wild: Two Examples of What Happened
Source: Federal Reserve Board of Governors, Strategic Economic Decisions, Inc.

equities, and (2) the reserve requirement of the entire banking system—arguably the principal lever of Fed power when the Fed was established in 1913.[12] Note also that the result of both of these deregulations was to generate a much more leveraged economy.

The margin requirement, expressed as a percentage, is the difference between the market value of the securities being purchased, or carried, and the maximum loan value of the collateral as prescribed by the Board of Governors. The reserve requirement (or required reserve ratio) sets the minimum reserves that each bank must hold relative to customer deposits and notes. Please note that, due to slight variations in reserve requirements across regions and changes in the banking structure over time, the reserve requirement line represents a weighted approximation of historical data.

To bring this story to life, consider what happened to the stock market margin requirement in 1958. The first graph shows how it was tightened in only three months from 50 percent to 90 percent due to a stock market bubble. The message to investors was: "We are strapping on your seat belt for your own protection, folks." Contrast this with the recent 2004–2007 housing bubble: As house prices soared, home owners were allowed and indeed encouraged to put ever less down on their houses. Millions of homeowners ended up with virtually infinite leverage on their investments. Even my Labrador retriever knew this was idiocy.

In commenting upon the abandonment of using changes in margin requirements to rein in equity market speculation in the United States, Yale economist Robert Shiller wrote:

> Why did the Fed abruptly abandon its active margin-requirement policy in 1974? An important reason was the influence of the new Efficient Market Theory, the idea that markets always work extremely well. Eugene Fama's highly influential academic article "Efficient Capital Markets" appeared in 1970, and Burton Malkiel's book *A Random Walk Down Wall Street* was first published in 1973. Ever since, the Efficient Market Theory has been a powerful influence. Most of our leaders who might feel like commenting on the level of the market have retreated from doing so, thinking that such an action might be viewed as rash and irresponsible.

In applying his analysis to the tech bubble that was peaking when this article was published in 2000, Shiller goes on to point out:

> If the Fed were to follow the same (margin-requirement) procedure today as in the past, then given today's very high price/earnings ratios and recent equity price increases, margin requirements would probably be over 90 percent today. The absence of such a reaction from the Fed board members today, the abandonment of their old concern about speculation, and the reluctance of national leaders to say anything about speculation in the market, must be part of the reason why the current boom is bigger than any before.[13]

To further understand the impact of the new "markets-know-best" philosophy, consider then–Fed Chairman Greenspan's explanation of his refusal to "interfere" in either of the two celebrated U.S. bubbles of the two most recent decades: the high-tech *and* housing bubbles. Despite his admission that both reflected "irrational exuberance," Greenspan did little to curtail the rise of either. He proffered the lame excuse that "it is hard to know whether there is a true bubble until after it bursts."

Really? Was the chairman not familiar with the statistical mean reversion that characterizes every known asset class, with the singular exception of contemporary art where, the worse the art, the higher the price *ad infinitum*? But the Fed was not the only culprit here. Consider the abject role of the SEC in permitting the leverage afforded to broker dealers to rise from around 12:1 to over 35:1 in 2004. How dare the regulators involved have permitted such levels of leverage given the obvious consequences of doing so? What is important to understand in all of this is that a new *philosophy* arose during the Thatcher-Reagan-Greenspan era—one that legitimized this markets-know-best view of the world. Once again we see that philosophies matter. They hatch ideas. These in turn hatch policies. And bad ideas hatch bad policies.

Emergence of a Pathological Incentive Structure

The excesses and resulting societal distress precipitated by these philosophical developments were exacerbated by a perverse change in the incentive structure operative throughout the financial community. Bluntly, it became rational for mortgage brokers and bankers to develop and peddle ever more complex and opaque products. These "enhanced yield" securities promised suspiciously high returns for an amount of risk that was either deliberately or carelessly underestimated.

Moreover, in a low-yield world, there was a huge demand by investors of all stripes for high-yield instruments. After all, without sufficiently high returns, investment managers got fired by clients who had become used to 12 percent indexed returns throughout much of the 1980s and 1990s. Finally, large fees were garnered by those who produced and marketed such securities. Even worse, the story was not restricted to new-fangled securities tailored to the alleged needs of sophisticated institutional investors like pension funds. It trickled down to normal home owners to whom bankers peddled subprime mortgages with negligible down payments and teaser interest rates—insanely risky loans.

Exacerbating matters was the reality that many of these new instruments were inherently complex and thus, opaque. When this is the case, it becomes partially forgivable for a banker selling such instruments to exaggerate their true risk/return appeal. Nonetheless, "buyer beware" takes on a new and ominous meaning when the underlying risk and embedded leverage cannot be understood by the very quants that created the products in the first place, much less by anyone else.

Anyone who doubts the importance of this comment need only note the recent advent of so-called "mark-to-model" asset valuations— valuations of complex assets reflecting the failure of traditional mark-to-market valuations to exist at all! This is an entirely new phenomenon in applied finance, one *unthinkable* within the dominant paradigm of classical Efficient Market economics. And this is another reason why I spent a good bit of time discussing the new theory of risk developed at Stanford University, since it can accommodate such phenomena in a rigorous manner.

What can be said about the behavior of product originators and investment bankers who peddled those sophisticated and opaque securities that have collapsed in value and are now regarded as a bad joke? Do we assume that there was an increase in the percentage of bad guys *per se*? Not necessarily. For to some extent, this behavior stemmed from the advent of new incentives and new technologies that made it rational for bankers to do what they did. In the past, their behavior would have been different due to the different incentive structure that prevailed, and due to the fact that financial engineering had not yet come of age.

One final point should be made about the role of pathological incentives in helping to create the global financial crisis. Consider the scandal whereby banks could bundle many mortgages together into "securitized packages," and then sell these to yield-hungry investors as almost riskless. Outrageously, banks were free to do this without retaining any ownership of the products peddled. If they have no skin in the game, so to speak, then why would they bother to do their homework when creating such packages? No wonder the quality of loans turned out to be much lower either than was advertised, or expected.

The same point about a lack of skin in the game applies to the structure of today's investment banking firms. These were once partnerships where the partners had every reason to be cautious about how *their* own capital was deployed. The buck stopped with them. This was no longer true once Goldman Sachs and many other firms became limited liability corporations, and could play a Heads-I-Win, Tails-You-Lose game with the taxpaying public.

Who is to blame when undesirable behavior results from pathological incentives? It is easiest to blame the immediate perpetrator for his or her behavior. But is this really fair? The incentives that drive all of us to do what we do in our lives are best viewed as "given by society" and not chosen by any of us individually. To this extent, bankers themselves were perhaps not as blameworthy as they appeared to be in the recent crisis. The moral is that, if society does not like the behavior that results from an existing set of incentives, then legislators and regulators must change and improve the incentive structure. Instructing people to act "better" given unchanged incentives is hypocritical and will not succeed. This is as true at the level of the family as it is of entire societies.

Excess Societal Leverage

The fourth and final box appearing in Figure 4.1 contains the title "Excess Leverage." I have already stressed the all-important role of leverage in amplifying distress during a Perfect Storm. I have also stressed the fact that the only policy-relevant control variable in Figure 4.2 was leverage. The other three Perfect Storm variables are state variables that are not controllable. Finally I mentioned that it is possible to determine the optimal amount of leverage both for individuals and for society as a whole. This will be a function of people's degree of risk aversion, and of the probabilities of gains and losses they think they face when making an investment. Once we can determine what is optimal, we can also determine what is excessive.

What I did not do was to make the case that *government* should not allow excess leverage since it is a "public bad" or "external-ity" which must be reined in. It is important to *prove* this because, if we don't establish this from first principles, then markets-know-best dogmatists can oppose leverage regulation as unnecessary and "meddlesome." At a much deeper level, I also want to show that excess leverage is problematic above and beyond its role in amplify-ing Perfect Storms. For even without any such storms, excess leverage remains a drag on public welfare. Fortunately, the required proof can be explained with the help of a simple diagram.

Consider a society in which it is legal for people who wish to leverage way up to do so, borrowing as much as they wish to or can. Suppose that some subset of the population avails itself of this abil-ity, typically players in the financial sector. Suppose that the remain-der of the population does not wish to leverage up, other than to assume normal (and often optimal) amounts of household debt. Might a nonmarket "externality" arise here to the extent that those who choose to leverage up can cause significant harm to those who choose not to? If this is the case, then there is an *a fortiori* right for government to regulate leverage. But do those who leverage up highly harm the general public, and if so, how? This is the root question, and one that is rarely addressed.[14]

The answer is that yes, they do. An informal proof can be given by discussing Figure 4.4. The solid line or "turnpike," as economists call it, represents that "natural" rate of growth of wealth and living standards of an economy over time. The greater the slope of the line, the more rapid wealth growth becomes. This growth rate depends upon such factors as the growth of the work-force, of the capital stock, and of labor productivity. In classical growth theory dating back to the work of scholars such as Frank Ramsey and John von Neumann early in the twentieth century, lever-age and uncertainty played no role in determining the nature of this turnpike.

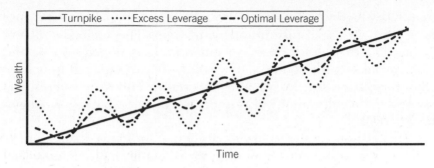

Figure 4.4   **Explaining the Wealth Growth Paradox**
Source. Strategic Economic Decisions, Inc.

When classical theory is extended to include uncertainty, and the ability to leverage, the economy gets somewhat riskier. Let the dashed line in Figure 4.4 represent the trajectory of the economy in this setting in which everyone is assumed to leverage "optimally" as described earlier on in the chapter. For example, a normally risk-tolerant person might assume a mortgage representing 70 percent of the cost of their house—certainly not 95 percent! And no fund managers exist who would leverage up other investors' money by factors of 10-, 50-, or even 500-to-1, not even for a single, 10-minute, "once in a lifetime" trade. The curving dashed line in the figure represents normal business cycles in this regime of optimal leverage, and of correspondingly greater cyclical risk.

Now allow a subset of investors (and indeed institutions) to leverage *way* up. This will give rise to the much riskier ride for the entire economy, as depicted by the dotted line in the figure. The analysis of Figure 4.2 comes into play, and thus we have the Full Monty of endogenous risk, and possibly even a Perfect Storm or two. Business cycles become much more extreme, as indicated in the figure by the dotted line. Remarkably, the first fully formal model showing how gyrating bouts of collective optimism and pessimism ("animal spirits") in tandem with debt cycles generate business cycles of this kind was published by Kurz, Motolese, and Jin in 2006.[15] The underlying ideas go back to Keynes, and more recently to the late Hyman Minsky with his brilliant theory of credit cycles. But a theoretically correct model pulling it all together—along with statistical testing—is only six years old.

Now in this rough-and-tumble new world, there will clearly be huge winners who reap millions and indeed billions from their highly leveraged positions. Others will lose and go bust, and may take down financial institutions with them. The societal problem is that, due to leverage-fueled speculation, to endogenous risk, and to financial sector fragility, *most* citizens will not only fail to benefit from these excesses, but will almost certainly end up worse off. Just ask those tens of millions of workers worldwide that lost their jobs to the GFC!

This is how average citizens are hurt, and this is the central point of the argument for reining in excess leverage. It turns out that excess leverage does nothing to increase the long-run growth rate of the economy as a whole, or the wealth of workers. That is, it does not increase the slope of the "turnpike" in the figure. It just creates a much riskier environment with far more pronounced business cycles.

Yet it is axiomatic in economics that society should only assume more risk if the expected returns (average wealth growth) rise appropriately. But this is not the case with excess leverage, as is known within the theory of economic growth. The reason is intuitively clear: Periods of economic boom due to excessive optimism and leverage are inevitably offset by subsequent periods of busts. The long-term average rate of growth (the turnpike) is not impacted.

To conclude, the dashed line is far superior to the excess-leverage-driven dotted line. It delivers the same end result with much less risk. Excess leverage is indeed a public bad, and must be checked. The case for government intervention to limit leverage is thus well grounded in first principles.[16]

This completes our discussion of the contents of the four boxes appearing in Figure 4.1 that summarize the four origins of the credit market crisis of 2007–2010: the advent of poor economic theory, of a markets-always-know-best deregulatory environment, of pathological incentive structures, and of excess leverage that greatly amplifies the impact of mistakes. We now discuss the two kinds of policy reforms needed to redress today's state of affairs.

Requisite Policy Reforms

To complete this chapter, and keep things simple, let me just summarize two types of financial market reforms that should make Perfect Storms much less likely in the future. Both proposals stem from the foregoing analysis of what causes such storms to occur.

The behavior of interacting agents in an economy can always be represented as a "game," as is done within game theory. A game has two main components: its *payoff matrix* associating a payoff to each player corresponding to any choice of strategies by all the players; and a *feasible set* of the strategies available to each player. In Figure 4.5, Type I reforms are policy changes whereby the payoff matrix is altered in a way that incentivizes the players to act in a way that is better for social well being. More specifically, these payoff-changing reforms specify new carrots and sticks intended to persuade players to choose new strategies that are collectively beneficial to society as a whole. Type II reforms are different. They alter the feasible strategy sets of the players, imposing outright restrictions as to which strategies are legal (feasible) under what circumstances, and which are not.

For the sake of brevity, the principal Type I reforms are simply listed in Figure 4.5 rather than discussed, with one exception: the need to rethink the concept of "risk assessment and risk management." Most of the other proposals are well known, and to some extent have been incorporated in new legislation, such as the Dodd-Frank Wall Street Reform and Consumer Protection Act. In the case of Type II reforms, we zero in on the need to limit leverage throughout the financial system, and to reduce the size or at least the riskiness of banks.

Type I Reforms

These are the types of remedies that have been discussed in the financial press, and in some cases acted upon by Congress and by the regulatory authorities. Among the reforms that are most needed are:

- Products must be made much more transparent, with much stiffer penalties imposed for peddling deceptive and/or non-transparent products.
- Securitization must be altered so that those who originate loans are compelled to retain some stake in the loans they originate— a measure originally proposed by former Secretary of the Treasury John Snow.

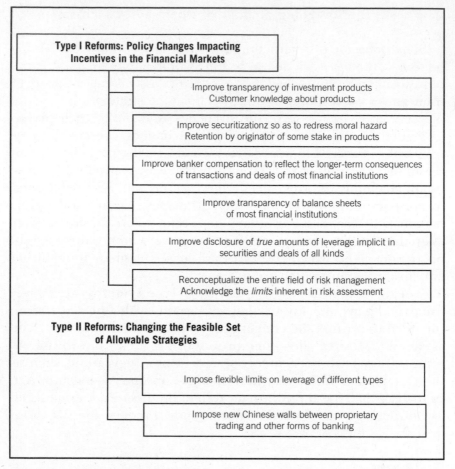

Figure 4.5   Type I and Type II Policy Reforms
Source: Strategic Economic Decisions, Inc.

- Banker compensation should be altered to depend upon the longer-term consequences of transactions and deals— not simply the volume and value of such transactions up front.
- Balance sheets of a wide variety of financial institutions must be made much more transparent so as to avoid any further structured investment vehicle–type deceptions.
- The true amount of leverage explicitly or implicitly embedded in securities and "deals" of all kinds must be better assessed and explained to clients.

- The field of risk management must be completely rethought, and with it the training that so-called quants and risk-assessors receive.

This last reform merits special discussion. What is needed is a radical change in what it means to assert that "risk is being properly managed." To begin with, it must become understood that superior risk management logically *presupposes* superior risk assessment of the risk being managed. More specifically, any meaningful claim that a given strategy or product will successfully manage risk must be backed up by a demonstration of how the strategy successfully transforms the probability distribution of resulting gains/losses into one with less risk. Why is this necessary? Because the entire purpose of risk management is to permit a transformation of the original distribution into a post-risk-management distribution that is less risky and more acceptable to the client. Therein lies the essential value of risk management. Obvious as this may seem, few risk-management customers are ever shown the true transformation of risk that they are purchasing. For example, fat tails are rarely identified as a possible risk.

However, wholly new training in risk assessment is needed if superior risk management is to be possible. Why? Because there will be environments in which the dominant risks are endogenous, and therefore not amenable to assessment by traditional quant statistical analysis at all. Even worse, such risks will often be fundamentally nonknowable, for reasons stressed previously. As a result, the very concept of optimal risk management becomes problematic: How can risk management exist if the underlying risks cannot be described, much less quantified?

Such limitations inherent in risk management should be explained to clients. In the past two decades, risk management technology centered on value-at-risk (VAR) models. As is now finally recognized, the theory underlying VAR completely sidesteps the endogenous risk story, and with it the very kinds of risk that recently brought down the world financial system. My own view is that an entirely new program of risk assessment and risk management is needed. Its basic premise would be that both classical exogenous risk and endogenous risk must always be taken into account, even though they must each be assessed differently.

Trainees in the new program would learn that "fat-tailed" events are not simply random, but are rather *caused* by factors that generate them (e.g., by the four drivers depicted in Figure 4.2). They must learn how to quantify and monitor the probabilities of these drivers on an ongoing basis and, as a result, to assess the probabilities of fat-tailed events to the extent possible. I described a simple process for doing so in greater detail in endnote 11. This is just a start.

A good place to kick off such a rethink would be in the curriculum of the CFA Institute. The material it requires investment management trainees to master for certification is studied by students all over the world. The institute has a genuine monopoly, for better or worse. As someone who has lectured at CFA events worldwide, I find the content of today's CFA program stale and dated: classical efficient market-type theories, enlivened with an overlay of behavioral finance. This content needs to be completely reworked given the disaster of the GFC, given the fall from favor of all efficient market theories, and given the advent of new theories that can make sense of Perfect Storms. I tried a few years ago to interest the powers that be at the Institute to proceed along these lines, but met with no success. Hopefully this will change, as the CFA Institute is in a position to move the entire financial profession forward in a long-overdue and useful manner.

Type II Reforms—Limiting Leverage and Breaking Up the Banks

The Type I reforms just cited amount to rearranging the sticks and carrots (the payoff matrix) of the existing game. They will help reform the financial system, but they do not go far enough. Restrictions must also be imposed upon the types of strategies that are legal (feasible) in the first place.

Limiting Leverage   This is by far the most important policy in the entire panoply of Type I and II reforms. But to listen to pundits of most persuasions, reducing leverage somehow ends up being of secondary or tertiary importance. They put far more emphasis on mitigating self-dealing, greed, and incompetence—all worthy goals. I personally find this remarkable. But then again, I have been steeped like a tea bag in the new theory of endogenous risk, so I am particularly sensitive to the role of excess leverage in nonlinearly amplifying financial disasters.

The comments by Martin Wolf on the opening page of this chapter are typical of the current attitude toward leverage. Wolf cites conflicts of interest and rampant incompetence as the true culprits behind the mortgage crisis. He does not seem to view leverage *per se* as the true villain, much less the regulatory authorities that permitted and indeed encouraged such leverage: the Fed, the SEC, Fannie and Freddie Mae, and so forth. He does cite NINJA loans, but cites them as proof of incompetence by bankers rather than as one more manifestation of excess leverage that never should have been allowed in the first place. To be fair, Wolf may have written elsewhere about the perils of excess leverage, as he surely understands these.

Yet deep down, almost everyone intuits that excess leverage lies at the heart of the GFC. What explains why this topic is skirted as much as it is? Why is leverage a phantom variable that is duly acknowledged but then ignored? I can think of four reasons:

1. There is no sense that an "optimal" amount of leverage is a meaningful concept, much less one that can be quantified at both the individual and societal level. And without such a benchmark, who can determine what leverage is excessive? So why focus on it? Yet the concept is indeed meaningful, and can be quantified, as was pointed out earlier.

2. There is no awareness of the role of endogenous risk in dramatically amplifying the damage wreaked by excess leverage. I know of no commentator on the housing crash, much less on the resulting GFC, who has ever cited or utilized this new concept. Instead, we are treated to endless discussions of the "mysteries" of Black Swans and fat-tailed events. But there is no longer a mystery here given the new theory of Kurz and his colleagues. There are reasons for when and why highly improbable and damaging events occur.

3. Given the fools that regulators, bankers, quants, and Nobel laureates in financial economics have made of themselves, it is simply irresistible for the financial press to go after these parties rather than to discuss a highly complex subject such as optimal leverage. The press should set its sights much higher, and delve much deeper.

4. There is a sense that it is hopeless to try to reduce leverage given the opposition to doing so by financial behemoths, and by hedge fund managers and traders. This sense is magnified by the patchwork nature of banking and regulatory supervision.

If we are to seriously limit leverage, exactly who is going to lead the charge to do so against the self-interests of banks and other investors?"

A Radical Proposal—Need for a Leverage Czar   At present, the principal steps taken to reduce leverage are those Basel III (and related) Accords requiring increased bank capital to support loans, and thus to reduce bank balance sheet leverage. Financial institutions have been fighting these, are dragging their feet in implementing them as of this writing, and are discovering new ways to dilute their force. In the United States, the Dodd-Frank Wall Street Reform and Consumer Protection Act places regulatory authority in these matters inside the Fed. I share the view of Sir Mervyn King of the Bank of England and of Paul Volcker in New York that the measures being proposed and implemented fall far short of what is needed. Indeed, some analysts believe that equity capital of 20 percent of the balance sheet is needed, roughly double what is being proposed. But this higher percentage would significantly reduce bank profitability. Guess who will prevail in this tug of war?

Yet I have a related concern. The Fed is the wrong institution in which to vest regulatory power over the banks. It is well-known that, within the Fed, power and prestige are located in the area of monetary policy, not in regulatory activities that are much lower profile. Given this reality, along with the Fed's failure to display much concern with the leverage issue, I believe an entirely new arrangement is needed. Specifically, I would like to see the creation of a Department of Asset Market Leverage whose *sole* job it would be to deal with market-by-market leverage in a novel manner. It would be headed by a Leverage Czar known for his or her integrity and independence, for example, a Paul Volcker of sorts.

The proposed name of the new department bespeaks the problem being addressed. It is asset market bubbles and the leverage ("financing") that propels them that has always been the root problem, a point stressed often by the late Hyman Minsky in his celebrated work on debt cycles. But if asset market bubbles tend to be the problem, and if excess leverage amplifies the boom and its subsequent bust, shouldn't leverage be *explicitly* targeted and controlled, and not always play the role of second fiddle? Recall that excess leverage is an externality, and a big one. But now a new problem arises: Which asset markets should be regulated as regards leverage, and when? There should not be one leverage policy for all since assets markets often move independently of one another. Bubbles in different sectors thus rarely coincide. Moreover, since different asset markets are prone to bubbles of different sizes.

The solution is to have independent regulation for the different asset markets in which bubbles occur, in particular the stock market, household real estate, commercial real estate, bonds, and commodities. There would be a separate regulator for each asset class. Extensive use would be made of "mean reversion" evidence, the tendency for prices to rise above and then below some long-term mean value. For example, price/earnings valuations of stocks average 15 over the long run. As this valuation rose to over 30 during the late 1990s, a large stock-market bubble was clearly underway. Optimal policies would raise/lower legal leverage ceilings depending on the deviation of current valuations from mean-reverting trends, and would do so on a market-by-market basis.

Furthermore, it would not be banks alone that are regulated. Rather, institutions of every kind ranging from individual speculators to hedge funds to commodity brokers and to banks would be subject to the appropriate leverage limits, with extremely severe penalties for dodging these. To be sure, different limits would apply to different categories of investors.

Would such a policy amount to "meddlesome government interference" as apologists for markets-know-best economics would probably argue? Must it become politicized? No. Policy could take the form of well-publicized "rules" known by all in advance, just like the Taylor rule formerly utilized in setting Fed policy. Transparency and predictability would thus be achieved. The rules would be quasi-robotic, driven by *objective* considerations of deviation from trend values. Political interference would be minimized, just as it is in the Fed's Open Market Committee decisions.

To be sure, many commentators have proposed dynamic regulatory adjustment rules, although these rarely target leverage *per se*. I am going somewhat further, partly because everyone now acknowledges the harmful role played by asset bubbles, and partly because we understand the all-important role of leverage in amplifying endogenous risk and creating Perfect Storms. Never forget the most important point about Figure 4.2: Leverage alone is a control variable that can be changed at will. The other variables are state variables. Learn to live with them and focus instead on the control variables. An irresistible analogy: While the courtiers of King C'nut allegedly railed against the waves crashing upon the shores of Denmark many centuries ago, their wise king counseled them to construct seawalls instead of bewailing the state of nature.

Macro-Controllability   There is one last virtue in the proposal to regulate leverage on its own, and it is a very important one stemming from the foundations of macroeconomic theory. Many observers blame the Greenspan and Bernanke Fed for causing the technology-stock bubble of the late 1990s and the housing bubble of 2004–2007 by keeping interest rates too low. "The Fed could and should have used interest rates to prevent these asset market bubbles." But this is not true: Even if higher rates would have prevented bubbles (and this is not at all clear), the Fed should not necessarily have used its interest rate tool. This is because the Fed's mandate is to use monetary policy to regulate employment and prices on Main Street—no more—and both could have been adversely impacted by much higher rates.

The problem here is that asset prices *per se* were never explicitly targeted, partly because it was not understood how adversely asset market bubbles could impact Main Street. Suppose, however, that the Fed now does wish to better control asset prices. If it does, can it do so? Here we run into a problem known as "controllability" in macroeconomics. It happens that the correlation between asset prices and consumer prices is very low, along the order of –0.05 during the past two decades.[17] Thus, in using conventional monetary policy to impact consumer prices and the state of the economy, its mandate, the Fed would have a hard time in also controlling asset prices. Looked at in reverse, the Fed could *attempt* to prevent an asset bubble by raising rates to, say, 12 percent, but doing so could cripple Main Street and cause deflation, thus violating its mandate.

What can be done? The theory of controllability tells us that the government needs a new and independent "policy instrument" to help regulate asset prices. That new instrument would be the policies of the proposed Department of Leverage with its robotic, dynamic regulation of asset market leverage. Happily, controlling leverage and hence asset prices would not impact consumer prices due to the lack of correlation between goods and asset prices. The policy mandates of the Fed and the Department of Leverage would in this sense be independent of one another. An important point of economic policy arises here, and is discussed in an endnote for the interested reader.[18]

Breaking Up the Banks

The last reform I would propose is one championed by many, notably Mervyn King and Paul Volcker. There are two different ways in which to break up banks that are "too big to fail," and these are often confused. First, there is the proposal that existing banks shed their "proprietary trading" activities of investing and speculating with their own capital. The bank that remains would be a less leveraged if less profitable entity. A different reform would be to permit banks to continue their proprietary trading, but require them to hold much higher capital reserves to back up such activities, again making them less leveraged and less profitable. The remaining bank would be spared the vicissitudes of large gains and losses generated by large trading bets of the kind that cost UBS over $2 billion in September 2011.

The second main proposal would require the large commercial banks to be split into many smaller banks, thus mitigating too-big-to-fail concerns in a different direction. Completely aside from the prop trading issue, there is growing concern that there are now even fewer huge banks than before controlling far too large a share of total bank assets.

I believe both proposals have merit and should be implemented. In the case of prop trading, there is clearly a conflict of interest in large firms when prop traders within a bank assume leveraged positions (long or short) at odds with what the banks' own customers are being advised to do. It is not so much that this is bad *per se*, but that it stokes public cynicism about banks and thus undermines the confidence in the financial system that is so important for its credibility. Additionally, prop trading as we know it has increased the riskiness of institutions that engage in it.

As for breaking up the banks themselves into many smaller pieces, this should have the beneficial role of reducing "systemic risk." Recall that it was the collapse of confidence in the huge banks right after the Lehman Brothers fiasco that precipitated the GFC to spread like wildfire from the United States and United Kingdom to the entire world. I have been told that such contagion would be much less likely to happen in a world of many smaller banks. Frankly, I am not sure this is true.

Yet there is a deeper reason for ridding ourselves of too-big-to-fail banks, and this reason is moral and political-philosophical in nature. The public quite rightly believes that, during the recent crisis, the large banks got away with murder. People rightly believe that large banks are playing a game of Heads-I-Win, Tails-You-Lose. They come out ahead no matter what happens. In good times, the big banks reap and keep all the benefits of success. But in bad times, the risk of contagion is so great that government *must* bail them out to prevent panic and collapse. It is the taxpayers—the voters—who end up holding the bag, and they have every reason to be indignant about the current system. Cynicism is heightened by the highly inflated pay commanded by bankers and traders at "big" institutions, in contrast with the much more modest compensation at local banks that enjoy widespread local support. In sum, the game has been rigged in a manner that rightly undermines confidence in the entire financial system. And confidence in the financial system itself is a *sine qua non* for true capitalism to deliver the goods that justify its very existence. Public policy must thus ensure that such trust is in place.

For these reasons, I support fundamental revisions to today's banking system of the kind currently being implemented to one degree or another, independently of the matter of leverage. However, if the issue of leverage itself is properly addressed, it may not be necessary to actually break up the big banks. In this regard, it is noteworthy that big banks dominate both the Canadian and Australian banking scene, yet virtually all of these institutions emerged from the GFC unscathed. What did they all have in common? They all had balance sheets whose leverage was a fraction of that of the large U.S./UK banks. India offers an even better example, where regulators were dead set against the "excesses" of the Western banks for two decades. The financial system there proved very resilient as well.

Sharing a Dirty Little Secret

This concludes the chapter on preventing Perfect Financial Storms in the future. I support all the reforms listed in Figure 4.5. But of these, the Type II reform of controlling leverage is the most important.

I am often asked why this obvious point is not more widely recognized, and why leverage reform is so vigorously opposed. I offered four reasons earlier, and I would now like to offer a fifth, a dirty little secret virtually never discussed.

The powers that be in Greenwich, Connecticut, on Wall Street and in the City of London enjoy very, very, very large incomes. They are very powerful and contribute heavily to political campaigns. Moreover, their spouses are used to such incomes, incomes that have become entitlements of sorts. But what these players will not tell you is that their stratospheric incomes are due in large part to leverage. Nor will they confess that talent has less to do with their success than they might think, notwithstanding that brilliant fund managers do indeed exist, as is true in any calling. Leverage, financial sector cartelization, and luck play a larger role than skill. The two Type II reforms that I have proposed squarely confront leverage and cartelization. As for the role of luck in life, and its implications for optimal tax policy and redistribution, please see Chapter 6. If you are a fund manager, your head may spin.

CHAPTER 5

Bargaining Theory 101

How *Not* to Deal with China

We are living in the age of economists—the Age of Larry Summers, as it were. These high priests sit at the right-hand side of presidents and prime ministers, dominate cabinet meetings, and help explain "the economy" to a benighted public. Indeed, they do more. With the advent of Economics Imperialism during the past few decades, economists have confidently utilized their analytical prowess to become spokesmen on topics ranging from date rape, to demography, to financial system reform, and to the pursuit of happiness, not to mention the future of the world economy.

Yet there is a paradox here. Despite the appeal of their models, economists have less and less to say about the most important issues of our time. For these issues are political in nature—indeed political philosophical—not economic. Attacking these problems in a satisfactory manner cannot be achieved with the tools of micro- and macroeconomics. As a result, when economists do discuss such issues as how to prevent welfare state bankruptcy, the results are superficial and piecemeal. Strangely enough, the same can be said of the analyses of most political scientists. Their discipline is highly problematic as it never found a "core model" around which to organize the pastiche of insights it offers, interesting as many of these insights are.

In this chapter, I attempt to offer such a core model, and to apply it to a case study involving the growing rivalry between China and the United States. More specifically, I argue that the root problem of political science has been its failure to adopt as its core model the concept of politics as *multilateral bargaining behavior* between overlapping interest groups. After all, this is what social life is all about—with a single notable exception: economic behavior within an "invisible hand" market economy where prices coordinate human activity, and where no concept of bargaining is either required or in fact possible. Given today's absence of a bargaining perspective on matters political, the analyses of today's most pressing political issues are often half-baked.

For example, consider how little both political scientists and economists have had to say about *the* central problem confronting most all governments of the West during the next several decades: How can democratically elected governments be prevented from continuing to mortgage our children's future? This problem is rarely identified in the policy journals or op-ed pages, much less addressed in a serious manner. To be sure, commentators on both the Left and the Right often *complain* about the future insolvency of many welfare states, but to complain about a problem is not to analyze it, much less solve it. Without the right core model around which to organize our thinking, it is unlikely that much progress will be made in doing so.

The great irony here is that a suitable core model does in fact exist, a model of multilateral bargaining that is ostensibly unknown to most social scientists, and that astonishingly is neither discussed nor referenced in most political science textbooks. The model stems from John F. Nash Jr.'s remarkable theory of bargaining set forth in the early 1950s. Many of you will know of Nash from the book and movie about his life, *A Beautiful Mind*. In two papers published in 1950 and 1953, Nash posed and deduced an axiomatic solution to the problem of how two people compromise their differences and arrive at a mutually acceptable compromise during bargaining.

Another game theorist, John Harsanyi, would give a much deeper source of support to Nash's bargaining solution in two papers published in 1956 and 1963. In the second paper, he also extended Nash's theory to games with any number of players and coalitions. Because of the pioneering work of these two scholars on bargaining theory, it finally became possible to clarify such concepts as "relative power," "balance of power," "political economy," "credible threats," and "interest group politics." For this and related work, both Nash and Harsanyi would receive the Nobel Memorial

Prize in Economic Sciences in 1994, notwithstanding that neither was an economist proper.[1]

This chapter has two goals. The first goal is to introduce the Nash-Harsanyi bargaining paradigm in very simple terms. In doing so, I show how this framework makes possible a precise definition of the all-important concept of relative power, and how it advances analytical social science in several other ways as well. Bargaining behavior turns out to be the magnetic north of politics, and the Nash-Harsanyi model is the missing "core model" that could play a unifying role in political science analogous to that played by the law of supply and demand in economics.

The second goal is to apply the Nash-Harsanyi model to the ongoing bargaining game between China and the United States as these two powers begin to duel for global primacy. The analysis here is intended to suggest a new way of thinking about power, conflict, and conflict resolution. The "historically inevitable" loss of power by the United States to China emerges as a half-truth, and the real story lies in the arrant incompetence of the United States in its bargaining with China, as contrasted to the consummate skill of the Chinese in getting what they want from us. This situation can be remedied if the United States (and by extension the West) starts to properly protect its turf rather than yield it time after time to an aggressor. The Nash-Harsanyi logic makes clear how to do so, and why it should be done.

To sum up, there exists an unfortunate and unnecessary imbalance today between *res politica* and *res economica*, a distinction apparently introduced by Aristotle. Economics does not and should not rule the roost. Indeed, properly understood, free-market economics turns out to be no more than a limiting special case of multilateral bargaining, as the Nobel laureate Robert Aumann proved formally, in a remarkable result we will review later in this chapter. This confirms Aristotle's insight that politics trumps economics, and that politics is indeed the master discipline. The time has arrived for this truth to be recognized if we are to forge meaningful solutions to those political problems that are becoming the dominant issues throughout the West.[2]

The Origins of Economics Imperialism

The phrase "Economics Imperialism" has been in use for nearly three decades. The term was coined by the late economist Kenneth

Boulding of the University of Colorado at Boulder. It captures the reality that, of all the social sciences, economics has emerged as the most relevant, most useful, and most rigorous discipline. Its perspective on social behavior and its analytic methods have invaded most every branch of sociology, political science, and social psychology. The success of such books as *Freakonomics* is proof of this point, as its authors Steven D. Levitt and Stephen Dubner have emphasized. Finally, if any further proof is needed, just consider the surging enrollments in economics and finance courses at major universities worldwide during the past few decades.

The same phenomenon is true in the field of public policy analysis. There was a time when the cabinet of the U.S. president consisted of lawyers, businessmen, political scientists, and economists. Economists in fact were latecomers to the game. It is often forgotten that they were few in number prior to World War II since neither the data nor the theory they needed yet existed. Lawyers dominated policy since the time of President Lincoln, as did gentlemen farmers before that. But this is no longer the case. We are now living in an age when economists such as Martin Feldstein or Lawrence Summers or Ben Bernanke dominate public policy discussions. With their well-honed analytical skills (lacking in other fields), they sound off with credibility on any number of topics, and often have the last word.

But do they deserve such credibility? At a time when ballooning government deficits are issue number one throughout the West, and when the prospect of "red ink as far as the eye can see" is supported by the most reputable of economic projections, can you think of a single economist who has asked, much less answered, the Great Question of the day: "How can we pass a constitutional amendment preventing the government from further mortgaging the future of our children and grandchildren, and in doing so spare the United States further credit downgrades, and potential bankruptcy in the long run?" This is a question of political theory, one that economists understandably are hesitant to address. But since welfare state solvency will be *the* principal issue for Western democracies during the next 50 years, their specific expertise will become less interesting and less relevant.

Five developments explain the advent of Economics Imperialism:

First, the discipline of economics is indeed highly analytical and rigorous, and this imparts credibility to it.

Second, as a scientific endeavor, economics can both describe and explain a wide range of phenomena. Armed with these capabilities, it can also help to forecast the future. Of course, these forecasts are not always accurate, and it is easy to laugh at them. But it may be better to laugh at the fruitless attempts of physicists to predict where a scrap of paper will land when dropped from five feet above the floor. The "standard error of estimate" of their forecasts is much higher than those of economists predicting the path of the economy! Forecasting is difficult in any field, but that does not render it useless, and economic forecasting has become indispensable in today's society.

Third, the analytics of economics are not mere abstractions, but are transformed into testable models via the linkage between economic theory and econometrics. In an age when the objectivity of analysis is prized, it helps a policy maker to be able to trot out extensive statistical backup for his case, regardless of how flawed the underlying statistical methodology might be.

Fourth, economics was the first discipline to capture and recognize the all-important concept of "incentives." When they make decisions, consumers, producers, investors, and indeed politicians respond to given incentives. This point is extremely important for two reasons: (1) the concept of "incentive structure compatibility" is arguably the most important concept ever set forth in analytical social science, and can be utilized to assess the performance and viability of entire social systems (e.g., capitalism versus communism) as I demonstrate in the next chapter; and (2) incentives can be changed by government policy—in particular, changed for the better via superior policies. This second point has permitted economics to be linked to public policy in a very compelling manner. By knowing the consequences of rerigging the incentive structure, a policy analyst can better predict the outcomes of various policy changes, and thus can identify a better policy.

Fifth, beginning students of economics are presented with a powerful analytical model that is as compelling to economics as the law of gravity is to physics: the law of supply and demand. Imagine economics without this core model!

The Contrasting Failure of Political Science

Now contrast these selling points of economics with the state of political science today. To begin with, there is no organizing paradigm or "model" of any kind. The field is often described as unrigorous and mushy. Consider the field of international relations, and journals such as *Foreign Affairs*. Some very good articles appear, representing the considered views of highly knowledgeable people. But the reader looks in vain for clear, rigorous definitions of concepts such as optimal threats or balance of power or self-interest or rationality. Moreover, crucially important issues of incentive structures are either suppressed or confused. Worse yet, the most fundamental perspective cross-cutting all forms of politics is usually given short shrift, namely "Politics: Who Gets What, When, and How," the perspective memorably proposed by Harold Laswell back in 1935.

All in all, the paradigm of politics as the process of multilateral bargaining between competing interest groups is either absent from the pages of most political science books and op-ed articles, or else is present in an ambiguous way. Accordingly, a core model centered around bargaining is truly needed.

Why the Paradigm of Economics No Longer Suffices

There are several different reasons why political science can now be viewed as more fundamental than economic science.

First, as economic theorists such as Robert Barro at Harvard have shown, the proper functioning of free market economics is completely dependent upon the assumptions of the rule of law, of nonbribable judges, of sanctity of contract, of transparency, and so forth. That is to say, proper political institutions are a *necessary* condition for the virtues of a free market system to deliver the outcome society wants, namely an efficient allocation of resources and risk. These underlying institutions come first, and we surely need a rigorous discipline to make sense of these political prerequisites of economics.

Second, the ability of a free market capitalist system to deliver the goods requires much more than the basic institutional setup just described. Specifically, whenever issues of "public goods," "externalities," or "imperfect competition" arise, interest groups that are impacted must determine via multilateral bargaining exactly what gets provided to whom, and who is to pay how much of the bill. In a more general global context, issues of coping with misaligned currencies, vast trade imbalances, and theft of intellectual property rights will only be resolved politically via multilateral bargaining between the impacted interest groups. This is part and parcel of a well-functioning capitalist system. Alas, there is no invisible hand to settle these issues without bargaining there is to determine the daily price of fresh produce in the marketplace.

Third, we are living in a world where the price, quantity, and allocation of important commodities like oil were once determined by a free market. But they no longer are. We are now witnessing a dangerous "politicization" of the oil, gas, copper, and other markets. We will see the day when China may well determine the allocation of certain natural resources whose supply they have tied up via long-term bilateral contracts with nations throughout the developing world. Should this occur, then markets *per se* will no longer allocate resources as they have in the past. This role will have been assumed by bargaining.

Fourth, most of the important issues that could stymie future world growth and precipitate war remain quintessentially political in nature. For starters: Who gets how much water at what price? Who will pay how much for global warming? How much will tomorrow's youth be taxed to pay for the elderly? How high a tax bill will they be willing to pay before defaulting upon the debt they inherit? What is their threat strategy? Which nations will be "allowed" to go nuclear? The list goes on.

In short, our future will depend upon the quality of governance. But what exactly do we mean by "success in governance?" Is there a yardstick of good governance in politics analogous to that of "efficient resource allocation" in economics? More broadly, is there an organizing paradigm or model that could prove as useful to *res politica* in the future as the Law of Supply and Demand has proven useful to *res economica* in the past? Happily, there is. Yet this model is completely unknown to most political scientists and philosophers. As an aside, there is a thriving group of "rational choice theorists" within the political science community who have gone part way in creating analytical models and rendering their discipline more rigorous. Nonetheless, their models are largely silent on the root issue of bargaining power as defined later in this chapter, and are thus somewhat bloodless in my own view. Their principal limitation is that they cannot properly deal with the role of *relative intensity of preference* in bargaining.[3]

The Possibility of the Hegemony of Political Science: The Nash-Harsanyi Pluralistic Bargaining Model

In the opinion of scholars familiar with it, the Nash-Harsanyi model of multilateral bargaining is one of the marvels in the history of analytical social science.[4] Before its development during the period of 1950–1965, concepts like "power," "democratic pluralism," "bargaining equilibrium," and "balance of power" were problematically elastic concepts lacking precise meaning. Accordingly, such variables could not be measured quantitatively for the purpose of model building. Additionally, without this model, the notion of relative bargaining *ability* could not be defined. For absent a model predicting an optimal bargaining equilibrium between symmetrically rational and skillful players, the degree to which one player could be said to bargain better than another in the real world could not be determined.

By extension, it was also impossible to assess the relative competence of different governments in striking bargains on behalf of their citizens without the yardstick made possible by an idealized model. For example, how can we assess how incompetent the U.S. government was in permitting Chinese mercantilism to boost employment in China, while costing millions of "good jobs" over here?

The Building Blocks of the Model

The building blocks of the model are players, strategies, payoffs, and preferences. More specifically, we have:

1. The set of n individual players
2. The set of all possible pairs of players that could come face to face with each other in any number of overlapping coalitions that might include them both (you and I are both members of the Sierra Club and of the Classical Music Association)
3. The set of possible coalitions that these players can form and oppose one another (e.g., the environmentalist lobby versus the timber industry)
4. The set of strategies available to each player individually, and available to each and every coalition that might form— including those threat strategies that any individuals and/ or coalitions utilize, should negotiations break down and no compromise be reached
5. The resources available to each individual player and to each coalition—including economic and military resources alike
6. The "dividends" each player receives from any coalition he joins—a payoff proportional to his "relative contribution" to each coalition

7. The preferences of each player for what is at stake, including his willingness to take risk in pressing for his demands. This latter feature is often called a player's "risk tolerance," and while it is only one type of preference, it plays a very important role in bargaining.[5]

The Logic Utilized to Arrive at a Rational Bargaining Compromise

Nash modeled bargaining behavior as a two-stage game played by two players. In stage 1, the two players each announce the optimal threat strategies which each would deploy should no compromise be agreed upon during the second-stage game, the bargaining game proper. The "threat payoff" associated with these threat strategies serves as a point of reference whereby each player knows what his fate will be should no deal be reached by the time when the opportunity to bargain further expires. (It is assumed that there is a negotiation expiration date.) A bit further on, I will explain the logic by which each player selects his optimal threat strategy. The impetus propelling each player towards a compromise is that both know that they will end up worse off without an agreement (where they receive only the threat payoff) than with one.

Nash showed that, in every such game, there will be a unique solution, that is, a unique compromise between the players. If the game is a simple one consisting of two players attempting to divide the pie, the solution would represent the agreement whereby player 1 would receive, say, 65 percent of the pie, and player 2 would get 35 percent of it. But why would they not each get 50 percent? What *differences* between the players cause an unequal outcome to be agreed upon? Nash himself did not really answer this question convincingly as his approach was too abstract to do so, but John Harsanyi did in 1956.[6] He modeled the bargaining game as a bargaining process consisting of a sequence of "concessions" by both sides—just as we observe in real life. At first, each player demands most of the pie. "If I don't get 90 percent, I'll screw you." As time goes on, both reach a "sticking point" at which it is irrational for either to concede further, and bargaining stops. This sticking point is the solution in Harsanyi's model.

For any game, there will be one and only one such sticking point, and it happens to be the Nash solution, arrived at via a very different logic from Nash's own logic. Harsanyi provided a convincing explanation of why the sticking point would generally be *asymmetrical* in the sense of awarding an unequal division of the pie to the players. The reason was that the players typically had different preferences towards risk. This reveals itself during bargaining by the fact that a player with less risk aversion than the other is willing to press his demands harder than the other during the process of bargaining. In doing so, he is more willing to run the risk of receiving the threat payoff than the other is. In game theory parlance, his "fear of ruin" is lesser.

The Solution Itself

But where does this process stop? What exactly is the unique sticking point of any game? What makes both players refuse to make further concessions? Harsanyi showed that there is a unique sticking point corresponding to the point in the bargaining process where both players individually have reached their "risk limits." More specifically, for each player, the loss to himself from a further concession to the other would exactly equal his gain of reduced "fear of ruin" risk that results from making the concession. Once again, fear of ruin risk is simply the risk each player faces of receiving the threat payoff, and of going home empty-handed. In sum, the sticking point is the point where the risk limits of both players are reached, and remarkably this solution is always the Nash solution.[7]

Harsanyi's concept here is as subtle as it is powerful. It can be summarized by claiming that pie is awarded in proportion to risk tolerance: Each player will receive a slice of the pie whose size is larger than the other's slice to the extent that he has a greater tolerance of risk than the other. Interestingly, there is another, newer justification for the same solution: Pie is awarded in *inverse* proportion to the players' *relative need* for it. More specifically, a player will receive a slice larger than the other's to the extent that he is "less needy" for it than the other. Thus, a player that just ate a hot fudge sundae and is not hungry can bargain down another player who has not eaten, and who has two hungry children to feed. It may not seem "fair" that the needier settles for less, but it is the way of the world. The relative needs version is perhaps the more intuitive of these two rationales for the Nash-Harsanyi solution. No complex concept of risk limits is required. This solution was introduced and shown to be formally equivalent to the Nash solution in 2004.[8]

The Case of More Than Two Players, and of Coalitions

In 1963, Harsanyi extended the entire Nash-Harsanyi logic to the case of more than two players who were free to form coalitions, indeed "overlapping" or "pluralistic" coalitions. Any player could be a member of as many interest groups as desired. His model was necessarily quite complex, given the need to model rational bargaining behavior both by all possible coalitions, and by all pairs of individuals that confront each other inside and outside of the various coalitions to which they might belong. Here is a simple summary that should prove useful since I will draw on this model later in discussing the United States versus China game.

Like the two-person game solved by Nash, the *n*-person game consists of two stages. In stage 1, all coalitions form and announce optimal threat strategies against one another. In a corporate labor dispute, the company's optimal threat might be to fire all workers whereas the workers' threat might be to go on strike and maximize bad publicity for the company. Then in stage 2, a consensus is arrived at specifying how much of the overall pie each of the players will receive in light of the relative bargaining power of all the coalitions of which he is a member.

The outcome that is reached by all players who bargain in this manner is known as the game's *multilateral bargaining equilibrium*. It formalizes previous concepts such as the political scientist David Truman's notion of "pluralistic politics," where pluralism reflects the reality that we are all members of different yet sometimes overlapping coalitions advancing the variety of overlapping interests we have as human beings. The outcome that is arrived at will accurately reflect each player's (and each coalition's) relative power. But what exactly *is* each player's power? Can this be formalized? And how do individuals and coalitions select threats against one another that are credible, much less optimal? What do these terms mean? These are two loose ends to which I now turn. In passing, I will explain the interrelation between free market behavior in economics in which there is *no* bargaining at all, as opposed to bargaining behavior in general.

Optimal Threat Strategies That Are Credible

As was discussed informally previously, the concept of threat strategies plays an important role in determining the outcome of bargaining.

But how does each player (whether an individual or a coalition) determine which of many possible threat strategies is the optimal one? What exactly does "optimal" mean here? And finally, how will his opponent know that this threat is credible—not just a bluff—and thus be effective in orienting the bargaining game? Nash and Harsanyi provided answers to all three questions.

In selecting a threat strategy, each player (and each coalition in the case of n-person games) will want to trade off two different entities, X and Y. X refers to the damage he can do to the other player in selecting his threat. You might think that his optimal threat will be to wreak maximal damage upon the other. But this is incorrect because it ignores the role of Y, which denotes the damage he inflicts upon himself in exercising the threat. Accordingly, a given player (or coalition) will want to select that threat that maximizes the *spread* between the damage it can inflict less the cost to himself of doing so, that is, the spread X–Y. But the other player (or the opposing coalition) will look at the problem in reverse: He will select a threat strategy maximizing the mirror image spread Y–X.

But as Nash showed, this is equivalent to minimizing X–Y. Thus, the threat selection game between any two players (or coalitions) ends up being a kind of zero-sum "MaxMin" game in which the entity that one party wants to maximize is the entity that the other party wants to minimize. Nash proved that there will always exist a unique pair of threat strategies—one for each player—that solves this MaxMin problem.[9] This is true even though the particular threat strategies available to each player are different, as are the potential values of X and Y for each player. This is a remarkable result.

Let me show an intuitively appealing and simple example of this logic at work. Suppose you and I are two neighbors living in wooden houses 50 feet apart. We both get very angry at each other over a dispute concerning my decision as to where to construct a new fence between our houses. We each pull out a box of matches and say to one another, "If I don't get my way, I will use these to burn down your house." We would each thus *appear* to have symmetrical threat power over each other. But this is incorrect. For I remind my neighbor: "The wind always blows from my house towards yours. So if you burn down my house, you will burn down yours as well. The reverse is not true. So stop bluffing!"[10]

Will such threats be credible? The answer is yes insofar as any other pair of threats will be mutually irrational and each player will know this. Are they likely to be utilized? No. They are never to be played. Their role as in real life is to "orient" the game and provide a strong motivation for the players to reach a deal—a deal leaving everyone much better off than they are with the threat payoff. It is precisely when the players do *not* know the disagreement payoff that confusion results, cooperation breaks down, and threat strategies end up getting played. The advent of World War I offers a good example of such an outcome.

There is one last important point here. As Nash originally pointed out, the threats must be "enforceable" so that all players know *for sure* what happens if they do not reach a compromise and negotiations break down. They must be "binding." For a good example of this logic, just recall the Doomsday machine of the Cold War. This machine represented the binding threat strategy that compelled compromise between the United States and Russia during the Cuban Missile Crisis. A very important point here is that, when the threats are credible and enforceable, neither player will have any reason to think that that opponent is bluffing when announcing his optimal threat.

The Meaning of Relative Power

The simplest way to think about the relative power between players in any bargaining game is to start off with the special "symmetrical" case in which all players will have equal relative power. This will occur if each and every player is strategically identical in terms of his resources, his preferences including his tolerance of risk, his contributions to all coalitions that might form, and his strategy sets—including his potential threat strategies as an individual, or a member of any coalition. If all players are strategically equal in this regard, their relative power is the same, and each ends up receiving an equal share of the pie at stake.

Differences in power will thus reflect differences in the strategic endowments of the players. Our fundamental result is: A player will have greater relative power than other players to the extent that:

1. He has greater resources than other players (money, military prowess, athletic prowess, intellectual capabilities).
2. He has greater threat power than other players as defined earlier.
3. He contributes more "worth" to the coalitions that he joins (e.g., an MVP has more power than other players because he contributes the most to his team).

4. He joins coalitions that are more powerful in opposing other coalitions than are the coalitions that other players join— that is, he has greater "coalitional muscle."

5. He has greater tolerance for risk in pressing his demands than other players have, or equivalently, he has less "fear of ruin."

Harsanyi formulated a *power index* measuring the relative power of different players in a manner that captures all five of these strategic dimensions of power.

Free Market Economics as a Special Case of n-Person Bargaining

The relationship between free market exchange theory and bargaining theory is remarkable, and this brief discussion of it will reinforce my thesis of the primacy of politics over economics. Market-based economic exchange can be analyzed as a very simple *bartering* game in which a consumer's only threat strategy is not to buy an available product at the terms offered. "I want four cucumbers for my two squashes," says one player. The counterparty shouts, "No way. I will only give you two cucumbers for those mealy squashes of yours." They settle on an interim exchange rate of, say, three cucumbers for two squashes. Note that in bartering games of this kind, market prices do not exist and thus play no role.

Now consider a very special case of this bartering game in which (1) there are a very large number of players, (2) no individual player has any strategic power at all, and thus has no ability to create or to join any coalition of other players, (3) no player has any threat power at all against any other player except to decline a particular exchange offer, for example, "two squashes for two cucumbers is unacceptable, thank you," and (4) prices do not exist to coordinate behavior.

When economic behavior is modeled in this manner, then the allocation of goods and services to every player that results from bartering will exactly coincide with the allocation awarded by a classical free market. In the latter case, a price system exists and coordinates who ends up with how much at a supply/demand equilibrium. The two different models are strategically equivalent in that *every player takes home the same allocation of goods and services.*

This was the celebrated result of the Israeli economist and Nobel laureate Robert Aumann cited earlier. It makes clear how "economics" in the sense of free market exchange with prices is a very limiting special case of the Nash-Harsanyi bargaining model of "politics." The bargaining model will apply in *any* context, whatever the number of players, and whatever the setting, whether economic or political. Conversely, the market model will only apply in the extremely special circumstances of a perfectly competitive free market. In short, the bargaining model is the master model within which models of competitive economic markets only exist as special cases. So much for Economics Imperialism!

This concludes our summary of the Nash-Harsanyi theory. In my view, this offers the core model that should form the foundation of much political science. It rigorously addresses the fundamental question of who gets how much and why, along with subsidiary concepts like threats and power. What follows is a case study that demonstrates how applied bargaining theory can shed wholly new light on a very important issue: dealing with China.

An Application of the Bargaining Model to Today's United States versus China Game: How *Not* to Negotiate with Thugocracies

As an American traveling the world, I find it ever more discouraging to witness the decline in the power and influence of the United States. On the economic front, it is now taken for granted that the Chinese economy will surpass that of the United States by around 2035, although estimates vary widely. But economic concerns about China far transcend the differential rates of growth. There is growing anger at China's aggressive theft of intellectual property, the ongoing suppression of its exchange rate, and other long-standing mercantilist policies that continue to chafe.

In the longer term, there is the threat that China's growing web of bilateral resource agreements with nations throughout the emerging world will subvert the concept of free markets in natural resources, thus putting the West at risk. For the better part of a century, the world has benefitted from free markets in most all resources, with aggregate supply and demand determining prices and allocations. Will this be replaced by a system of bidding for Chinese "allocation permits"—with permits primarily being granted to nations that play ball with China, a system almost certain to trigger a resource war? Anyone doubting this possibility should recall Russia's behavior in cutting off natural gas supplies to the Ukraine when the latter's government did not play ball with Putin, or recall China's more recent threats of limiting "rare earth" exports to friends of the state. Both of these actions should serve as warning signs for the future.

China's Growing Belligerence

On the political and military front, 2010 was the year when China came out of the closet and let it be known that it was gunning for various global spheres of influence. Not coincidentally, this was the year that the Obama administration canceled the U.S. F-22 as well as the space shuttle, and sharply introduced its reliance upon "cheaper" drone missiles. These moves signaled that the United States would follow in the footsteps of its European allies in devoting an ever-smaller share of its resources to defense, in exchange for an ever-greater share going to entitlements. Additionally, President Obama's explicit forfeiture of U.S. leadership in the Libyan campaign offered additional proof of U.S. disengagement from global leadership.

The Chinese government had predicted much of this, of course, and is rapidly filling the growing power void with annual increases in military spending of an official 12.6 percent. A more believable estimate is probably around 14 percent. By introducing some reasonable assumptions, China could surpass the United States militarily within 25 years. Its excuse, of course, will be the need to protect its growing empire of overseas investments that will span the globe both east-to-west and north-to-south. China is a relatively resource-poor nation, and its government is understandably obsessed with its need for resources, given the size and the aspirations of its population.

The Chinese political and military expansion does not stop with its defense budget. There is growing truculence of every kind: its aggressive claims to the islands and underwater oil reserves throughout the Pacific Rim, its increasingly aggressive deployment of its navy, its plan to construct a naval base at Gawar on the coast of Pakistan, its ever-expanding claims to control over the South China Sea, and more. Nearly all of its neighbors are alarmed. Upset by the proposed Pakistani port, India is being drawn closer to the United States than it has been for years. The Vietnamese government is involved in an ongoing dispute over its claims to the Spratly and Paracel Islands. On June 22, 2011, China ordered the United States not to get involved in this dispute, typifying its new truculence. Vietnam for its part is so upset by bullying from China that it apparently has invited the U.S. navy to return to Cam Ranh Bay to protect it. Singapore, South Korea, Japan, the Philippines, and Taiwan are also increasingly concerned, and are speaking out.

Additional disturbing developments are taking place on the domestic political front. Increasingly, reformers in China are under attack as being "capitalist roaders" and next-generation Communist leaders are reviving Mao Zedongs's musings, tactics, and memories. A disturbing internal power struggle is underway in this regard, with liberals losing out to conservatives. In a recent essay, General Liu Yuan, son of Mao's earliest comrade-in-arms Liu Shaoqi, argues for a strengthening of the military over the cultural in China, praising war as the foundation of nation building, and expressing admiration for the 2001 terrorist attacks on the U.S. World Trade Center.

Others, fearful of future challenges to the Communist Party, are coalescing around Mao and his beliefs. Mr. Xiao in Hunan points out, "they seek the most powerful symbol of the Party, and Mao is the only thing that stands for that." He argues that the members of the "princeling faction" take a dynastic view of political power, caring about ideology only to the extent that it can help them gain and maintain control. Current Chinese behavior certainly supports this appraisal.[11]

Must the United States Decline?

Does the reality that China is becoming an economic and military powerhouse seal the longer-term fate of the West, as is increasingly assumed? In particular, is it true that the United States is in rapid decline relative to China? Must it be? Is it as simple as extrapolating the contrasting growth rates of GDP and military spending, and then predicting China to be the victor? These forms of power cannot represent the whole story given the surprising successes in the past of such lesser entities as the Athenian republic, Macedonia under Alexander the Great, Portugal, Singapore, Hong Kong, and Holland. Each of these successes were unexpected in their time. Conversely, numerous big powers that by rights should have dominated lesser powers failed to do so throughout history. The Chinese empire between 1550 and 1980 arguably falls into this category.

In all cases, skill, determination, and leadership played a far greater role in establishing power than did size alone. But what in turn might such skill consist of? Is it ability to innovate? Here the West is at no ostensible disadvantage to the East, at least not yet. Is it superior productivity growth more generally? Certainly not in the case of the United States versus China, where available (if problematic) data suggest that the United States maintains its lead.[12]

Bargaining Skill

Is there some other advantage that plays an important role in the tug-of-war between the United States and China, and between the West and the East more generally? Yes, there is, and it is one that is virtually never cited: the ability of one side to outsmart the other in terms of its bargaining ability. I am now going to draw upon the Nash-Harsanyi theory to suggest that both the United States and its Western allies merit a grade of D in Bargaining Theory 101, whereas China merits an A. Of course, this suggestion is vacuous without understanding exactly what "bargaining ability" means. Intuitively, poor negotiators are those who fail to utilize their resources as effectively as they could, and vice versa for good negotiators. But all this is a bit vague, and I want to utilize the Nash-Harsanyi theory to clarify the deeper meaning of *relative bargaining ability*.

To begin with, the theory makes it possible to determine the outcome from bargaining that *would* be agreed upon by symmetrically rational players of *equal* skill. As a result, we have a concrete benchmark making it possible to rank players in any real-world game by their relative bargaining ability, and to do so in two different ways. First, a player who receives less than he ideally "should" according to the model will be said to be a less skilled bargainer, whereas one who gains more than he should is a more skilled bargainer. It is that simple. Second, and more subtly, if one player has more relative power than another in reality, then the real-world difference in their two degrees of power should conform to the Harsanyi power index described previously, assuming that both players have equal bargaining abilities. This is true because the Harsanyi power index is derived from and is consistent with the Nash-Harsanyi bargaining model that defines the outcome the underlying game. If their real-world difference in power differs from their Harsanyi power index scores, then a difference in bargaining skill must explain why.

We can thus identify differences in bargaining ability in either of two ways: First, we can compare the actual outcome of the game with the theoretically ideal outcome that parties of equal bargaining ability would arrive at. Second, we can assess the actual versus the theoretical amount of relative power of each party, and thus determine whether the actual power of one versus the other approximates what it ideally should be, or whether it differs. If it differs, the reason why will be different skills in bargaining.

In what follows, I shall pursue the second approach, and contrast the sources of relative power of China with those of the United States. The conclusion is that the United States has had far greater power than China has along most every dimension of relative power in recent decades, but has fared far worse than it should have in the deals it strikes. That is to say, the United States has bargained very poorly with China, and has repeatedly been taken advantage of to a degree inconsistent with the true power structure of the two nations.

Opportunity for the United States to Improve Its Bargaining Skills

This conclusion results from applying the deductive logic of the Nash-Harsanyi theory to the United States-China rivalry. The deductive nature of the theory with its emphasis on causality permits us to know *why* the United States and its allies have received less than a fair shake in their negotiations with Beijing. Armed with this understanding, the nation can in principle do a better job when bargaining in the future. The United States can learn how to bargain so that it achieves payoffs commensurate with its true power. In doing so, the United States and its allies should be able to slow down the relative decline of the West.

This message of hope for the West is altogether different from the more familiar message set forth by those who are banking on a Chinese implosion, much like that of post-1990 Japan. Their view stems from concerns about fraudulent Chinese statistics that overstate the nation's growth and wealth, concerns about forthcoming Chinese resource shortages, worries about bad loans disguised on the balance sheets of dozens of regional banks, concerns about China's own demographic crisis, anticipation of fighting between ethnic factions, and so forth. I shall not join this debate. For what it is worth, my own belief is that China will in fact emerge as the dominant economic power on earth because China possesses arguably the greatest asset on the planet: the attitude and ability of the Chinese worker. Nonetheless, its ascent will be slowed by its two principal flaws: a very poor legal system, and wide-scale corruption which is a corollary of a poor legal system.

The Determinants of Relative United States/Chinese Power

There are five different dimensions of power in the Nash-Harsanyi theory. I now attempt to show that the United States has been and remains more powerful than China along almost all of these dimensions, with the exception of perhaps the most important one: *relative risk tolerance*. Whereas China is highly risk tolerant ("determined") in pressing for its agenda, the United States and its allies have become extremely risk averse, making threats that are vacuous, adopting supine policies, and rarely exacting a meaningful price from China for its egregious violations of international trade law. Since this risk aversion does not mirror the preferences and risk attitudes of most Americans, especially those millions who have lost their jobs to Chinese mercantilism, the behavior of the U.S. government can only be regarded as derelict. The relative risk aversion dimension of power will be discussed last. We will start off with the relative resource power of China and the United States.

1. Resource Power—Economic and Military The United States has had, and still has, an overwhelming superiority over China as regards resources, although the gap has narrowed and will shrink at an accelerating rate over the next two decades. Let's start off with economic resources of various kinds. No matter how it is measured, U.S. GDP is still far greater than Chinese GDP. This difference is far more pronounced when contrasting GDP per capita. Likewise, the net worth of the United States is estimated by the Federal Reserve Board to be $58 trillion whereas estimates of the net worth of China run from $15 to $25 trillion. In the latter case, however, no relevant data are published by Chinese economic authorities, so no one really knows China's net worth. But this figure can be approximated since it is known that the net worth of a nation is usually 3.4 times its GDP; in China's case, $5.87 trillion GDP times 3.4 = $20 trillion.

A nation's debt burden represents a different dimension of resource power, but the logic is a bit trickier. Debt is a form of negative power to the extent that too much debt becomes a strategic encumbrance that can limit a nation's options in the case of conflict. Thus, we increasingly hear that "the United States can no longer afford to intervene overseas and must focus on reducing its own deficit instead." As for domestic debt, total federal debt in the United States is currently nearly 100 percent of GDP whereas the total debt of China is officially stated to be 20 percent of GDP, a very low number.

So at first glance, China has an edge over the United States in this regard. But as a Chinese government study published on June 27, 2011 demonstrated, the regional governments have additional debt equal to 27 percent of GDP. But this figure only includes debts that are explicitly guaranteed, and when provisions for bad loans by regional banks are added in, then total Chinese *explicit* debt is around 70 percent of GDP. But as Victor Shih of Northwestern University points out, "if you take a broad view of the Chinese government's contingent liabilities rather than explicit debt on the books, then the number rises to well over 150 percent of GDP in 2010."[13]

As for foreign debt—the debt owed by each nation to all other nations—the United States is in the doghouse, owing some $3.5 trillion more than it is owed. China on the contrary is the world's largest net creditor nation. These imbalances pretty well amount to the sum of each nation's trade balances over time. Thus, the total external debt of the United States is the sum of its past annual trade deficits with the world, and vice versa for China, which has run large global trade surpluses for a long time. In terms of bargaining power, external debt only matters as an encumbrance, just as was the case with domestic debt.

All in all, therefore, the economic resources of the United States currently give it considerable net power over China—for the moment. Yet looking forward, any such advantage will ebb away due to developments we have already cited. Not only will the GDP and net worth gap narrow and ultimately be reversed, but the United States debt status is almost certain to worsen, especially as regards domestic debt. The most serious risk for the United States lies in its tens of trillions of unfunded welfare benefits, especially medical benefits, as emphasized so starkly in Chapter 3. China will experience similar problems due to its own forthcoming demographic crisis, but it is taking a leaf from the West in not promising unrealistic entitlements benefits to its people.

As for military resource power, while the Chinese can boast of a huge standing army, their air and naval defenses are far inferior to those of the United States. These are the sources of military power that matter most in today's world. All in all, the United States could prevail in almost any military engagement with China at the present time. But this U.S. advantage will ebb rapidly. There are two reasons why. First, China is determined to gain a first-class military capability, and it will have the financial and technological resources with which to do so. Second, the United States for its part has already begun to disarm because of existing fiscal demands. I fear an acceleration of U.S. disarmament as entitlements spending and rising interest expense on the debt soar in the decades ahead. The United States will join its European allies who decades ago disarmed so as to be able to finance cradle-to-grave security. Politicians can easily cut defense spending without losing votes, but they find it nearly impossible to cut unaffordable social benefits that never should have been promised in the first place.

The Obama administration's cancellation of the development of the F-22 project is the most telling sign of what lies ahead, along with the dismantling of the U.S. space program. The F-22 decision guts the hope that the United States will maintain air superiority. Already, new Su-27 Chinese fighters will soon match our stealth bomber capability, and two such planes recently chased an American reconnaissance plane over the Taiwan Strait. The cost/benefit analysis used by the administration to justify its F-22 decision was badly flawed, apparently taking little account of the great benefit of maintaining absolute air superiority. Moreover, the cancellation of the F-22 was precisely the signal *not* to send to the Chinese at the very time they were becoming more belligerent on every front. To be sure, the F-22 program has had development problems. So did the stealth bomber for many years, but look at the results of persevering. The United States has remained unassailable for decades due to its superior air power.

2. Threat Power   For purposes of judging the outcome of the United States-China rivalry to date, this is perhaps the most interesting and also misunderstood of the five dimensions of power. Therefore I devote considerable time to threat power, both military and economic. Remember in what follows that what matters in assessing threat power is not how much damage a player can do to his opponent, but rather how much damage a player can do *net the cost to himself* of doing so.

Military Threat Power   With its extensive short- and long-range missile capabilities, and its air and naval cover, the United States could inflict terrible damage on China at virtually no cost to itself, whereas the reverse holds true for China. The United States thus has and has had far greater military threat power than China. But for reasons just stated, this differential will shrink rapidly. The one area where China may already have a relative advantage over the United States is in cyber-espionage. The 2007 incursion into the office of Secretary of Defense Robert Gates and more recently into Google and Morgan Stanley are highly disturbing. The possibilities here are truly frightening, as cyber-espionage can easily morph into cyber-warfare.

To date, neither the United States nor China has had to issue threats and flex its military muscles against one another. There has been no source of military conflict between the two powers save for ongoing saber-rattling over Taiwan. This will no longer be the case in the future were China to deny the United States (or her allies) access to markets for those global resources in emerging markets it increasingly tends to control. This would be a new form of threat power that is quite probable looking forward.

To begin with, China's weak spot is its lack of resources. To cope with this, the nation is developing a global supply chain that is requiring huge investments of manpower and capital across the globe. The great question lurking here is: Will these resources be added to what we normally think of as "global supply" that can be "globally demanded" by any buyer willing to meet the market price? Or will the supply be preempted for Chinese consumption via long-term contracts negotiated bilaterally between China and its investment partners? In the latter case, the threat of resource wars will loom large. The failure of the United States and its allies to develop their own supply of future resources all but ensures that resource wars will occur.

A good example of the failure of the United States to act in its own interest in this regard has been the abject performance of the U.S. Department of Energy. A Harvard Business School case study should be written about the money that has been wasted on this bureaucracy. Its ineptitude and inaction has made the all-important concept of "U.S. energy independence" a joke around the world. President Obama's State of the Union address in January 2011 risibly equated energy independence with the production of more solar panels. The point was not lost on anyone.

The truth is that, with proper leadership and appropriate supply-side policies, the United States could easily be gaining energy independence from those thugocracies on whom we now depend. In doing so, the United States would not only achieve energy independence, but by reducing its trade deficit, would boost GDP as well. Most important, its threat power would increase since energy producers like Iran and Venezuela could no longer threaten to cut off their supplies. By stymieing energy independence at every turn, the Obama administration is reducing the nation's future threat power. This may well leave U.S. military action in the form of resource blockades as the only viable option for gaining increased resource supply from overseas in future decades.

Economic Threat Power   The area of trade is where the differential threat power of the two nations has been most important to date. Up to five years ago, it would perhaps have been necessary to defend the view that China has to a very significant degree cheated its way to its balance-of-trade hegemony via decades of hypermercantilist policies—policies never effectively opposed by those impacted in the West. These policies included currency-rigging in the extreme, violation of any number of covenants intended to foster free and fair trade, outright theft of intellectual property worth hundreds of billions of dollars, the large-scale production of counterfeit goods, and so on. But within the past few years, most observers have conceded that China has gotten away with murder in its trade relations, and that something has to be done about it. Please bear with me here, as several of the issues that arise are inherently counterintuitive, and thus widely misunderstood.

A very interesting "big picture" article on this subject was written in 2004 by the late Paul Samuelson of MIT, America's first Nobel Laureate in economics.[14] In a phone conversation I had with Professor Samuelson just after he published this essay, he told me that proving the case of currency manipulation by China was the easy part of the story. The more important part was that China's behavior had undermined the entire basis of free trade, namely the Ricardian principle of advantage, by means of its unprecedented policy of intellectual property theft.

Intellectual Property Theft   Suppose Country A has an advantage over country B in producing, say, maple syrup, because Country A was endowed with maple forests whereas country B was not. And vice versa in the case of whatever natural endowment country B possesses that Country A does not. As a result, it is in both nations' interest that they trade. Samuelson commented that China had changed the rules of this game for the worse by demanding that, in order for country A to sell its maple syrup to China, it would have to export its forest of maple trees as well. Otherwise, there is no deal.

I have often been infuriated to read that Intel or some other such company can only manufacture inside China if it hands over a large number of what used to be known as "trade secrets," that is, the very basis of the competitive advantage U.S. companies achieved by decades of hard work and innovation. I have been ever more infuriated by the supine response of the U.S. Department of Commerce and other agencies in almost never exacting a price from China for its transgressions. All we seem able to do is to protest, ineffectually. We rarely if ever retaliate and give China some of her own medicine despite the reality that we possess much more relative threat power than it does, as will be seen later in this chapter.

Currency Manipulation Proper   Bad as China's policy of intellectual property theft may have been, it is still important to understand the magnitude of Chinese currency market manipulation in recent decades, and its true impact. For this is the arena in which the issue of threat power has arisen most dramatically, and in which the West has abjectly failed to utilize the threat power advantage it had. The result was lower GDP growth, an excessive loss of jobs, and decreased wealth. What is important is to contrast what "should" have happened to the yuan/dollar according to the theory of free and fair trade, versus what did happen.

Broadly speaking, when a newcomer to the world economy soars from rags to riches as China has since 1980, its currency will and should appreciate very significantly relative to the currencies of stodgier, older economies. This statement assumes free and fair trade of the kind endorsed by the covenants of the World Trade Organization. Figure 5.1 makes clear what actually happened in this regard. I have also included the behavior of the Japanese yen for purposes of comparison.

The astonishing fact that the Chinese yuan relative to the dollar was repeatedly devalued—not revalued upward—is a dirty little secret known to very few. I will never know why. Perhaps this results from living in an era of foreshortened memories, where databases typically go back only five or ten years. We regularly hear about China's willingness "finally" to let the yuan appreciate by some 27 percent between 2005 and today. But what actually matters is

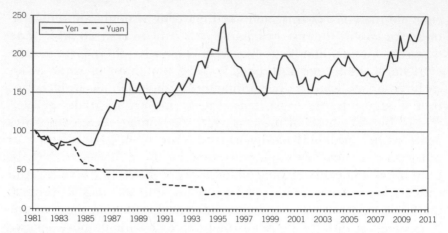

Figure 5.1 The Dirty Little Secret about the Chinese Yuan
Source: Bloomberg, and Strategic Economic Decisions, Inc.

that, even after this act of generosity by the Chinese government, their currency is worth *well under half* what it was worth when the Chinese economy was in shambles as late as the early 1980s. And between 1990 and 2011, the yuan/dollar has depreciated by 46 percent. Depreciated! It is hard to believe that this could have happened, much less that no one ever mentions it. Please study the figure.

Part of the explanation for this devaluation concerns what happened in the mid-1990s. China's currency policy before 1994 must be viewed differently from the period after 1994 because, prior to 1994, the yuan traded at two different exchange rates: an official and an unofficial rate (the latter for preferred customers). In 1994, these were aligned via a devaluation, as seen in the figure. What is remarkable is that, having devalued the official rate significantly via the alignment, the currency never appreciated thereafter until late 2005, and very slowly after that, always remaining far lower than its earlier pre-1994 value. The explanation for this outcome was full-scale currency manipulation as many scholars have noted.

To grasp the true magnitude of what happened, contrast the case of China with that of Japan as shown in the figure. To begin with, Japan's rise during 1970 to 1990 was much less spectacular than China's more recent rise, partly because Japan was already a wealthy economy. Theoretically, this predicts that the rise of the yen should have been much *less* than that of the yuan. To be sure, Japan fought fiercely for its cheap (devalued) yen throughout the 1970s and 1980s, but the United States and her allies strongly jawboned the nation to let its currency appreciate, which it did. The yen more than *doubled* against the dollar as the figure makes clear. Nothing comparable was done to force China to revalue as successive U.S. administrations let China get its way, and failed to make any credible threats against it.

Two Reasons Why the Yuan Should Have Appreciated   In the context of free and fair trade, how exactly does economic theory predict that the currency of a winner like China will appreciate hugely? There are two reasons, both rarely cited. First, consider a simplistic model in which trade in goods and services is the only kind of trade permitted. Trade in assets is forbidden. Then in this case, there can be no trade deficits at all since such deficits are financed by asset sales. Accordingly, the currency value must change so as to keep the trade deficit at zero. A rising star like China would find that, with its newfound productivity and cheap labor, the United States (and other established nations) starts to buy far more Chinese goods than China wants to buy U.S. goods. The result: The demand by Americans (and others) for the yuan with which to buy Chinese goods will far exceed the demand by China for dollars with which to acquire U.S. goods. As a result, the Chinese currency must appreciate by the law of supply and demand, and by a lot over time. The higher yuan permits the trade deficit to remain at zero, as required, because a stronger yuan encourages the Chinese to buy more foreign goods, and it discourages foreigners from buying Chinese goods.

Matters become more complicated when we extend this simple model to include trade in assets, whether in real estate, T-bills, or whatever. The main story here, known as the Belassa-Samuelson effect, is that trade in assets should cause a *further* appreciation of the currency of the emerging economy. Why is this the case? Assuming that China enjoys the rule of law and transparent investment policies, foreigners will want to invest in rapidly appreciating Chinese assets far more than the Chinese will want to buy the assets of slower-growing, more established nations. This translates into greater demand by foreigners for the yuan than Chinese demand for dollars (or whatever), since foreigners must acquire yuan to invest in China, and the Chinese must acquire dollars to invest in the States. As a result, the Chinese currency is pushed up yet again by the simple law of supply and demand.

By taking both of these stories into account, a case can be made that between 1980 and 2010, the Chinese currency could well have *appreciated* by some 300 percent, if not even more, had China let the currency market function freely. But due to an astonishing level of open market purchases of dollars, accumulating over $3 trillion in foreign exchange reserves, by keeping its capital account closed, by permitting corrupt judicial and administrative practices to frighten away foreign investors like myself, and by endorsing a raft of other unfair policies, including the sale of counterfeit goods and intellectual property theft, the Chinese currency is valued at roughly half of what is was some 20 years ago. That is an exchange rate of one-sixth of what it arguably should be.

Certain academic economists sympathetic to China make the case that we should ignore the United States/Chinese trade imbalance and by extension the yuan/dollar exchange rate, and focus instead on China's trade balance with the entire rest of the world, a balance that has shrunk. This is very unconvincing. Exchange rates are binary by nature, and these binary rates matter. After all, they constitute *prices* of a very important kind. The United States was China's primary target market for exports for two decades. What Figure 5.1 makes crystal clear is that, while we should have experienced a soaring yuan, and accordingly a much lesser outsourcing of jobs than we did, the United States experienced the reverse to its great detriment, while becoming the world's largest net debtor in the process.

Failure to Utilize Our Relative Threat Power Superiority—A Political Disgrace The supine response of the United States to China in matters of trade would have been understandable had China had a significant threat power advantage over the United States. But it did not, as a Nash-Harsanyi analysis of optimal threats makes crystal clear. To begin with, the Chinese government has depended hugely on its ability to export manufactured goods to the West. During the past two decades, it understandably felt obliged to create hundreds of millions of new jobs to prevent unrest, if not outright revolution, and China's leaders have acknowledged this throughout the past two decades. Had the United States (in conjunction with other Western powers) said "enough" and issued an enforceable threat of large import tariffs unless they played fair, it would have hurt the Chinese gravely. But what would have been the offsetting cost to us of doing so?

The standard reply is that Americans would have suffered for two reasons. First, the government would to some extent have denied U.S. workers some of those extra-cheap Chinese imports that have raised U.S. living standards. To be sure, many *consumers* did benefit, but consumer well-being is not the appropriate measure of what is good for the nation as a whole. Don't millions of lost jobs enter into this calculus? And what about growing indebtedness to foreigners due to financing huge trade deficits? Second, the U.S. inflation rate would have been driven higher. This could have happened, to a limited extent. But the econometric evidence shows that the link between trade and the inflation rate has become very tenuous during the past two decades.

Remember that, to assess relative threat power, we must assess the situation when viewed from China's perspective as well as from our own. Had the United States played tough, what could China have done in retaliation? What was its threat power? It had virtually none. Of course, they could have refused to export their "cheap goods" to us, but doing so would have hurt them far more than us, as just explained. Additionally, they could have stopped funding the U.S. trade deficit by cutting back on purchases of U.S. Treasuries, as they recently have. U.S. interest rates then get driven up, damaging the domestic economy. This, at least, is their standard threat, but it is vacuous. As will be explained, the U.S. deficit will get funded *regardless* of the size of Chinese purchases of Treasuries. All China would end up achieving by not buying U.S. Treasuries is a lower value of the dollar, not higher U.S. interest rates. But a lower dollar is good for the U.S. economy, and arguably bad for China.

To sum up, the Chinese had a fraction of the relative threat power that the United States possessed during the two-decade-long period when we continually rolled over and gave them everything they wanted. From a Nash-Harsanyi standpoint, this represented extreme bargaining incompetence on the part of five successive U.S. administrations. There is a lesson in all this for how differently the United States should act in future confrontations with China.

What the United States and Its Allies Should Have Done a Decade Ago   The United States and its allies should have made China's admission to the World Trade Organization in 2001 conditional upon abandoning their hyper-mercantilist policies. The Chinese would have been told five years in advance that their admission was dependent upon opening their capital account and permitting the yuan to appreciate, upon ceasing to steal intellectual property rights, upon ceasing to sell counterfeit goods (e.g., fake Gucci bags), and so forth. The price to them of not doing so would be not only rejection from the WTO, but also stiff punitive tariffs enacted by all the major Western allies. The reason for advance notice is important. In bargaining theory, you should never back a player into a corner. This could have been avoided by articulating credible and enforceable penalties that China would incur in the future by failing to adhere to globally accepted concepts of free and fair trade. China would then have had the time required to make suitable adjustments.

But what did we do? The United States acted *as if* China possessed the threat power, whereas we did not. Our government sold our own population's interests right down the drain. The United States also failed to create a coalition of other nations such that China would have had no alternative but to play ball. Instead no coalition was organized, and the Chinese government pursued a divide-and-conquer strategy, isolating potential Western allies from each other. They gained WTO admission on their own terms, and that was that. How dare our policy makers have let this happen, perpetually apologizing for China, and exhorting domestic manufacturers to be patient and accommodate China's "period of reentry" into the global economy? Exactly whose interests should our representatives in Washington have been defending?

Four Fallacies about Relations with China   First, it is easy to misinterpret the gist of my main argument, and to conclude that it is anti-Chinese in spirit. It is not. I have no objection to the rise of a great trading partner whose success causes an ongoing outsourcing of jobs here at home. Everyone should welcome the return of China to the world fold. What I and many other observers are concerned about is the *excessive* rate of U.S. job losses, of GDP loss, and of foreign indebtedness growth that excessive Chinese mercantilism has brought about. I know of no definitive analysis of the difference between the number of good jobs that United States and Europe have lost versus the lesser number we *should* have lost had China played fair and square, and let the yuan appreciate significantly rather than fall nearly half in value. But estimates in the range of 5 to 7 million jobs are often floated.

In a 2010 Briefing Paper of the Economic Policy Institute,[15] Robert Scott examines extensive evidence on the subject of job losses to China, and concludes that the United States alone lost 2.4 million jobs since 2001. Add in losses during the 1990s, and losses suffered by other nations, and this total of over 5 million seems reasonable. Also, Scott's numbers do not apparently include job losses from exports to China that would have materialized were it not for China's currency policy, and its other forms of mercantilism.

The second fallacy concerns those alleged benefits to United States and other Western consumers that cheap Chinese imports made possible. As indicated previously, this is at best a half-truth. Let's tally up the costs of these alleged benefits. To begin with, some economists claim that the cheap yuan encouraged the excess consumption that has imbalanced and damaged the U.S. economy during the past two decades. Additionally, those ever-so-cheap Chinese goods that we consumed caused a ballooning trade deficit. By elementary economic theory, such deficits result in growing indebtedness to foreigners (debt that must be serviced, thereby reducing future living standards), reduced levels of GDP growth, and increased unemployment due to excessive outsourcing. So all in all, there was nothing "free" at all in the cheapness of these goods. As we all learn in Econ 101, there really is no free lunch in economics.

The third fallacy centers on the oft-cited claim that the Chinese could drive up our interest rates by not funding our fiscal deficit. This is the single most widespread fallacy that I know of in international economics. It involves what is known as "the adjustment process" whereby, when a surplus nation (China) ceases to buy the assets (T-bills) of a debtor nation (the United States), then either the dollar falls, or the interest rate rises, or both. Over 90 percent of the time, it turns out that the dollar falls and the interest rate does *not* get driven up. This fact can be substantiated both in the data, and at a theoretical level. If the interest rate is not driven up, but the dollar falls as usually happens, then Main Street U.S.A. will *benefit*. Its factories will export more, and its hotels will be full. Moreover, since China pegs its currency to the value of the dollar, should China drive down the dollar and thus the yuan with it, the rest of the world would be even more irate with China's currency policy than it already is. In sum, China has virtually no threat power over the United States in this regard. What about the ancillary threat that U.S. deficit would no longer be "funded"? It turns out that that, too, is a concept with no meaning, and it cannot happen for reasons explained in endnote 16.[16]

The fourth and last fallacy concerns the misplaced belief that any retaliation against China's currency policy would somehow have been "protectionist" and thus wrong on our part. But as Paul Samuelson has stressed, there is nothing protectionist in retaliating against protectionism already initiated by another nation. The concept of "free and fair trade" is a *symmetrical* relationship between nations. More specifically, the benefits from free trade presuppose that *all* parties play by the rules of the game—not all parties except for a few that choose not to for their own benefit. In the latter instance, those who cheat can and should be made to pay a stiff price until they either agree to play ball, or are tossed out of the fold with much reduced access to global markets.

Economic Threat Power in the Future   Looking forward, the position of the United States has been badly damaged by letting China get away with its mercantilist agenda. We have transferred (or permitted to be stolen) priceless intellectual property rights, become a huge net debtor, and permitted China illegitimately to become dominant in many markets. Regaining lost share in these markets would be very difficult. Additionally, as time has gone by, supply chains have become linked in such a way that punitive tariffs would not only hurt China, but also the economies of the West.

3. United States versus China—Coalitional Worth   This is the simplest dimension of relative power to analyze in a United States-versus-China context. It addresses the relative value a player contributes to such coalitions as he joins. The United States is the richest, most productive, and most powerful nation on earth. The worth it brings to any coalition of other nations is greater than the value that China can bring to any coalition it might join, with rare exceptions. But the gap here will shrink as China becomes bigger and more powerful, develops its own middle class, and permits consumption spending to rise from 35 percent of GDP today to over 50 percent, as it ultimately will.

As this happens, China can offer ever more benefits to any coalitions it might join, in particular preferential access to its own growing markets. But for the moment, the United States is MVP to team Earth. This reality is strengthened by the belief that the United States is a reliable and reasonably benevolent partner, as well as one endowed with a high-quality legal system. China lacks both of these attributes.

For all this, there is one area in which China possesses growing coalitional worth that outstrips that of the United States and almost every other nation. This is its willingness and ability to invest in the economic development of problematic emerging economies, economies that most Western nations may wish to steer clear of. China overlooks those issues of corruption, poor environmental standards, and human rights violations that may trouble most other investors. China asks no questions, takes control, and consents to build turnkey plants, projects, and even cities—largely on its own terms and often with its own labor. In such circumstances, China can emerge as a more valuable partner to the host countries involved than the United States and its allies can. Its coalitional worth is higher.

Regrettably, while China often disguises such investments as economic in nature, they are becoming increasingly political and disruptive. Nowhere is this clearer than in its growing involvement with Pakistan. "The pattern of trade and investment between China and Pakistan suggests that the United States has little chance of retaining its status as Pakistan's major ally," suggests James Brazier, an analyst at HIS, a U.S.-based political risk consultancy. He goes on: "Pakistan's relationship with China could soon resemble that of Myanmar (Burma), another former part of British India which is now closely dependent upon China."[17] Increasingly, Pakistan's feared ISI intelligence agency has closer ties with its Chinese counterparts than it does with the U.S. CIA. In India, New Delhi's politicians and military command frequently voice their concerns about the nature of China's assistance to Pakistan. They point to the port at Gwadar on the Arabian Sea built by the Chinese Harbour Engineering Company, to dams built on sensitive sites, and to the sale of sophisticated military hardware including jet fighters, helicopters, frigates, and "civilian" nuclear assistance.

4. Coalitional Power   Coalitional power will reflect the relative strengths of the coalitions that the United States and China respectively are apt to join, or to create. Here the United States would seem to hold the upper hand for two reasons. First, for reasons of history, the United States has succeeded in forming any number of fruitful alliances with powerful nations during the past century. Coalitions that have included the United States as a member, like NATO, have had lots of muscle. Additionally, the United States befriended its former enemy Japan immediately after Japan's surrender in 1945 at the end of World War II. The resulting United States–Japanese alliance ruled the Pacific theater for many decades thereafter. Finally, there was the Marshall Plan in Europe which is universally considered to have been a benevolent and successful venture by the United States.

China's situation is quite different. In recent years, it has largely kept to itself, and has not forged alliances with powerful nations, with the possible exception of Russia. Nor has it needed to, given the nature of its ambitions. However, now that the nation is becoming rich and powerful, is maturing, and is flexing its military and political muscles, it may well seek to form coalitions. However, it would seem as if it is more interested in two-party partnerships based upon recip-rocal economic needs than it is in multiparty political coalitions. Even then, China's "partners" inevitably express concern about the hard terms China drives in its bargains, and in particular the degree of control it seeks. Pakistan's explicit concerns cited earlier offer a good case in point at present. All in all, the United States should continue to possess greater coalitional power than China.

5. Relative Risk Tolerance—The Big Story   This determinant of power along with relative threat power is the most important variable for assessing relative power in the United States versus China bargaining game. As mentioned previously, the Nash-Harsanyi theory establishes that the players' relative risk attitudes are very important in determin-ing which player gets how much of the pie at stake. With equal risk tolerances, the pie gets divided 50/50, abstracting from issues of threats and coalitional muscle. The greater the risk aversion of one player relative to that of the other, the lesser his share of the pie as the result of bargaining.

When this logic is applied to the United States versus China bar-gaining game, the conclusion we arrive at is very disturbing. What we have just seen is that, in four of the five other determinants of relative power, the United States has greater power than China. This was particularly true in the case of relative threat power in matters of economics and trade. But if this is true, *why* has China virtually always prevailed over the United States during the past three decades, and why did the United States never retaliate in an effective manner? There are only two possible explanations. If you assume that the United States behaved rationally in the sense of bargaining theory, then the *only* reason it buckled was because of extreme risk aversion. We simply would not risk rocking the boat, and we did not do so. The decision was always to roll over and "give the Chinese more time." The Chinese, on the other hand, were relentless in pressing their agenda, and they prevailed, especially as regards their currency value and their trade practices. They were willing to assume large risks. They felt that they needed to win, and they did.

Assuming that extreme risk aversion on the part of successive U.S. State Departments and administrations was the reason for the outcome of the bargaining game, a subsidiary question arises: What entitled our elected representatives to sell the United States down the drain, along with millions of outsourced jobs? Did they assume that the citizens they represented were themselves completely risk averse, and that we did not mind losing millions of good jobs and becoming a huge net debtor nation? I don't recall being polled as to my views on this subject. Nor to be sure does anyone else.

Additionally, where were the media, and economic commentators for that matter? Until recently, most assumed the risk-averse position of the *New York Times*. In commenting on punitive Congressional legislation proposed in early 2007, a lead *Times* editorial of August 13, 2007 stated: "We have consistently argued against such punitive legislation, which could harm America's economy by unleashing a trade war." In his essay cited earlier in the chapter, the late Paul Samuelson exposed the fallacy of this view. It is only when free and fair trade exists across *all* nations that no one player should adopt punitive measures and thereby risk a trade war. But in the real world, China never played free and fair, so the United States and all other nations had every right to defend themselves via retaliation at any point they might have chosen. They chose not to do so.

Now assume that the U.S. government was *not* in fact very risk averse. What then could explain the weak position it assumed in conflict after conflict with China, keeping in mind that the United States was much more powerful than China? The only remaining explanation would be an abject lack of bargaining ability. In my opinion, this lack of skill partly stems from a widespread misconception about the role of threats in bargaining. It seems to be very politically incorrect for the U.S. State Department to make credible threats. Instead of making credible threats, it expresses "concern," whatever good that does. "But couldn't making threats lead to war?" is a constant refrain from self-styled doves. The answer, in fact, is *no*. This is a central point of the Nash-Harsanyi theory that very few people grasp: When threats are made that are optimal and credible in the sense I have explained, they rarely ever get played. A cooperative agreement is reached, largely induced by the articulation of credible threats. Today's mantra of "being diplomatic" and not rocking the boat may have it all backward. The ancients were right when they said, "If you wish for peace, prepare for war."

The net result of this case study is that the United States enjoyed much greater power than China along every dimension of power except for relative risk aversion. Yet it buckled in most every confrontation with China, at least in matters of trade policy. The United States thus receives a D in Bargaining 101, whereas China receives an A. The foregoing case study can perhaps be criticized for being too retrospective, and not focusing enough on the future. But this is not primarily a chapter on bargaining with China in the years ahead. My main goal has been to use a real-world case study drawn from the past to showcase how the imperatives of bargaining theory can help us avoid the kinds of mistakes we have made in the past, and thereby do a better job in the future.

Looking forward, the principal economic imperative is that the United States should form Fair Trade coalitions with its Western allies, and utilize its coalitional power to force China to redress its unfair practices under penalty of large tariffs, should it fail to do so. Any such threat strategy must be credible and binding, and should give China time to adjust. On the military front, the United States should forge Free Passage coalitions with Vietnam, India, Brunei, Malaysia, Singapore, the Philippines, and other nations now being threatened by China in international waterways, especially the South China Sea and the Indian Ocean. In late July of 2011, a Chinese warship confronted an Indian navy vessel shortly after it left Vietnamese waters. The Chinese warship demanded that India's INS Airavat identify itself and explain its presence in international waters shortly after it completed a scheduled port call in Vietnam.

China's blatant disregard for international law and the right of free passage in international waterways reflects its determination to seize *de facto* control of the entire South China Sea, and to intimidate free passage in the Indian Ocean as well. New Delhi is understandably up in arms at these bully tactics, but this is what we can expect from China unless it is properly checked by appropriate superpower action. The United States in particular should guarantee free passage to any legitimate voyage. Further appeasement of China will lead only to worse confrontation later, as both history and game theory predict.

The Remarkable Power of the Bargaining Model in Political Science and Beyond

Having completed the case study of the United States-versus-China bargaining game, let me conclude this chapter by summarizing six different ways in which the Nash-Harsanyi model of politics represents a powerful platform for a reconstruction of political science.

1. Incorporating the Right Mix of Cooperative and Noncooperative Game Theory

In searching for the right paradigm with which to make sense of strategic interaction, game theorists during the past six decades believed that they needed to choose between two very different kinds of games: noncooperative versus cooperative games. In the former case, every player individually and in isolation adopts a strategy that is optimal against every other player's strategy. This requirement must hold true in a binary manner for all pairs of players. Coalitions of players advancing their common interests do not exist in noncooperative games. No threats or binding agreements can be made. No cooperation is possible between people. Bargaining as we think of it does not exist. It is all unrealistically *atomistic.*

Nonetheless, the noncooperative game can be very useful in special circumstances. The most celebrated example is the Prisoner's Dilemma game, a noncooperative game that is studied in virtually all branches of the social sciences. Two prisoners are kept in isolation from each other. Since neither prisoner can get together with the other and make a binding agreement not to tattle on the other, no gains from cooperation are possible. In this case, the noncooperative solution of the game is for each prisoner in isolation to tattle on the other in hopes of receiving a shorter prison term. The result: Both tattle, and both serve a longer term than they would have served had they been able to communicate and agree not to tattle on each other.

Interesting as this example may be, most real world games are not like the Prisoner's Dilemma. People are not isolated. They cooperate and make binding agreements to advance their mutual interests. Nonetheless, the noncooperative perspective has dominated game theory for the past few decades. Previously, the cooperative paradigm had been dominant. In this latter case, players enter cooperatively into coalitions for the purposes of adopting coordinated strategies that end up leaving all members better off. In other words, bargaining takes place. Threats can be made. Cooperation is central. Yet a problem with many classical cooperative game models was that they could not properly incorporate the role of optimal threats as a prelude to a "final settlement" in bargaining, nor accommodate players' different intensities of preference for the stakes in the game.

The first great virtue of the Nash-Harsanyi theory is that it overcame both these limitations, and emerged as the most persuasive of all cooperative game theories. Its second virtue was that it integrated the paradigms of both cooperative and noncooperative theory into a single integrated theory, one that could be deduced from very fundamental axioms. Noncooperative behavior is captured in the stage 1 threat game ("If I don't get my way, I'll see that you pay dearly"), whereas cooperative behavior is captured in the stage 2 game ("Let's all end up better off and split the gains from cooperation fairly"). In the process of integrating these two perspectives, these game theorists also showed how the stage 1 and stage 2 games are logically interdependent: One cannot be solved without solving the other.[18]

2. Ridding Political Science and Economics of the Anthropomorphic Fallacy

Throughout much of political and social science, it has been implicitly assumed that groups of diverse people with divergent and competing goals can be analyzed as if they were a single person. Political analysts were traditionally forced to adopt the anthropomorphic conceit that society could be modeled as a single group, namely "the people" or "the public." The preferences of diverse people could be represented by the "social preferences" of the group. In economics, the concept of a "representative consumer" was introduced to represent a host of individual consumers of differing tastes. But as would eventually be realized in both disciplines, such aggregations of individuals into a fictitious group called "society" possessing "social preferences" are almost always logically illegitimate, and cannot be made without paradoxical implications.[19]

In the Nash-Harsanyi model, and in many other game theoretic models, there is no need to carry out such aggregations. The anthropomorphic fallacy is dispensed with at the outset. When policies are adopted, nothing is being "maximized." The concept central to economics of a person attempting to maximize his utility by selecting the best mix of foods for dinner or the best mix of assets for a portfolio is replaced by a radically different concept: *The achievement of an optimal compromise* between individuals and groups with different goals. This tectonic shift was of such importance that the great "Johnny" von Neumann who originally created and mathematized game theory in the 1940s would regularly boast that, in game theory, nothing is being maximized. He contrasted this with the case of physics, in which almost every law can be stated as the solution to a particular maximization/minimization problem. He viewed this as a great advance in science, which indeed it was.

3. Highlighting Why Credible Threats Are Required for Peace

The bargaining model highlights a very important insight for public policy analysis: If policy makers in different nations really want peace (the cooperative solution), they must articulate very clearly *exactly* what will happen should the cooperative solution not be reached, and should they have to fall back and play their optimal threat strategies. If they do not do so, and are confused about what will happen if negotiations break down, the result can be needless misunderstandings leading to, say, war. As we stressed earlier, threats must be crystal clear, credible, and enforceable. Contrast this theoretical requirement with today's soft-power environment in which it is politically incorrect in the extreme even to mention the word threat, much less the term "binding and enforceable threat."

The point I am making is not theoretical at all. The role of explicit, binding threats was critical in the development of the doctrine of mutual assured destruction (MAD) that governed the balance of terror during the Cold War with the Soviet Union. The concessions made by the Russian government that prevented war when it backed down during the Cuban Missile Crisis would not have been made had Russia not understood that thermonuclear annihilation would have been the result of not compromising.

4. Providing a Yardstick for Measuring Bargaining Ability and Political Competence in General

In the absence of a compelling definition of a rational bargaining outcome, it is difficult to say whether a given party bargained competently or incompetently during its negotiations with others. By extension, with no yardstick in hand, there can be little accountability by government to its citizens regarding the quality of the bargains it strikes on their behalf. Happily, the Nash-Harsanyi model provides precisely the missing yardstick, as was hopefully clear in our analysis of the United States/China game.

5. Offering a Simple, Graphic Representation of Politics

Political science will never be a "science," much less a successor to economics as the dominant paradigm without some intuitively appealing core model that can be summarized by a couple of intuitively appealing graphs. In economics, that model is the concept of "market equilibrium" graphed by intersecting supply and demand curves. The Nash-Harsanyi theory can and should play an identical role within political science, and it, too, can be summarized graphically. It is outside the scope of this book to exhibit this here, but I hope you will take it on faith that an intuitively appealing pair of graphs exist that could render a new concept of political science as intuitively appealing as supply = demand is in economics.[20]

6. Offering a Unifying Framework for the Moral Tripos of Politics, Economics, and Philosophy

There is one last way in which the Nash-Harsanyi theory is remarkable. It can be shown to unify at a very deep level the fields of Moral Philosophy, Economics, and Political Science. More specifically, consider such disparate topics as the theory of fair representation in political philosophy, the question of how to allocate the "pie" in proportion to the relative contribution made by those baking the pie, the problem of allocating pie in proportion to people's needs, the issue of measuring different people's relative power in a conflict situation, the problem of assessing people's relative social status, the concept of a political balance of power (multilateral bargaining equilibrium) as previously discussed and finally the concept of a supply/demand market equilibrium in classical economics.

It turns out that the equations of the Nash-Harsanyi theory can be restated in many different ways, yielding appealing solutions to the central problems of all seven of these topics. You have already learned about one of these results, namely Robert Aumann's discovery that a competitive market economy corresponds exactly to a degenerate bargaining game in which no agents have any power with which to form coalitions. Back in 1978, I proposed that a formal unification of multiple disciplines would one day be possible, assuming that certain theoretical problems were solved first.[21]

These problems have now been solved, and I hope to demonstrate a complete unification of the Moral Tripos of Economics, Politics, and Philosophy in a future book. In the next and final chapter, I will sketch a second example of the proposed unification: how deep-rooted problems in the subject of distributive justice can be solved using a bargaining theoretic framework.

CHAPTER 6

Beyond Democratic Capitalism

An Idealized Political Economy, with Distributive Justice

Throughout this book, I have been quite critical of Western political economies, the United States in particular. But in the latter case, I have tried to be constructively critical, proposing concrete solutions to practical problems. In this final chapter, I want to go deeper and address several philosophical questions that matter because our views on these issues impact how we think and thus how we act: What might an *ideal* political economy consist of? How does today's form of democratic capitalism compare with such an ideal? Does it deserve its tarnished reputation? At a more fundamental level, what properties do people truly value and seek from their economic and political systems? Is the capitalist norm of economic "efficiency" enough, as an economics textbook might well suggest? Or are there other norms? In particular, is there room for justice and fair sharing of the pie along with economic efficiency? Finally, what about privacy and freedom? Can these be accommodated as well? As will be seen, the answer to this last question is yes. All these norms can be accommodated side by side. Thus, just as the five previous chapters do, this final chapter conveys a strong message of optimism.

While it is currently unfashionable to pose "big" questions such as the nature of an ideal social system, the need to do so has arguably never been greater. There is a sense that democratic capitalism is now failing to deliver the goods, at least in Europe and the United States. Living standards are falling for the middle and lower classes. Unemployment is high and failing to come down. Perceived maldistributions of wealth are causing protests and riots throughout the West, and this is just the beginning of what will happen as overstretched welfare-state governments start to renege on their promises to an aging population of unaffordable pension and medical benefits.

Do you know anyone who is not concerned about the future, regardless of his or her political leanings? There is widespread recognition that today's elected politicians are unable to arrive at compromises that will solve our problems. Polls in many nations rate politicians at the bottom of popularity lists. Few people believe that Right-wing or Left-wing candidates have meaningful answers to today's most important questions.

In the West, questions are beginning to be raised about the long-term viability of democracy itself. If today's dysfunctional system leads to further financial crises, to soaring debt and credit downgrades, and to falling living standards, how long will it be before we elect that "strong man" who promises to make the trains run on time once again? And once he is in power, how long will it be before a one-party state emerges and civil liberties are curtailed? Such a question was unthinkable in the West during the decades since the defeat of fascism during World War II, and since the implosion of communism in 1989 that was celebrated by Francis Fukuyama's book *The End of History and the Last Man.* After all, we liberal democratic capitalists were the victors, at least so we were told. But was ours a Pyrrhic victory?

Overview and Summary

I shall start off explaining why *true* capitalism properly understood represents one of the great institutional innovations and successes of history. As the eminent *New York Times* journalist David Leonhardt wrote in his economics column published on July 27, 2011:

> Economic truths may not rise to the level of certainty of two plus two equals four, but they are not so different from the knowledge that the earth is round, or that smoking causes cancer. When it comes to economics, we know that a market economy with a significant government role is the only proven model of success. The United States has outgrown Europe

because of our greater comfort with market forces. . . . On the other hand, unencumbered market forces often lead to disaster, as 1929 and 2008 made clear.

But what exactly is Leonhardt claiming here? What are the various economic, institutional and governmental preconditions for successful capitalism? What are the precise circumstances under which Adam Smith's concept of the "invisible hand" really does work as advertised, and under which it fails? As we review these, we will see that true capitalism does not represent some libertarian alternative to a system with a strong government. For strong and good government has been presupposed by capitalist theory from the time of Adam Smith, a point many self-styled conservatives seem to have forgotten.

This section culminates with a definition of the public good as given in classical economics. This makes clear what the market *and* the government should each do to maximize the public good, or in economics jargon, to achieve an efficient allocation of private and public resources. This ideal provides a yardstick to demonstrate the extent to which real-world "bastardized capitalism" falls so short of the mark. In this regard, I introduce a unified explanation of why real-world capitalism often lets us down.

The second section of the chapter builds on the classical results of the first, but delves much deeper. It investigates the concept of *idealized social systems*. More specifically, we investigate those properties above and beyond economic efficiency that might characterize an ideal economic resource allocation system. For example, do not most of us value the properties of freedom, justice, and equality, informational efficiency, stability, and privacy, along with classical efficiency? Drawing upon the brilliant work of the late Nobel laureate Leonid Hurwicz, I explain how "snow-white capitalism" alone is consistent with *all* these norms. By this term, I mean the perfectly competitive free market backed up by the rule of law.

The chapter then shifts to the polarizing issue of justice, and in particular the subject of distributive justice, which concerns the optimal distribution of wealth and income. My principal goal is to show how issues of redistribution are not "outside" of free market economics, but in fact integral to it. In particular, I demonstrate how a belief in the principles of true capitalism logically *requires* a belief in redistribution. This is a theorem based on the role of luck in life, not a speculation, and it is one that will make many anti-redistributionists do a double-take!

Fortunately, great progress has been made in the past few decades in clarifying the topic of fair distribution, and it has been a focal point of my own research for several decades. I want to bring readers up to date and argue once again that the issues here are neither Left wing nor Right wing in nature, but much more fundamental. Anyone doubting the relevance of the topic of distributive justice should remember that Harvard's Michael Sandel has become *the* rock star of international academics largely because of his focus on this issue.[1]

Students worldwide recognize justice to be the most fundamental of all topics. They like being made to think about it, and to argue about it. The rest of us largely sidestep the issue, Republicans and Democrats alike. Holding a belief about "repealing the Bush tax cuts" does not amount to possessing a theory of justice. For starters, no one has even tried to demonstrate that tax rates either before or after the Bush cuts were fair in any sense. Heaven help us if our stance on this issue is supposed to proxy our political philosophies!

The chapter concludes with a sketch of what an ideal political economy might resemble, one that far transcends classical concepts of the public good by explicitly integrating within it the two fundamental strands of distributive justice: to each according to relative need, and to each according to relative contribution.

True Textbook Capitalism, and the Correct Role of Government

When Bill Clinton went to Oxford as a Rhodes Scholar, he studied the traditional Moral Tripos known at Oxford as PPE (Philosophy, Politics, and Economics). There, he and his fellow Rhodes Scholars presumably learned that Adam Smith's original analysis of market capitalism was in fact an investigation into moral theory in a broad sense. Indeed, the ideas underlying Smith's *Wealth of Nations* of 1776 were rooted in his predecessor treatise *A Theory of Moral Sentiments* of 1759. Accordingly, as economic theory developed during the next two centuries, emphasis was often put upon such morally pregnant concepts as nonwastefulness (now known as "efficiency"), and distributional equity.

In short, the links between capitalist economics and moral philosophy were deep and abiding from the start. It is easy to overlook this tradition when, in today's ideological environment, a belief in capitalism has degenerated into a belief that "markets know best," that the principal virtue of free markets is that they result in maximal efficiency, and that the role of government should be as limited as possible. To be sure, many people who have studied and understood Econ 101 know that the government must redistribute income since it cannot avoid doing so—as when it raises revenues to fund public goods, just as it must intervene to remedy "market failures" such as pollution and the excess leverage we have discussed earlier.

Nonetheless, this is acknowledged in an increasingly grudging manner—as an agenda that can be ignored as we celebrate the role of decentralized free markets in generating an efficient allocation of resources. This bias distorts the truth about genuine capitalism, namely that it is a social system in which government *and* businesses *and* consumers work hand in hand to maximize the public good, always subject to such constraints on unfettered free enterprise as are required to reach this maximum.

What exactly are the prerequisites for a capitalist economic system that seeks to maximize the public good? There are three kinds:

1. **The Rule of Law:** For free markets to function correctly, the rule of law must prevail. Citizens must benefit from the sanctity of contracts, nonbribable judges, transparency in commercial relations, and the protection of intellectual property rights. Without such protections, capitalism morphs into crony capitalism in which deference to the concept of "free markets" is hot air at best.

2. **The Economic Preconditions for Decentralized Free Market Transactions to Maximize the Public Good:** As students learn in their textbooks, the following five requirements must be met for the full promise of the invisible hand to be fulfilled.

   i. Perfect competition—in particular the absence of any bargaining power by any group whatsoever whether cartels, labor unions, or oligopolies. This first assumption requires that product and labor markets must be fully deregulated and highly competitive. Every individual producer and consumer takes prices as given by the invisible hand and has no ability to set prices, or otherwise rig markets.

   ii. Diminishing marginal utility for all goods and services, the property whereby your fourth Coke during a hot afternoon satisfies you less than your third Coke, which satisfies less than your second Coke, and so on.

iii. The existence of complete markets for hedging, that is, insurance markets permitting all risk averse agents to hedge every and any risk by creating appropriate portfolios of derivative securities.

iv. The absence of nonmarket phenomena or "externalities" such as pollution, where the price system either fails to operate, or else misallocates resources.

v. Diminishing returns to scale on the part of most (but not all) industries.

If all of these conditions are met, then it can be proved that a decentralized free market system will generate the largest "pie" possible out of the resources available. That is, the outcome will be efficient and nonwasteful. This is the principal result of Microeconomics 101, first proven formally by Kenneth Arrow in his 1953 paper that extended invisible hand economics to include uncertainty about the future, and in doing so identified requirement number (iii) on hedging. Note that the role of government and "politics" is absent from this simple model, except for the presupposition that the rule of law is in place. I shall refer to such idealized microeconomies as *snow-white economies.*

Next we add the prerequisites required to provide public goods, and to deal with externalities and with the lack of perfect competition.

3. Governmental Preconditions to Cope with Externalities, Imperfect Competition, and the Provision of Public Goods
    The following four requirements must be addressed:

i. Need to regulate business cycles and financial market crises via appropriate fiscal and monetary policies.

ii. Need to redress market failures or "externalities" (e.g., pollution) and to provide basic public goods (e.g., a legal system, a military system, etc.).

iii. Need to enforce perfect competition and to prevent the formation of cartels to the extent possible.

iv. Need to address any issues of distributive justice that arise within the economic system and cannot be wished away.

As for distributive justice, once the need for public goods arises (e.g., an army must exist, sewers must be built), a decision must be made by government as to who should be taxed how much to pay for it. This is a political decision made by a very "visible hand," not a market decision made by an invisible hand. Thus issues of taxation that are fair inexorably arise within capitalist theory.

Classical Definition of the Public Good

To recap, a world of true capitalism is one in which all three of the previous sets of conditions are satisfied.[2] The result will be an efficient allocation of resources, and one which is fair assuming that government explicitly addresses the issue of fair distribution. We shall define such an outcome as one that maximizes the public good in a classical sense.

This concept of the public good provides a yardstick against which any nation can ascertain how far it is from the ideal, and can determine how to improve upon the status quo given the political will to do so. Be sure to note how far this ideal lies from today's presumption that capitalism is all about the unfettered play of free markets. It is not, and never was, even though the healthy functioning of markets is indeed central to its success.

The Bastardization of Capitalism

The arguments I have made earlier in this book should make it clear that today's U.S. political economy lies far away from this ideal. This is evidenced by sluggish growth, an inequitable distribution of wealth and income, a preposterous system of health care, an over-leveraged financial system, an excess of consumption over investment—especially nonexistent public sector investment, unchecked cartels making a mockery of perfect competition, lobbyists buying access in Washington, and a system of entitlements skewed towards the interests of today's elderly at the expense of future cohorts of the elderly.

At a much more abstract level, what goes wrong is the *politicization* of economics. As I discussed in Chapter 5, Robert Aumann's 1977 theorem showed that, in a truly capitalistic world of perfect competition and the invisible hand, no agents possess any bargaining power at all. To restate his result, the allocation of goods and services resulting from free-market behavior is untainted by any form of bargaining power (i.e., of politics). In such a world, there will be no K Street lobbyists, no self-dealing, no cartels, no rock-bottom "carried interest" tax rates for millionaires and billionaires in finance, no regulatory decisions not in the public interest, and so forth.

Well, the real world is a far cry from Aumann's idealized world of "strategically inert" market participants. It is one where *lots of bargaining power exists* so that the final allocation of resources is the result of multilateral bargaining behavior. Powerful interest groups attempting to achieve their goals utilize credible threat strategies. Their most common threat strategies are threats *not* to make campaign contributions unless regulatory decisions go their way. As a result, "might makes right" all too often. This is the genesis of the corruption and distortion in the resource allocation that is causing increased consternation by the public at large, and by the Occupiers of Wall Street most notably at this writing.

In some idealized fantasy world of snow-white politics, the machinations of all these interest groups would be replaced by the deliberations of some philosopher king who would arbitrate every regulatory decision on the basis of "maximizing the greatest good for the greatest number," or some related politically neutral norm. What a far cry this would be from today's world of K Street lobbyists!

How bad is today's bastardized form of capitalism? Should we get discouraged and seek an alternative form of a resource allocation system? No, we should not, for as we are about to see, capitalism on balance works very well and is much too precious to throw out, warts and all. To understand this, it is necessary to understand the seminal work of Leonid Hurwicz.

Beyond Efficiency: The Eight Ideals of an Optimal Social System

One wintry morning in Cambridge, Massachusetts in the early 1970s, when I was an applied mathematics graduate student, I visited the economist Kenneth Arrow in his office at Harvard, seeking some advice from on high. He mentioned that I should not miss taking a course from an old friend of his who was visiting Harvard at that time and was known within the economic theory community as a brilliant original thinker, Professor Leonid Hurwicz. I knew little about Hurwicz, but took Arrow's advice and took the course. It was the single best course I have ever had. To begin with, Hurwicz was a superb and patient teacher who explained very complex things very simply.

But most important, Hurwicz was a very big thinker. He generalized economic science in a breathtaking manner. Traditionally, most economists had simply investigated how to tweak an economy so that it could deliver an efficient allocation of resources, which was until then the Holy Grail of economics. Hurwicz, by contrast, focused not on a given economy, but rather on the set of all possible economies or resource allocation *systems* (e.g., capitalism, communism, socialism, whatever). And he asked not merely which system was most efficient, but how each system ranked according to numerous other norms that will be discussed shortly. His colleagues came to call his enterprise the theory of "mechanism design." Hurwicz mathematized it, and thus transformed previous thinking about alternative social systems into a proper branch of science. For this contribution, he would earn the Nobel Memorial Prize in Economic Sciences in 2007.

I will start off by setting forth the norms an ideal political economy should satisfy, and then cite his main analytical result about the status of capitalism. Think of each of the following eight norms as a property that almost everyone would like to be satisfied by their social system.[3]

Eight Idealized Properties of an Optimal Political Economy

An initial caveat is in order. Hurwicz originally restricted himself to the case of what I have dubbed "snow-white" economies, that is, resource allocation systems satisfying the first two groups of prerequisites identified previously. Accordingly, while the rule of law is assumed, there are no issues of externalities or public goods to be arbitrated by government. While more recent work permits these to be included, the exposition will be clearer if we stick to his simplest and earliest results. Here are the properties we might all hope for in a resource allocation system:

1. **Classical Efficiency:** A resource allocation system is classically efficient if the outcome is the largest pie possible given the endowments (skills and wealth) of the citizens, and given the state of technology of the day. Another way of defining efficiency is to require that, if any one agent is to be made better off by virtue of some reallocation of goods and services that were produced, then at least one other person must be made worse off. There is no "waste" in this sense. There is no slack in the system. As a norm, efficiency is like apple pie or motherhood: Who could be opposed to it? Who wants waste?

2. **Dynamic Stability:** The stability of an allocation system refers to the degree to which the system is stable once it is subjected to shocks. The shock could be a market crash, a hurricane, or whatever. If the system is stable, then after a finite period of time, things will return to the way they were. Most people equate stability with a sense of security, and value this property.

3. **Optimal Growth of Wealth and Income:** Independent of Hurwicz's work, research by T. Koopmans and E. Malinvaud in the 1950s permitted pure capitalist theory to be rendered dynamic rather than merely static. As a result, the concept of economic growth over time could be studied and, more important, the concept of *optimal* growth could be defined. Other things being equal, people prefer a system in which wealth and living standards rise rather than fall, and do so in an optimal manner. Who doesn't want a better tomorrow? I am taking liberties in adding this norm to those Hurwicz himself proposed, because he easily could have added it, and because this norm matters to people.

4. **Informational Efficiency:** This particular norm emerged from a debate that raged during the mid-twentieth century between free-market theorists and central planners. As early as the 1920s, socialists and communists believed that an efficient allocation of resources could be achieved by central planning. Planners could, in principle, determine who should produce how much, and who should consume how much of every commodity produced. No invisible hand price system was required.[4] What Hurwicz and others show is that *decentralized* invisible hand pricing without the bureaucracy of central planning is much more "informationally efficient" than central planning could ever be. That is, far fewer data about individual people's endowments, preferences, and firms' modes of production are needed in a market-based system than in a centralized system to arrive at an efficient outcome. Hurwicz deemed this kind of efficiency desirable, especially because of its close relationship to the next two norms.

5. **Decisional Decentralization or Freedom:** This norm represents the degree to which an agent can make decisions on his own in order for the system to function efficiently. Does someone else (e.g., the state) need to tell him what to do?

Does he require permission slips from Big Brother before making a decision as to what to order for dinner? This is a very reasonable norm since most people prefer the freedom associated with decisional privacy to a lack of such freedom.

6. **Informational Decentralization or Privacy:** This norm refers to how much information different agents need to know about each other's preferences or production processes in order for the resource allocation system to function. When I decide to manufacture my firm's metal vessels using my own technology and resources, need I know how other manufacturers are making their vessels, and how many vessels each is making? It certainly facilitates my life if I have no need to obtain data about others. Analogously, when I decide what to serve my guests for dinner, need I know what all other hosts are serving their guests? Most people like privacy, and the less we need to know about other people's business, the better.

7. **Equity, Including Distributive Justice:** Most people prefer systems and outcomes that are fair, or equitable. The reason they do is that each of us has experienced being treated unfairly, and we do not like it. The problem, of course, is to know what the term "fair" means. In some contexts, this is easy: We all want to be tried by a jury that is unprejudiced so that the deck cannot be stacked against us. The more difficult context is that of distributive justice: What distribution of the pie is fair? The seemingly zero-sum nature of this deepest of all questions makes the answer all the more difficult to arrive at. The final two sections of this chapter will focus on precisely this issue.

8. **Incentive Structure Compatibility:** This norm was the crown jewel of Hurwicz's work. Now the concept of incentive compatibility is somewhat abstract and thus deserves an explanation of why it qualifies as a desirable norm. Briefly, let us identify alternative resource allocation systems (capitalism, communism) by the *rules of the game* that define each. These rules consist of all the penalties, rewards, and regulations that incentivize people to make the decisions they do. I use the term incentive "structure" in order to stress that, for any resource allocation system, the rules of the game consist of *all* incentives impacting the decisions of *all* agents.

For a long time, everyone has known what Steven D. Levitt and Stephen Dubner stressed in their delightful book

Freakonomics, namely that incentives strongly impact individual behavior. Just think of the impact on smoking of cigarette taxes and other penalties. Or recall the old saying "Spare the rod, spoil the child." What Hurwicz did is to investigate the impact of the incentive structure *in its entirety* on system-wide properties like efficiency, freedom, stability, fairness, and so forth. His work made it possible to "grade" alternative sets of rules of the game on the basis of how favorably they impacted the performance of the social system as a whole. To understand the power of this contribution, suppose we ask whether or not private property ownership is good for society. Hurwicz taught us to answer this question as follows. Consider the differing impact on system-wide efficiency of two different sets of rules of the game, one set permitting private property ownership, the other preventing it. All other rules are held constant so as to focus on the impact of property ownership alone. Now which of the two systems is more efficient as measured by the size of the pie that gets baked?

If the answer is that private property ownership incentivizes people in the society to act in ways that end up producing the biggest pie possible, we can then state the institution of private property ownership is *incentive compatible* with the goal of economic efficiency. And so forth for any or all of the six other norms we value above and beyond efficiency. The important point here is that there must be clearly specified *goals* (e.g., efficiency and stability) with respect to which a given social system is or is not incentive compatible in order for the term "incentive compatibility" to be well defined. This point is both subtle and brilliant!

The Principal Result

Hurwicz's main result was to prove mathematically that the rules of the game in a snow-white market economy as defined earlier are incentive compatible with all of the norms we have identified, excluding norm 7 (equity), which requires a consensus as to what is fair, and government intervention to achieve it. In other words, individuals acting selfishly in a snow-white economy will unknowingly act in such a way as to fulfill *all* these ideals except for norm 7. The first intuition that this might be true (for the case of the efficiency norm) was Adam Smith's conjecture that decentralized free-market behavior by selfish individuals would achieve the greatest possible efficiency when such behavior was coordinated by the invisible hand of the price system.

Kenneth Arrow, Gerard Debreu, and others would demonstrate the precise conditions under which Smith's conjecture about efficiency would hold true. Hurwicz's contribution was to extend these classical results to encompass *all* the above norms, not merely norm 1 (classical efficiency). Perhaps more important, he demonstrated mathematically why almost no conceivable resource allocation system *other* than free-market exchange will satisfy many of these norms. It is in this sense that we can now fully understand why free-market capitalism is far superior to any other system yet proposed. Moreover, Hurwicz demonstrated all this in a scientific manner devoid of ideological prejudice and thus defused what had previously been an extremely ideological debate between the Left and the Right.[5]

In concluding this review of Hurwicz's contribution, I want to stress that the concept of incentive structure compatibility (norm 8) is one of the most powerful concepts ever introduced into social science. It provides the missing link between the motivations and actions of individuals on the one hand, and the performance of the entire society on the other. It made it possible to measure the true performance of alternative social systems and to do so merely by contrasting the rules of the game operative in each. An endnote explains this remarkable contribution in greater depth for the interested reader.[6]

Relevance of Snow White Capitalism to Bastardized Capitalism

Given that we live in a world of bastardized capitalism, as David Leonhardt of the *New York Times* suggested, why have I discussed Leonid Hurwicz's results concerning an idealized world of snow-white economies? Of what possible relevance are these findings to the realities of our own flawed social system? The answer is that they could not be more relevant. The reason lies in the fact that, problematic as real-world capitalist economies might be, they contain within them *subeconomies* that very closely approximate the ideal described by Hurwicz. To understand how this is true, think of our economy as partitioned into two quite distinct sets of industries that coexist within one system: those riddled with cartelization and cronyism, and those that are very competitive.

Fortunately, the latter set is far larger than the former. Indeed, near-perfect competition and an absence of bargaining power typify most small businesses, most consumer electronics, agriculture, retailing, restaurants, hotels, the global auto industry, consumer products, and so forth. Competition is fierce—which is exactly why average risk-adjusted returns are modest, and why it is hard to get rich. A firm like Goldman Sachs is not representative of business at large. By far the majority of businesses do not have the bargaining power and cannot earn the returns that Goldman Sachs does. We the consumers end up the principal beneficiaries of high levels of competition.

Now ask yourself how well such highly competitive sectors perform. Each and every year, most of us enjoy better bedding, better and safer cars, a greater variety of foods, better consumer electronic products, a wider choice of restaurants, better hearing aids, better prosthetic limbs, better access to the movies and music of our choice, better cruise-ship destinations, and so on. The list is nearly endless. *Even better, the after-inflation price of such goods tends to drop.* The point is that a large part of the economy pretty well replicates the kind of snow-white competitive economy whose virtues Hurwicz captured so brilliantly.

Now contrast the performance of these competitive sectors with that of highly cartelized, noncompetitive sectors that deliver public education with negative productivity growth, decrepit mass transport systems, and "financial innovations" created by bulge bracket financial firms that have made bankers very rich while causing widespread distress on Main Street. In a different direction, note how impressively the rate of innovation in the telephone sector accelerated once the AT&T monopoly was broken up. The result was much better service for a fraction of the cost per calling minute.

The Moral of All This

So remarkable are the fruits of snow-white capitalism, or the real-world approximation to it we enjoy in many economic sectors, that we should do our best to preserve it and to build upon it. Government should strive to render uncompetitive sectors competitive, and should prevent competitive sectors from becoming uncompetitive. More generally, we must never throw capitalism out with the bathwater just because of our distress over malfeasance on

Wall Street. It is tempting to do so, and people have every reason to be outraged about today's crony capitalism that violates the predicates of true capitalism. But we must not strike back in the wrong manner lest we end up hurting ourselves.

Distributional Equity

The conviction of the have-nots that they are unfairly taken advantage of by the haves has often been cited as a primary determinant of social and political upheavals throughout the ages. The names of Spartacus, Robespierre, Marx, and Mao come to mind when we recall cries for redistribution across history. This redistributive impulse is far from dead. The outcome of the next U.S. presidential election will surely reflect widespread outrage over today's inequalities in wealth and income.

The purpose of this section is to demonstrate how various forms of distributional equity are part and parcel of economic theory, and of capitalist theory in particular. This claim will surprise many people who have always believed that free-market economics focuses solely on matters of efficiency, not equitable distribution. But this is not true. I now show that there are five ways in which issues of distributive justice are lodged within free-market theory. I do not address the problem of what the *correct* distribution of wealth and income is, and how this might be determined. This larger issue is addressed via a comprehensive theory of justice sketched in the concluding section.

In reviewing how the issue of fair distribution arises within free-market economic theory, it is important to separate at the outset the two different and competing ethical norms that arise in discussions of distributive justice. On the one hand there is the contribution principle according to which each agent should receive a wage that is equal to his relative contribution to the organization paying him or her. On the other hand, there is the needs principle, according to which resources should be allocated to people in proportion to their relative needs. Further on in this chapter, I will discuss the thorny relation between these two concepts, and the question of whether both can be satisfied at once within an idealized polity.

Interestingly, both principles of distributive justice arise within classical market theory, as we will now see.

The Contribution Principle

In an idealized competitive economy, each worker will be paid a wage equal to what he contributed to the enterprise he works for. His wage will equal his "marginal product," or contribution to his firm, as has been known for many decades. The proof of this is simple: A company that pays its workers a wage exceeding their contribution will be driven out of business because it will make losses, under perfect competition. A firm that pays workers less than their contribution will be unable to retain employees. Every manager of a business knows that importance of respecting the contribution principle. If an employee is underpaid relative to his contribution, say to corporate sales, *he* will know it all too well. If an employee is overpaid, *everyone else* will know it, and the issue of compensation will rankle and cause morale problems.

Suppose we are interested in the applicability of the contribution principle in a much broader class of environments than that of economic markets, for example, political or non-governmental organization (NGO) environments where "correct market wage rates" cannot be defined, so that the contribution principle applicable in a market context cannot be invoked. Is there a way in which contribution fairness can be respected? Remarkably, there is. Suppose that in these nonmarket environments, resources get allocated via multilateral bargaining of the kind described in the previous chapter, as they usually do. Then as John Harsanyi first demonstrated, the payoffs from multilateral bargaining satisfy a more powerful and abstract form of the Contribution Principle than the more familiar "wage = marginal product" version known from microeconomics.[7]

The Trade-Off Between Efficiency and Equity

Many people believe that the two norms of equity and efficiency are intrinsically at loggerheads because of "incentive effects." If the tax code is too progressive, then the wealthy and productive will reduce their contribution of labor and capital such that the pie will grow less rapidly, or possibly shrink. While there is some evidence to support this view, it is highly controversial except in extreme cases where wealthy and productive people are excessively penalized. But for game theoretical reasons demonstrated in an important paper by Professors Robert Aumann and Mordecai Kurz, punitively high tax rates rarely should be and rarely are imposed in the real world.[8]

But there is a different and much deeper way in which equity and efficiency concerns are commingled in capitalist economics. The dominant virtue of an invisible-hand economy is that, given the initial endowments (wealth and skills) of each agent, the outcome of market exchange will be an efficient allocation of goods and services. Now suppose government wishes to make the resulting distribution of income and wealth more equitable. For example, it could institute a lump-sum transfer from some agents to others. Can it do so without destroying the efficiency of the allocation that results? To state this differently, will there exist an efficient allocation *regardless* of any forced transfers made between agents?

The answer to both questions is yes, and this is known as the Second Fundamental Theorem of Welfare Economics, first proved by Kenneth Arrow and Gerard Debreu in the very early 1950s. What this established from first principles is that market-based capitalism with its virtue of efficiency is fully compatible with fairness-based redistribution. This was an extremely important result for the moral philosophical basis of capitalist theory, for we learned that equity and efficiency need not be at loggerheads at all.

Bad-Luck-Based Redistribution Due to Missing Markets

To me, by far the most important and indeed improbable link between equity and market capitalism was discovered in 1953. This was the year that Kenneth Arrow extended classical invisible hand economics to incorporate uncertainty about the future. Until then, no one had figured out how to make sense of concepts like supply, demand, price, equilibrium, and efficiency in a world where agents did not know the location of their future supply and demand curves, and thus could not forecast future prices.[9]

Remarkably, Arrow proved that all the main concepts and results of classical economics (e.g., market efficiency) still hold true when agents are uncertain about future supply, demand, and price variables provided one fundamental modification is made to the classical model. Once uncertainty enters the picture, an entirely new set of hedging markets would have to exist, "Arrow Securities" as they were originally known. These securities permit every agent to lay off every kind of risk about the future, and to do so in proportion to his or her risk aversion level. He could hedge against rain or shine at any future date, against war or peace, or against the success or failure of a new production process. Every unknown future "state of the world" could be hedged.

Given a complete set of such risk-spreading securities, risk-averse economic agents were not only permitted to spread their risks, but would wish to do so since it was in their self-interest. Assuming that these conditions were fulfilled, Arrow showed that—even with uncertainty present—the market will generate not only an efficient allocation of goods and services, but also an efficient reallocation of risk itself. Thus was born what many now refer to as the economics of uncertainty.

While Arrow did not comment on the revolutionary implications of his theorems for the seemingly unrelated issue of a fair distribution of wealth and income, others did. Here is the relevant logic. To begin with, the complete set of hedging or insurance markets required by Arrow's result do not and probably never will exist. This is the "missing markets" problem investigated by Robert Shiller at Yale, and many others, and this is what matters for the distribution of wealth and income.[10] This is because any insurance contract can be viewed as a redistribution of resources from someone *lucky* (his house did not burn down) to someone *unlucky* (your house did burn down). Therefore, as a result of the widespread lack of insurance transfers from the lucky to the unlucky due to missing markets, the *ex post* distribution of wealth and income in the real world ends up far more unequal and skewed towards the lucky (rich?) than it would be under a regime of *true* capitalism possessing complete markets.

One way of remedying this deficiency of missing markets would be to introduce a progressive tax code to approximate the net transfer payments that ideally would be made via complete insurance markets, but cannot be made in reality. *Viewed in this manner, the progressive tax code would be not an ethical construct, but rather a remedy for a market failure, just as pollution taxes are, in a different vein.* A progressive code would help restore the distribution of income and wealth to what it would have been in a world of complete markets.[11]

Of course there is a presumption here that wealthier people tend to have been luckier than others, and I believe this to be true to an order of approximation. Virtually any "successful" person I have known, or whose biography I have read, admits to having benefitted from lucky breaks on the road to success. As most of these breaks were events that could not be hedged, the outcome is a much greater degree of inequality than would have resulted with perfect self-interested hedging of all events. In the extreme, a winner-take-all-world emerges. The late Australian billionaire Kerry Packer put this to me better than any theorist ever has: "Woody, if you meet someone very successful who thinks he deserved his success, you know you have met a real jerk."[12] Bingo! Along the same lines, is hardly surprising how often we hear, "I would rather be lucky than smart."

The Oprah Winfrey Book Club Lottery The logic of luck-based redistribution is so compelling that I want to give a concrete example that really brings it home. Suppose you and I are both accomplished writers of exactly the same age and reputation. We have both sold about the same number of books, yet we both only make $75,000 per year because we write "serious" books. Now suppose a random event occurs: Oprah Winfrey opens up her book club. We both now face an equal chance that she might notice one of our next two books when they are published, read the book, and recommend it strongly to her audience. If I am the lucky one, then my income will soar from $75,000 to $5,000,000, and likewise for you if you are the lucky one.

What might we do to improve our welfare confronting this new possibility? Suppose that we are both risk averse, indeed equally risk averse. Then the Nash bargaining solution to the implied game between us will be to draw up an insurance contract whereby we split the extra $5,000,000 payoff *equally* should one of us luck out. Understand that this contract is motivated solely by our mutual self-interest, and not because of our beliefs about "fairness."

Given such a contract, our two incomes will remain equal should either or both of our books get endorsed by Oprah. *No "winner takes all" inequality arises.* But if we do not contract away the risk involved because we cannot draw up this mutually advantageous contract, one of us will walk away with a bonanza leaving nothing for the other. In this context, a progressive income tax would then help rectify the lopsided distribution of winnings resulting from a lack of insurance—*insurance required if economic efficiency is to result.* The tax would have the effect of "restoring" the distribution of income that true capitalism would have generated.

The moral here will be highly disconcerting for many self-styled conservatives and other devotees of capitalism who are doubtless unaware of Arrow's 1953 result. If you really believe in the free market, and worship at the high altar of market efficiency, then you had better rethink your position on distributive justice, and on the progressivity of the tax schedule in particular. What you have hopefully now learned is that capitalism not only implies an efficient allocation of goods and services, but also an efficient allocation of risk as well. I find it remarkable that this argument has never been exploited by self-styled liberals concerned about inequality.

One important point here is that there is nothing Left wing or Right wing about the logic I have set forth. Redistribution occurs because of acts between consenting adults wishing to pool and hedge their risks. As a result, today's shouting match between those on both sides of the redistribution debate should be much less shrill than it is. I now turn to still other ways in which issues of redistribution are intertwined with the theory of democratic capitalism.

Fair Tax Rates for the Provision of Public Goods

The need for and provision of public goods (e.g., the army and the law courts) lies outside of the scope of the market and its invisible hand. Government must provide these, and as a result must tax people to pay for them. But at what rate should it do so? Who pays how much of the freight? This is a straightforward problem of distributive justice. There are two basic ways in which it can be and is resolved. First, the answer could be dictated by politics alone, devoid of any ethical considerations. We are back to the Nash-Harsanyi theory of bargaining of Chapter 5. Interest groups flex their muscles, utilize their relative threat power, form coalitions, and reach a compromise as to who pays how much in taxes.

The second way to allocate the tax burden is more ethical and less economic in nature, and takes into account the relative ability of agents of different types to pay for public goods. It has long been accepted, at least within modern democracies, that the poor have a much more difficult time than the rich in paying their taxes if the same tax rate on total income, say 25 percent, applies to both. Accordingly, it is fairer for the poor to be taxed at, say, 15 percent and the wealthy at 30 percent of their differing incomes in financing government spending. This is one reason why, in reality, almost every nation has a progressive tax code. British utilitarians such as Jeremy Bentham and John Stuart Mill were the first to provide a formal logic as to why the poor *should* pay proportionately less than the rich for government services. Why did they claim it was harder for the poor to pay the same percentage on total income as for the rich to do so? What was their logic that implied a progressive tax code?

Their explanation lay in the principle of "diminishing marginal utility." This is the property whereby most people derive less utility (satisfaction) from the fourth ice cream cone they enjoy on a hot August afternoon than from the third cone, and less from the third than from the second, and so forth. Assuming that the government seeks to maximize the greatest good of the people when setting tax rates, the utilitarians proved that the principle of diminishing marginal utility implies a progressive tax code under which the poor pay a lower share. The philosophy that government should always select policies—including tax rates—that maximize the *sum of the utility payoffs* (happiness levels) of the people is now known as utilitarianism. What is important for our discussion about fairness is that the property of diminishing marginal utility is closely related to the ethically pregnant concept of relative neediness.

To see this, suppose that everyone derives more utility from their first $10,000 of income more than from their second $10,000 because the first $10,000 permits them to buy those staples their families need most, for example, basic food and rent. It is then an easy stretch to argue that a poor family with a total income of $30,000 "needs" its entire income to acquire the staples every family needs much more than a rich family with $300,000 of income does. If this is so, then a tax code that maximizes the public good will necessarily be progressive, and the rich will have a higher tax rate than the poor. This can be shown formally. In sum, a progressive tax code is much more consistent with the principle of to each according to his need than, say, a flat tax rate is.

Needs-Based Arguments for Redistribution

The four ways we have seen in which issues of fair distribution arise *within* economic theory bring us to the doorstep of the fifth way they arise outside of economic concerns. There is now an increasing demand for a no-holds-barred *moral* philosophical analysis of what distribution of wealth and income is fair, and why. In the debate over this issue, there has been a bias towards needs-based fairness as opposed to contribution-based fairness. More specifically, greater need on the part of the poor has been the touchstone for the theories of philosophers like the late John Rawls of Harvard. Rawls' magisterial

Theory of Justice created an explosion of interest in the topic of distributive justice when it was published in 1971.[13]

Following Rawls, and the utilitarian logic sketched previously, most philosophers have championed strongly redistributionist policies based upon the primacy of need by the poor. Furthermore, their attention has shifted from classical issues of how to fairly fund public goods to much deeper issues. For example, philosophers now question whether the highly unequal initial endowments of wealth and skills that people enjoy are "morally arbitrary" as Rawls called them, or not. If they are arbitrary and undeserved, then why not force wealth and income transfers to rectify the unfair starting point caused by unequal endowments? After all, the Second Fundamental Theorem of Welfare Economics sanctions doing so, with no loss of efficiency except for those incentive effects discussed earlier.

In another direction, the classical utilitarian criterion of selecting policies so as to maximize the sum total of human happiness has come under strong scrutiny because it is viewed as insufficiently redistributive. Indeed, Rawls' entire theory was a rebuttal to utilitarianism on these grounds, and his conclusions about tax rates are more egalitarian. We now turn to this subject in the final section in the chapter.

In closing this discussion of economic fairness, it is worth remembering that Adam Smith himself viewed economics as part of moral theory, and more generally of the Science of Man as he and his great friend David Hume dubbed their mutual investigations. Moreover, he had strong personal views about distributive justice, as any civilized person does. For example, he did not believe in inherited wealth, and he had little use for highly unequal distributions of income. In today's language, he thus believed in confiscatory inheritance taxes, and in highly progressive income tax rates. Imagine: Adam Smith of all people!

A Comprehensive Theory of Distributive Justice

For the 1992 *Handbook of Game Theory*, one of a number of volumes constituting the *Handbook of Economics* edited by Kenneth Arrow and Michael Intrilligator, John Harsanyi was asked to write the chapter on the subject of ethics, with a particular focus on distributive justice. His mission was to show how the advent of decision theory and game theory had impacted moral philosophy, and had made possible several overarching new theories of social justice.[14] Harsanyi was chosen to write this essay because he was the only game theorist who was also a moral philosopher and had made fundamental contributions to the theory of utilitarianism.

In his *Handbook* essay, he reviewed and contrasted three quite different theories of justice: utilitarianism, Rawls' theory, and a third quite formal theory that I developed in the late 1970s upon completing my PhD dissertation at Princeton.[15] Since this third theory was developed after the first two theories, I attempted to clarify several of the earlier arguments, and to extend moral theory in a new direction. Let me use a diagram taken from my original 1978 paper to clarify some of the issues involved, and to permit a comparison of the three theories. The issues here are utterly fundamental, very relevant today, and intrinsically interesting. Also, as with the results in Chapters 2–5, the logic utilized is strictly deductive in nature.

A "supergame" in game theory is just a game consisting of other games known as subgames. In Figure 6.1, the topic of distributive justice is modeled as a two-stage supergame. In the stage 1 game, members of society adopt some constitution setting forth

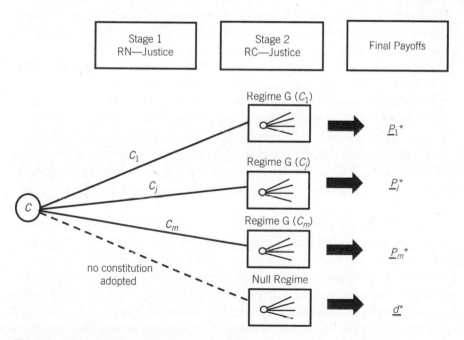

Figure 6.1   Modeling the Constitutional Choice Problem

the basic laws under which they will live. This constitutional choice problem can be thought of as that of selecting a set of "basic institutions" or equivalently an "incentive structure" that will constrain behavior in the second stage game. Then in the stage 2 game, people get jobs, compete, and do what is best for themselves and their careers. But in doing so, they are subject to the laws of the constitution selected in the stage 1 game. The black rays within each regime box indicate the set of all real-world strategies from which members of society will choose their best strategies during the stage 2 problem.

Appearing on the far right of the figure are the "payoffs" to everyone from doing what is best for himself or herself subject to the provisos of the constitution adopted. The capitalized letter $\underline{P}$ underlined is just shorthand for the fact that $\underline{P}$ consists of n different payoffs when there are n people involved, with one payoff specified for each person. Thus $\underline{P} = (P_1, P_2, P_3, \ldots P_n)$. There is one last detail. The dotted line at the bottom leading to a "null regime" with payoff $\underline{d}$ represents what happens if the citizens fail to agree on any constitution at all. This regime represents a non-cooperative game in the sense of Chapter 5. Its payoff $\underline{d}$ can be thought of as the payoff from a Hobbesian world devoid of laws and basic institutions, in effect a free-for-all of the kind witnessed today in Somalia.[16]

One assumption common to all three theories is that the payoffs $\underline{P}$ from all regimes possessing constitutions are high enough to permit all players to end up better off than they would be with payoff $\underline{d}$ in the null regime. This is not a restrictive assumption since, in a cooperative game, side-payments can be made from winners to any losers in all the games with payoffs $\underline{P}$. That is, the gains from cooperation of all those who benefit from the adoption of a constitution will far exceed any losses to losers, and the latter thus can be compensated via side payments.

Following in the footsteps of classical social contract theory, all three theories of justice that Harsanyi reviews adopt a two-stage structure like the one in our figure. For a real world example of this kind of social choice problem, consider the Constitutional Convention of 1787 when the U.S. constitution was hammered out in the summer heat of Philadelphia. Once adopted, its provisions would constrain behavior throughout society by setting out just what kinds of laws, tax rates, and penalties could be enacted.

The Two Fundamental Norms: Needs and Contribution

What moral norms should be respected in each of the two subgames pictured here? I took my cue from a paper sent to me by Professor Daniel Bell in 1976, a celebrated Harvard sociologist interested in issues of justice. The paper was by the Oxford philosopher Charles Taylor who stated something that neither Rawls nor the utilitarians had been explicit about: *the requirement that any acceptable theory of justice must take account of both needs-based and contribution-based fairness.* The importance of these two norms was stressed by Marx, and Rawls recognized the merits of both.[17] But neither Marx, nor Rawls, nor the utilitarians paid more than lip service to "to each according to his contribution." Needs-based justice always predominated, and everyone acknowledged that it was hard if not impossible to reconcile the two norms.

In this vein, recall Marx's memorable imperative: "From each according to his ability (ability to contribute), to each according to his need." The key phrase here is ". . . to each according to his need." The fruits of those who contribute more are presumably to be seized for those of lesser abilities who are more needy. Of course, those who contribute more may not like being used as pack horses for others, and might just decide to withhold their capital and labor so that less is left over for the needy. Indeed, it would be rational for them to do so, as Aumann and Kurz proved in their "Power and Taxes" paper cited earlier.

Unification of the Two Norms within a Comprehensive Theory

I did not accept the view that the conflict between these two different principles of distributive justice was intractable, and agreed with Professor Taylor that a proper theory of justice must accommodate both norms within a unified theory. In my theory, I argued that needs-based justice is appropriate in the stage 1 problem of constitutional choice, whereas contribution-based justice is appropriate in the stage 2 game of real life. The labeling in Figure 6.1 should make this clear.

Why might this be true? First consider the nature of the stage 1 game. There is an opportunity for everyone to benefit by agreeing upon the basic institutions required for a political economy to function well. No one contributes more than anyone else in this game, a game in which no actions of any kind enter the picture. Rather, what is at stake are the mutual gains made possible by agreeing upon a set of basic institutions at a constitutional convention. These institutions in turn make possible in the real-world stage 2 game the existence of an impartial rather than a biased judiciary, a progressive rather than a regressive tax code reflecting the differing abilities of people to pay, and an overall sense of fairness required for social cohesion and peace.

Some philosophers have deemed the ability of all members of society to gain from agreement on such basic institutions to be "manna from heaven." No claim based upon differential contribution can be made for this manna. Its existence is God given, just as is the possibility of enjoying a beautiful sunset, using waterfalls to generate power, or utilizing mass to create energy via Einstein's celebrated equation $E = mc^2$. The only way one member might contribute more than another in the stage 1 game lies in better conceiving and articulating the possibilities of constitutional choice than another does. But this particular talent seems irrelevant to the ultimate choice of a constitution. Overall, in manna contexts where no one contributes more or less than another, distribution according to relative neediness would seem to be the only morally acceptable criterion to invoke in arriving at the choice of a constitution. This conclusion is seen in the labeling of the two stages of the supergame in Figure 6.1.

Note that in speaking of a constitution, I refer to a set of "basic" institutions, not the set of all possible institutions. This is an important proviso. For the constitutions to be chosen from in stage 1 must be sufficiently minimalist in their constraints to permit sufficient freedom and flexibility required in the real-world stage 2 game. It would thus be counterproductive in stage 1 to determine who eats or wears what in the real-world setting of the stage 2 game. Agents in the stage 1 game know this, and know that they will value freedom in the real-world game. They thus settle upon a liberty-respecting constitution.[18]

Now consider the real-world stage 2 regime. The situation here is opposite to that in the stage 1 game. Here, individuals *do* contribute differentially to the creation of businesses, to writing books, to running restaurants, or other worldly activities. Here it is all about which team player is MVP, which firm had the highest return on the capital of savers/investors, which restaurants gained the highest recognition, and so on. In this real-world competitive context, distribution according to relative contribution is the appropriate moral criterion.

It is here in stage 2 that those virtues of the free-market system demonstrated by Hurwicz come into full bloom, virtues generated by the ability of agents to focus selfishly on maximizing their own risk-adjusted returns. And by extension, it is here that contribution-justice takes center stage (who *is* the MVP?), and that issues of needs-justice do not and indeed should not arise. Market behavior will *not* be efficient if agents are altruistic during their 8:00 a.m. to 5:00 p.m. jobs and focus on matters other than running their businesses to maximize returns. They can, of course, be altruistic after hours, as most of us are when we are with friends and family, or are assisting charitable activities.

Does this seem somewhat cold-hearted? In fact, it is not. This is because everyone knows during their 8:00 to 5:00 hours of self-interested behavior that issues pertinent to relative needs have *already been addressed* and dealt with by suitable provisos in the constitution chosen in the stage 1 game. These are the reasons why my theory requires that distributive justice in the stage 2 game respects relative contribution. In economic terms, the pretax remuneration to all agents should be in proportion to their marginal contributions.

What is remarkable in this regard is that the payoff from competitive market behavior under almost any constitution will *automatically* satisfy contribution-justice. Even more remarkably, in any non-market or political context where multilateral bargaining behavior is involved, the outcome will also respect the relative contribution principle. Both of these results follow from Robert Aumann's remarkable 1977 theorem cited previously.[19]

Overall, what this theory does is to disentangle the two fundamental distributive norms cited by Professor Taylor and apply them in the two totally separate domains where each is relevant. Needs-justice governs the choice of basic institutions and tax rates in the stage 1 game, whereas contribution-justice operates within whatever stage 2 game results from the constitution chosen. There is thus a clear division of labor between these two dimensions of moral theory.

The Princeton Philosophy Department

I tested these basic ideas in a case study I developed when I was a graduate student at Princeton years ago. Suppose the university's eminent Department of Philosophy must choose between two excellent professors in awarding tenure: Susan Stentley and Tom

Smith. Both have done excellent work, but Susan is thought to have a very slight edge professionally. Yet there is a complication. Tom is the more affable and popular colleague, and has an expensive illness as a result of which he would benefit much more than Susan from the added income and job security the tenured position would make possible. Which candidate will Princeton choose? Which should it choose?

The answer I received from every professor I asked—and most had very liberal views—was that they would pick Susan. "Our primary responsibility is to hold this department to the very highest academic standards possible." In my theory, this ostensibly heartless reply will be morally acceptable *provided* that the basic institutions of society chosen in stage 1 fund the cost of Tom's illness. This is the division of labor I just spoke of. To sum up, during their stage 2 game, the Princeton philosophers focus on the quality of their department and its reputation, and contribution-justice prevails. But they do so knowing that the most basic needs of their colleague Tom have been dealt with "elsewhere," via provisions of the constitution arrived at during the stage 1 game.

How to Measure Relative Needs

In both Rawls' theory and in Harsanyi's version of utilitarianism, the concepts of relative need and relative contribution remain somewhat murky. But why shouldn't they? Knowing how to measure and quantify both concepts has been a notoriously difficult problem for centuries. Peyton Young only determined how to correctly measure relative contribution in 1988, as already noted. Assessing relative needs is arguably more difficult than relative contribution. The reason is that doing so seemingly requires us to make what are known as "interpersonal comparisons of utility," or interpersonal comparisons of well-being to put it more colloquially. Let me further explain this difficulty.

Suppose Mother Teresa wishes to distribute $1 million between 20 supplicants of different needs, and suppose she wishes to do so in accord with the principle of relative need, as seems most reasonable.[20] Now how can she do so without an absolute yardstick of well-being whereby she can compare how much absolute well-being each claimant receives from each marginal dollar awarded? Who benefits the most? The second most? The third most? Rawls' theory requires a very basic comparison along these lines, and utilitarianism requires a much more demanding type of interpersonal comparison.[21] Many philosophers and economists object strenuously to the need to make such interpersonal comparisons since no one knows how to make them. This has always been a fundamental problem in moral theory.

The good news is that progress has been made in resolving this difficulty. In the case of relative needs, after being challenged by this issue for over 20 years, I demonstrated in 2004 that there is a unique measure of relative neediness that satisfies seven axioms. Remarkably, no interpersonal comparisons of utility are needed to arrive at this measure.

The result followed from discovering and proving that "relative risk aversion" so crucial in bargaining theory is formally equivalent to "relative neediness" in moral theory. Since bargaining theory awards pieces of pie in inverse proportion to relative neediness (the more risk averse you are, the more you get bargained down), the result implies that the relatively more needy you are, the less you receive. It thus turns out that the *inverse* of the ratio of sizes of the two pieces of pie awarded by bargaining is the appropriate measure of relative need. Finally, since no interpersonal comparisons of utility are needed in the Nash-Harsanyi theory to determine the sizes of the slices of the pie awarded by bargaining, none are required to determine relative neediness measured in this way.

To see this more clearly, suppose you get two-thirds of the pie and I receive one-third from bargaining. Given the logic just reviewed, the only reason for the outcome awarding twice as much pie to you as to me is that I am twice as risk averse—and equivalently twice as needy—as you are. Thus from a needs-based ethical standpoint, I should get twice as much as you do. Accordingly, the ethical allocation "flips" the bargaining allocation and I receive two-thirds of the pie, and you only one-third.[22]

Full Distributive Justice and a Theory of the State

If the supergame introduced in Figure 6.1 is solved, the result is *full distributive justice* in my theory. The two fundamental distributive norms of contribution and need are satisfied in the right order, in the right place, and in a very precise manner. Each applies in the context where it should apply, and there is no incompatibility between them. As a bonus, no interpersonal comparisons of utility are called for.

There is one last detail. The stage 1 game as I have described it is not in fact a game proper, but rather an arbitration scheme whereby a group of "founding fathers" collaborate to arrive at the fairest possible constitution. The decision problem within stage 2 is of course a genuine game. Thus it might seem that the super-game in Figure 6.1 is not in fact a supergame proper, but a hybrid of sorts. This is not in fact the case. For in determining the relative needs respecting constitution sought in the stage 1 problem, a particular Nash-Harsanyi bargaining game must in fact be solved, for the reasons described in endnote 22. So my construct can be viewed either as an arbitration problem, with an embedded stage 2 game, or else as a proper supergame. There is one last surprise: the two formulas for determining allocations that satisfy "to each according to his relative need" and "to each according to his rela-tive contribution" are themselves very closely related, the one being dual to the other.[23]

Comparison with Rawlsism and Utilitarianism

All three theories make use of an "original position" or "veil of Ignorance" or constitutional convention in which basic rules of the game are selected before we go out and play the game of life. So do most all historical theories of the social contract, for example, those of Rousseau and Locke. What the new theory offers is crystal clarity about previously murky concepts ("constitution," "needs," "contribution"). Additionally, ethics becomes free of the necessity of making interpersonal comparisons of utility. Finally, the theory does appropri-ate justice to both Relative Needs and to Relative Contribution.

Where these three theories differ significantly is in their treatment of the concept of relative needs. Rawls' stage 1 game, or his "original position" as he calls it, is one where every agent is assumed to be completely risk averse in the following sense: In the original position, every agent focuses exclusively on obtaining sufficient "primary goods" that he and his family can survive. Getting the minimal standard of living these goods bestow is of such momen-tous importance that he places no value at all upon upside risk, that is, upon the chance of ending up with more than his bundle of primary goods. An equivalent way of stating this is that everyone in the original position is assumed to act as if he was *certain* that he will be poor, blind, and disad-vantaged when he exits the original position. These strong assumptions lead people to select a constitution which is very egalitarian.

Harsanyi and many others viewed Rawls' exclusion of consideration for everyone except the worst-off members of society as confused and invalid. In his resurrection of utilitarianism, Harsanyi introduced a different and far more compelling scheme. Everyone in his original position is under a veil of ignorance. Everyone is ignorant as to what his characteristics will be when the stage 2 problem gets played, for example, poor and blind versus rich and well-sighted. More specifically, everyone is assumed to have an *equal chance* of ending up in anyone else's shoes. When a constitution is chosen under these assumptions, Harsanyi proves that it will be the one that maximizes the greatest good, or equivalently, it will be the utilitarian solution.

Harsanyi comes very close to arguing that the utilitarian outcome satisfies the norm of Relative Needs. And to an extent, it does. This is because of the role of diminishing marginal utility already discussed. We saw how utilitarianism logically implied a progressive tax code for this reason. Nonetheless, Harsanyi never clearly defined Relative Neediness, and did not show formally that the utilitarian decision rule does in fact allocate goods in proportion to relative neediness.

It has now been proven that the utilitarian allocation does not in fact satisfy the Relative Need norm, as my own theory does. Nevertheless, it can be shown that the prescriptions of the two theories will differ very little in many practical applications. Rawls' theory for its part is not consistent at all with Relative Need. Rather, he focuses on the absolute needs of the worst off.[24]

Conclusion

In writing this highly ambitious chapter, I hope I have been able to convey a sense of marvel at the progress that has been made in recent decades in clarifying a number of age-old concepts such as the nature of an ideal society, the status of democratic capitalism, and the meaning of justice in distribution. On the economic front, the work of Leonid Hurwicz arguably represents the most important step forward, since he dramatically generalized both the context and the concepts of classical economic theory. Nonetheless, while Hurwicz understood the importance of distributive justice as an important norm in the design of a social system, he wrote little about the subject and did not provide a theory of justice of his own. Interestingly, no economist has done so in recent decades. To be sure, scholars such as Arrow, Bergson, Samuelson, and Scitovsky greatly refined the quasi-ethical concept of the social welfare function introduced a century earlier by the utilitarians. But none of these economists produced an actual theory of distributive justice.

Two people did: John Rawls and John Harsanyi. It is these two who deserve credit for revitalizing this topic by introducing decision-theoretic arguments permitting concrete results about the nature of a fair distribution of wealth and income. This represented a milestone in the development of moral philosophy. Other nondecision-theoretic approaches have been advanced to clarify issues of distributive justice, but I have not found these compelling. For example, Harvard philosopher Thomas Scanlon published an important book on justice entitled *What We Owe to Each Other* in 1998.[25]

In his theory, Scanlon eschews the use of the highly analytic approaches reviewed in Harsanyi's *Handbook of Game Theory* article cited earlier. Rather, as is fashionable in current moral philosophy, Scanlon provides a very thoughtful if complex "account" of issues that arise in moral theory. What is odd is that, after reading his book, I had no idea how Scanlon would solve the simplest of all distributional problems, for example, how Mother Theresa should divide a pie "fairly" between people of different degrees of neediness. Indeed, Scanlon seems unaware that great progress has been made on this front

In the real world, *decisions* of just this kind must be made regarding what we really do owe to each other. In this regard, it is not surprising that the advent of decision theory and game theory has provided a tremendous assist to moral and political theory by permitting it to ascend from the murky level of philosophical "accounts" and word games about classical problems to the level of solutions applicable in the real world. This is the message I have tried to convey in the concluding part of this chapter.

Conclusion

My first goal in writing this book was to identify five challenges that the United States must confront because they matter so much to the nation's future. These ranged from extricating ourselves from a Lost Decade, to resolving the longer-run entitlements spending crisis, to preventing future Perfect Storms in the financial markets, to negotiating more effectively with thugocracies, and to confronting the thorny issue of distributive justice in seeking to create a more ideal polity.

My second goal has been to demonstrate how new theories based upon deductive logic can transform how we think about these difficult issues, and help us identify better solutions to the problems confronting us. Thus I have utilized unfamiliar concepts within macroeconomic theory to rethink the meaning of "government deficits." Doing so implies the need for a domestic Marshall Plan to redress the Lost Decade. As for the entitlements crisis, a new insight into the nature of the dynamics of total expenditure in markets implies a win-win solution to the problem of exploding health-care costs. In the case of financial market instability, the new theory of endogenous risk provided a completely fresh perspective on the true origins of Perfect Storms and how to prevent them.

As for dealing more effectively with thugocracies on the world stage, I drew extensively on the Nash-Harsanyi theory of multilateral bargaining, and the role of optimal threats in particular. The goal is to help U.S. policymakers rethink certain aspects of international relations so they can end up earning an A rather than a D in bargaining with other nations. Finally, I drew upon significant advances in normative political and moral theory to reformulate the concept of an ideal state—one in which the difficult subject of distributive justice is confronted, not sidestepped. The theoretical advances introduced originated in modern decision theory and game theory.

My third and final goal has been to show that these solutions to the five challenges are win-win in nature, and transcend the ideologies of the Left and the Right. In retrospect, I hope you will agree that ideology has played virtually no role in these pages, and that I have expressed strong reservations about the views of liberals and conservatives in equal measure. Indeed, the conclusions arrived at could be culled to form a syllabus for Common Sense 101, the course I hope to develop during my retirement.

How was all this possible given the inherent difficulty of the problems that are addressed? The answer lies in the nature of the deductive logic that has been used in every chapter. Once some simple axioms have been introduced and deemed "reasonable" by all involved, then the conclusions that are deduced from them *must* be accepted. Moreover, to the extent that the underlying axioms are simple and persuasive, so too will be the conclusions that follow, assuming that the reasoning process linking premise to conclusion is crystal clear and understandable.

The possibility of deducing win-win solutions to the problems posed in all five policy arenas is what inspired this book from the start. I see this as the best way to dampen way down today's deafening Dialogue of the Deaf, which has generated American gridlock of a very destructive nature. Each side repetitively recycles stale positions supported by cherry-picked data, utilizing inductive logic at its worst. The situation today is as intolerable as it is insulting to most normal people who sense that neither side is progressing toward a resolution of the nation's problems. It is no accident that politicians now rate lower than bankers and dogcatchers in U.S. public esteem.

While I can write a book heralding win-win solutions to many of the nation's problems, I am only scratching the surface in doing so. As I stress in Chapter 1, the next step is to enroll the media and the schools of government and public policy in a new cause: forcing a change in the way we expect policy makers to analyze policy choices and sell them to the public. I am dead serious about the need for a new game of political "Gotcha!" I really do want politicians, policy wonks, talking heads on cable news, and op-ed writers all "outed" for bad logic—the kind of logic that is preventing us from identifying solutions to major problems.

I want newly developed "idiocy indices" to be identified with White House economists who permitted a health-care bill to be formulated that was inexcusably supply light, with state department officials who sold the interests of millions of American workers down the drain by never standing up to China, with financial sector regulators who permitted an unconscionable tripling of broker-dealer leverage in 2004, with a president who arrogantly dismissed the best (Simpson-Bowles) proposals to date as to how to deal with the nation's long-term debt problems without giving a reason, and with a former Federal Reserve Chairman who permitted ever-lower down payments on houses during an unprecedented housing market bubble.

Pressing further, I want phliberals (phony liberals) exposed for their hypocrisy in supporting welfare state policies that lard today's elderly with benefits at the expense of tomorrow's elderly. Analogously, I want Right-wing fundamentalists who claim to have an open phone line to God to be forced to explain why they have no faculties of ratiocination at all, and as a result rely solely on faith, aka prejudice. Was there an Eleventh Commandment that I missed during theology class: "Thou shall neither reason nor think"? Enough is enough. Game over.

Despite the tribulations of this Dialogue of the Deaf, I am an ardent optimist. The good news is that solutions to all our problems exist. Moreover, I believe that many media spokespeople desperately want to elevate the standards of national debate. They, too, have had enough. My greatest fear is that more and more Americans are coming to believe that win-win solutions do not, in fact, exist. We must show them that they are wrong.

Supply/Demand Summary of the Patient Protection and Affordable Care Act

What follows is a bulletized summary of President Obama's Patient Protection and Affordable Care Act presented in a new way: The demand-side and supply-side provisions of the Act are clearly differentiated. This information strengthens the conclusions reached in the main text. This summary is included for the sake of completeness since few people know what the new Act consists of, or how it impacts demand versus supply for health-care services.

Demand Side

The Henry J. Kaiser Family Foundation recently published a helpful summary of those aspects of the new Act related to expanding insurance coverage. According to Kaiser, the Act will:

- Require most U.S. citizens and legal residents to have health insurance.
- Create state-based American Health Benefit Exchanges through which individuals can purchase coverage, with premium and cost-sharing credits available to individuals/families with incomes between 133 and 400 percent of the federal poverty level (the poverty level was $18,310 for a family of three in 2009) and create separate Exchanges through which small businesses can purchase coverage.

- Require employers to pay penalties for employees who receive tax credits for health insurance through an Exchange, with exceptions for small employers.
- Impose new regulations on health plans in the Exchanges and in the individual and small group markets.
- Expand Medicaid to 133 percent of the federal poverty level.

Additionally, to fully understand the demand side, it is helpful to summarize the three most controversial aspects of the legislation—namely (1) strict insurance mandates for individuals, (2) employer health-care insurance requirements, and (3) cost-containment provisions.[1]

1. **Individual Mandates:** To avoid the politically unpalatable concept of universal coverage through a single-payer system, the new Act instead requires all individuals (with limited exceptions) to buy insurance or face income tax penalties. In particular, the Act requires U.S. citizens and legal residents to have qualifying health coverage. Those without coverage pay a tax penalty of the greater of 2.5 percent of household income or $695 per year up to a maximum of three times that amount ($2,085) per family.
2. **Employer Requirements:** Perhaps no aspect of the new Act has garnered as much attention as its provisions *requiring* employers to provide insurance for its employees. In particular, the new legislature would:

   - Assess employers with 50 or more employees that do not offer coverage and have at least one full-time employee who receives a premium tax credit a fee of $2,000 per full-time employee, excluding the first 30 employees from the assessment. Employers with more than 50 employees that offer coverage but have at least one full-time employee receiving a premium tax credit will pay the lesser of $3,000 for each employee receiving a premium credit or $2,000 for each full-time employee, excluding the first 30 employees from the assessment.
   - Exempt employers with fewer than 50 employees from any of these penalties.
   - Require employers that offer coverage to their employees to provide a free-choice voucher to employees with incomes

less than 400 percent of federal poverty level whose share of the premium exceeds 8 percent but is less than 9.8 percent of their income and who choose to enroll in a plan in the Exchange. The voucher amount is equal to what the employer would have paid to provide coverage to the employee under the employer's plan and will be used to offset the premium costs for the plan in which the employee is enrolled. Employers providing free-choice vouchers will not be subject to penalties for employees that receive premium credits in the Exchange.

3. **Cost-Containment Provisions:** The Act's provisions to "contain costs" focus on the following:

- Simplifying health insurance administration by adopting a single set of operating rules for eligibility verification and claims status.
- Improving Medicare cost containment by:
  - Restructuring payments to Medicare Advantage (MA) plans.
  - Modifying the rebate system.
  - Reducing annual market basket updates for inpatient hospital care.
  - Establishing an Independent Payment Advisory Board to submit legislative proposals containing recommendations to reduce the per capita rate of growth in Medicare spending.
- Amending Medicaid by:
  - Increasing the Medicaid drug rebate percentage for approved drugs.
  - Reducing aggregate Medicaid DSH allotments.
  - Providing incentives for states to improve efficiency.
- Authorizing the Food and Drug Administration to approve generic versions of biologic drugs and grant biologics manufacturers 12 years of exclusive use before generics can be developed.
- Reducing waste, fraud, and abuse in public programs by:
  - Allowing provider screening.
  - Enhancing oversight periods for new providers and suppliers.

- Developing a database to capture and share data across federal and state programs.
- Increasing penalties for submitting false claims.

Supply Side

Let's now discuss how the new Patient Protection and Affordable Care Act, and changes made to the law by subsequent legislation, addresses the supply side of the equation. Broadly speaking, the supply-side provisions in the Act are intended to:

- Improve access by increasing the supply of needed health workers, particularly primary care practitioners.
- Increase efficiency and effectiveness by encouraging systems redesign.
- Improve the quality of care through improved education and training.
- Establish an infrastructure to collect and disseminate better data and information to inform public and private decision-making around the supply, education and training, and use of health workers.

The new Act includes several important provisions related to expanding the health workforce. In the following summary, I will highlight the Act's specific provisions that: (1) improve health system performance and quality and (2) strengthen and grow the health-care workforce.

1. **Improve Health System Performance:** The new Act includes several quality enhancement provisions, including:

   - Supporting comparative effectiveness research by establishing a nonprofit Patient-Centered Outcomes Research Institute to identify research priorities and conducting research that compares the clinical effectiveness of medical treatments.
   - Awarding five-year demonstration grants to states to develop, implement, and evaluate alternatives to current tort litigations.

- Increasing Medicaid payments in fee-for-service and managed care for primary care services provided by primary care doctors (family medicine, general internal medicine, or pediatric medicine).
- Developing a national quality improvement strategy that includes priorities to improve the delivery of health-care services, patient health outcomes, and population health.
- Requiring enhanced collection and reporting of data on race, ethnicity, sex, primary language, disability status, and for underserved rural and frontier populations.

2. **Strengthen the Health-Care Workforce:** The new Act includes several provisions to enhance and grow the health-care workforce, including:

- Establishing a multistakeholder Workforce Advisory Committee to develop a national workforce strategy.
- Increasing the number of Graduate Medical Education (GME) training positions by:
  - Redistributing currently unused slots, with priority given to primary care and general surgery and to states with the lowest physician-to-population ratios.
  - Increasing flexibility in laws and regulations that govern GME funding to promote training in outpatient settings.
  - Ensuring the availability of residency programs in rural and underserved areas.
- Establishing Teaching Health Centers, defined as community-based, ambulatory patient care centers, including federally qualified health centers and other federally funded health centers that are eligible for payments for the expenses associated with operating primary-care residency programs.
- Increasing workforce supply and support training of health professionals through:
  - Providing scholarships and loans.
  - Supporting primary-care training and capacity building.
  - Offering state grants to providers in medically underserved areas.
  - Training and recruiting providers to serve in rural areas.
  - Establishing a public health workforce loan repayment program.

- Providing medical residents with training in preventive medicine and public health.
- Promoting training of a diverse workforce.
- Advancing cultural competence training of health-care professionals.

■ Addressing the projected shortage of nurses and retention of nurses by:
  - Increasing the capacity for education, supporting training programs, providing loan repayment and retention grants, and creating a career ladder to nursing.
  - Providing grants for up to three years to employ and provide training to family nurse practitioners who provide primary care in federally qualified health centers and nurse-managed health clinics.

APPENDIX B

Dynamics of Total Health-Care Expenditure

In this appendix, we explore the dynamics of total expenditure under linear shifts to the supply and demand curves. The two principal propositions asserted in Chapter 3 are proven.

We begin with the case in which the supply curve shifts out faster than the demand curve. Subject to mild regularity conditions, this implies an eventual decrease in total expenditure. We consider two examples: first, the case of linear price-quantity relations, under which the time dynamics of expenditure assume a particularly transparent form. Second, we consider a pathological situation in which the supply and demand curves violate the regularity conditions and cause expenditure to increase without bound.

We also consider the situation in which demand shifts out more rapidly than supply. Very generally, this scenario results in a monotonic increase in total expenditure, without limit.

Assume that $s(P)$ and $d(P)$ are continuously differentiable supply and demand functions for some good with price P. Let supply increase and demand decrease with price, so that $s'(P) > 0$ and $d'(P) < 0$. Let equilibrium prices be defined implicitly by the market clearing equation $s(P^*) = d(P^*)$, so that equilibrium quantity is defined by $Q = s(P^*) = d(P^*)$ and equilibrium total expenditure by $E = Q P^*$.

Our primary interest is to understand the change over time in E as we shift out both the supply and demand curves at constant rates. Suppose we push supply and demand out at rates v_S and v_D, both positive. Then at price P and time t, we have effective supply and demand functions

$$S(P,t) = s(P) + t\,v_S$$
$$D(P,t) = d(P) + t\,v_D$$

Setting $S(P,t) = D(P,t)$ implicitly defines prices $P(t)$ and quantities $Q(t)$ that change over time, and these in turn define the time-varying total expenditure $E(t)$ that is the subject of this appendix. We assume that equilibrium prices are continuously differentiable for all t.

Lemma

If supply shifts out faster than demand, so that $v_S > v_D$, then prices must fall. In the opposite situation, prices will rise.

Proof

The equilibrium price $P(t)$ at time t is implicitly defined by

$$S(P(t),t) = D(P(t),t)$$
$$s(P(t)) + t\,v_S = d(P(t)) + t\,v_D$$

We may differentiate this expression to obtain

$$s'\,P' + v_S = d'\,P' + v_D$$

Rearranging, this yields

$$P' = (v_D - v_S)/(s' - d')$$

Because $s' > 0$ and $d' < 0$, the denominator must be positive. Thus the direction of price movement is determined by whether we push out supply or demand more rapidly. If we push out supply faster than demand ($v_S > v_D$), then the equilibrium price must fall. Prices will rise in the opposite case ($v_D > v_S$).

Proposition 1

Suppose that the supply curve shifts out more rapidly than the demand curve. Also, assume that the supply and demand functions have bounded first derivatives. Then expenditure must eventually decrease to zero.

Proof

In the proof of the Lemma, above, we found that

$$P' = (v_D - v_S)/(s' - d')$$

If supply and demand have bounded first derivatives, then there must exist some C such that

$$C < 1/(s' - d')$$

Since we are shifting out supply faster than demand, $v_D - v_S < 0$, therefore

$$P' = (v_D - v_S)/(s' - d') < (v_D - v_S)\, C < 0$$

Applying the fundamental theorem of calculus, we find that at time T,

$$P(T) - P(0) < T\, (v_D - v_S)\, C$$

or

$$P(T) < T\, (v_D - v_S)\, C + P(0)$$

Thus if $v_D - v_S$ is strictly negative, as it will be if the supply curve shifts out more quickly than the demand curve, there will be some finite T such that prices go to zero.

Because quantities are bounded, we then have that at some finite time T^*

$$E(T^*) = P(T^*)\, Q(T^*) = 0$$

This implies that if expenditure starts out positive, it must at some point decline to zero, perhaps after a period of initial increase.

Example 1

For our first example, we consider a case in which the dynamics of expenditure are particularly simple to understand. Suppose that supply and demand are linear. In the notation, this means

$$s(P) = a_S + b_S P$$

$$d(P) = a_D + b_D\, P$$

If we shift out the supply and demand curves at rates v_S and v_D, respectively, this means that

$$S(P,t) = a_S + b_S\, P + t\, v_S$$
$$D(P,t) = a_D + b_D\, P + t\, v_D$$

For supply to increase and demand to decrease with price, we must have $b_S > 0$ and $b_D < 0$. Equilibrium prices as a function of time are defined by

$$S(P,t) = D(P,t)$$
$$a_S + b_S\, P + t\, v_S = a_D + b_D\, P + t\, v_D$$
$$P = (a_D - a_S + t\, v_D - t\, v_S)/(b_S - b_D)$$
$$P = (a_D - a_S)/(b_S - b_D) + t\, (v_D - v_S)/(b_S - b_D)$$

By inspection, it's clear that if demand increases more quickly than supply so that $v_D > v_S$, prices will increase linearly, while if supply increases more quickly than demand, the opposite will occur. In the same way, we can express equilibrium quantities as

$$Q = (a_S + b_S\, (a_D - a_S)/(b_S - b_D)) + t\, (b_S\, (v_D - v_S)/(b_S - b_D) + v_S)$$
$$Q = (a_D + b_D\, (a_D - a_S)/(b_S - b_D)) + t\, (b_D\, (v_D - v_S)/(b_S - b_D) + v_D)$$

Expenditure then takes a complicated form which may be seen to reduce to

$$E = A\, t^2 + B\, t + C$$

With $A = \beta\, \delta/\varepsilon^2$, $B = (\beta\, \gamma + \alpha\, \delta)/\varepsilon^2$, and $C = \alpha\, \gamma/\varepsilon^2$, where

$$\alpha = a_S - a_D$$
$$\beta = v_S - v_D$$
$$\gamma = a_S\, b_D - a_D\, b_S$$
$$\delta = v_S\, b_D - v_D\, b_S$$
$$\varepsilon = b_S - b_D$$

As noted above, $b_S > 0$ and $b_D < 0$. This implies that $b_S - b_D = \varepsilon > 0$. Assuming that prices are positive at time $t = 0$, we have

$$P(0) = (a_D - a_S)/(b_S - b_D) + 0 = -\alpha/\varepsilon > 0$$

Combining this with the above yields $-\alpha > 0$ or simply $\alpha < 0$. Applying this assumption to quantities, we get

$$Q(0) = (a_D + b_D (a_D - a_S)/(b_S - b_D)) + 0 > 0$$

Equivalently,

$$Q(0) = -\gamma/\varepsilon > 0$$

and hence $\gamma < 0$.

The δ term must be negative, because v_S, v_D, and h_S are all positive, b_D is negative, and by definition

$$\delta = v_S b_D - v_D b_S$$

Finally, the sign of the β term comes down to whether the supply or demand curve gets pushed out more quickly. If supply shifts out faster, then $\beta > 0$. If the rate of demand shift is greater, $\beta < 0$.

We are now in a position to understand the exact dynamics of the expenditure function.

First, observe that the sign of the A term is governed by the sign of β:

$$\text{sign}(A) - \text{sign}(\beta \, \delta/\varepsilon^2) = \text{sign}(\beta)\,\text{sign}(\delta) = -\text{sign}(\beta)$$

If we push supply out faster than demand, then $\beta > 0$, $A < 0$, and total expenditure looks like a downward-opening parabola. In the opposite case, $\beta < 0$, $A > 0$, and total expenditure follows an upward-opening parabola.

It is sometimes possible to say more about the behavior of expenditure over time. Observe that

$$\text{sign}(B) = \text{sign}(\beta \, \gamma + \alpha \, \delta)$$

If we push out supply faster than demand, $\beta > 0$ and B is of ambiguous sign. However, when we push out demand faster than supply, $\beta < 0$ and B must always be positive. In this case, we also have A positive, so for all $t > 0$,

$$dE/dt = 2 A t + B > 0$$

As we saw above, in this case we can say definitively that when we push out demand faster than supply and initial prices and quantities are (naturally) constrained to be positive, total expenditure follows a strictly increasing parabolic path.

When we push out supply faster than demand, it is possible for expenditure to increase temporarily. However, as established in Proposition 1, it must always eventually reach zero, at the point T where

$$A\,T^2 + B\,T + C = 0$$

While the general expenditure function can be messy and non-monotonic, this linear/quadratic setting exhibits all of the most important large-scale behavior.

Example 2

We next turn to a pathological and somewhat artificial case in which demand explodes as price goes to zero. This requires a violation of the regularity conditions of Proposition 1 and results in expenditure that increases monotonically even while supply shifts out more quickly than demand.

Consider the following supply and demand functions

$$D(P,t) = 1/P^2 + 0$$
$$S(P,t) = 0 + t$$

Demand decreases with price and explodes as price goes to zero, and supply is perfectly inelastic. The velocities $v_D = 0$ and $v_S = 1$ indicate that we push out the supply curve by one unit per unit of time while leaving the demand curve where it is.

Setting supply equal to demand yields equilibrium prices:

$$1/P^2 + 0 = 0 + t$$
$$P = 1/\sqrt{t}$$

As in the Lemma, pushing out supply faster than demand implies that price must decrease with time. However, consider the expenditure function, which these prices and quantities imply:

$$E(t) = S(P(t),T)\,P(t) = t/\sqrt{t} = \sqrt{t}$$

One way to think about how expenditure can perpetually increase even as we push the supply curve out faster than the demand curve is that, although prices decline as time goes on, the quantity demanded blows up, driving an increase in total expenditure. If demand had a bounded first derivative, as in the hypotheses to Proposition 1, this behavior would be ruled out.

Proposition 2

Suppose that the demand curve shifts out more rapidly than the supply curve. Then total expenditure must strictly increase over time.

Proof

By definition, we have

$$E(t) = P(t)\ Q(t) = P(t)\ S(P(t),t) = P(t)\ D(P(t),t)$$

We may differentiate either term of this expression to get an expression for the change in expenditure over time:

$$E'(t) = P'\ S + P\ s'P' + P\ v_S = P'\ D + P\ d'P' + P\ v_D$$

From the Lemma, we know that if we shift out demand faster than supply, prices will rise. By assumption, supply and demand are always positive, so $P'\ S$ and $P'\ D$ terms of the above equations must both be positive as well. Prices and shift velocities must also be non-negative, so $P\ v_S$ and $P\ v_D$ must also have this sign. This leaves only the sign of the middle terms ambiguous.

The second term of the demand-based equation on the far right, $P\ d'P'$, must be negative because demand decreases in price. This leaves the change in expenditure over time as the sum of a mix of positive and negative terms, making this comparative static impossible to sign without information on relative magnitudes.

On the other hand, all of the constituent parts of the second term of the supply-based equation, $P\ s'\ P'$, will be positive and so must be their product. We may therefore express the change over time of expenditure as the sum of three positive terms, and therefore conclude that when demand pushes out faster than supply, expenditure must rise without limit.

Notes

Chapter 1: Dialogue of the Deaf

1. His 1932 physics treatise was *Mathematische Grundlagen der Quanten-mechanik,* Springer: Berlin. Von Neumann was much less known to the layman than Einstein, largely because he was not associated with any one big idea, such as Einstein was with theory of relativity. He was a peripatetic mathematician who invented game theory as we know it, and in 1928 proved its central theorem (the minimax theorem for zero-sum games). Shortly thereafter, he proved one of the most important theorems in the theory of economic growth. His work on self-reproducing automata in the late 1940s axiomatized the nature of human and machine self-reproduction in advance of the discovery of the double helix by Crick and Watson. Von Neumann also made one of the principal contributions to the invention of the modern "stored program" computer, referred to in earlier times as "the von Neumann machine." He rigorized and axiomatized quantum theory in physics in the late 1920s. He invented continuous geometry. Finally, he made major contributions to operator theory (von Neumann algebras), functional analysis, and ergodic theory, as well as to applied mathematics.

2. See Mendel Sachs, *Quantum Physics and Gravity* (New York: Springer Verlag, 2004). Sachs not only demonstrates the reasons why it will be impossible to "quantize" gravity, but he goes further. He reverses the logic of the standard model and shows how quantum theory can be obtained as a special limiting case of Einstein's theory of general relativity theory (of gravity), generalized to include both electromagnetism and quantum theory. Thus there is no need to quantize gravity at all. The ability to generalize general relativity to include electromagnetic theory within it came from Sach's generalization of the algebraic structure of relativity, analogous to Einstein's generalization of the geometric logic of space-time. In his theory, the field variables transform according to the laws of quaternion algebra. He shows that they must do so if the equations of relativity theory are to transform in accord with the irreducible symmetry group of relativity, a 16-parameter Lie group. His 16 equations (versus Einstein's

10) *factorize* into Einstein's original 10 equations of gravity, and 6 new equations that are in one-to-one correspondence with Maxwell's equations of electromagnetism, but that are more general than Maxwell's equations. Quantum theory can be obtained as a limiting case of the latter nonlinear formalism—a limiting case that can be approached, but can never be reached due to Noether's theorem. As a corollary, God does not need to play dice at all, and all the paradoxes of quantum theory disappear.

Chapter 2: Must There Be a Lost Decade?

1. By utilizing formal statistical analysis, you can learn that the decade-by-decade volatility of GDP declined by about 75 percent over the entire twentieth century (some of the earlier decades are not shown in the figure). There are five interesting reasons why this occurred. First, having been invented in the 1930s and 1940s, macroeconomic policy became utilized to stabilize business cycles from the late 1950s on. Second, the inventory cycle was tamed due to the advent of "just-in-time" inventory management techniques. Third, the manufacturing sector is inherently more volatile than the service sector, and the latter grew at the expense of the former, further stabilizing the economy. This is particularly true in the case of labor utilization, where an accelerating share of the workforce worked in services between 1945 and 2000. Fourth, family income was stabilized by the advent of two-income families. Fifth and last, both the level of household wealth and the access to credit increased. This provided a cushion that helped families to get through difficult times more easily so that consumption became less volatile.

2. Equation 2.1 is primarily useful for forecasting one- or two-year changes in GDP, and not much longer. This is because the terms in it refer to the sources of demand, not supply. More specifically, this formalism abstracts from changes in the productivity of labor, in the growth of the workforce, in total factor productivity, and in other longer-run supply-side factors that impact GDP growth along with demand. This point was stressed to me by Professor Benjamin Friedman at Harvard.

3. We are ignoring the issue of "statistical inconsistencies," such as unreported income, which often causes NI to be less than NP *ex post*. However, such discrepancies have little bearing on *ex ante* forecasts of either variable, which is why we shall ignore them.

4. The reader looking for a formal definition of National Income can now see that, by breaking out the Net Private Savings term in equation (2.3) into NI – Private Spending, and substituting this into (2.3), and then by rearranging terms within (2.3) so that NI ends up alone on the left-hand side, we arrive at an equation defining NI itself. The result here

is of no importance in this discussion. But this proves that (2.3) is in effect the equation of NI. This is disguised in the way I have written the identity.

5. For example, suppose that the U.S. trade deficit does not change over time. Then the dollar value of this net inflow will not change regardless of changing foreign asset preferences. For it must continue to equal and indeed to finance the unchanged trade deficit. Given this flow-of-funds constraint, known as the Capital Account = Current Account identity, it turns out that, when foreigners become disenchanted with buying more U.S. assets, the value of the dollar drops, whereas U.S. interest rates do not generally rise. At the new lower exchange rate, foreigners are spending less of *their* money buying U.S. assets, but they are spending the same amount in U.S. dollars. Thus, there is no reduction in capital inflows in dollars so that U.S. interest rates are not driven up, as is supposed will happen by virtually everyone. Rather, the value of the currency gets driven down to a point where reduced currency risk rather than higher yields is what attracts foreign investors. The currency does virtually all of the work. This is known as the interest-rate/exchange-rate adjustment process, and it is true in theory and in practice. It is highly counterintuitive, but very useful in real-world forecasting. A lower exchange rate as opposed to a higher interest rate will impact GDP growth in opposite ways, the former boosting growth, the latter depressing it.

6. See *Bold Endeavors: How Our Government Built America, and Why It Must Rebuild Now,* by Felix G. Rohatyn (New York: Simon & Schuster, 2009).

7. In what follows, I shall ignore monetary policy and focus on fiscal policy (taxes and fiscal deficits). For it is fiscal policy that is central to my proposed policies. Arrow and Kurz also only focus on fiscal policy, as the title of their book makes clear.

8. The model is that of optimal control theory, a discipline largely developed in the 1940s and early 1950s. There are two versions of the model: One is based on the Pontryagin maximum principle in optimal control theory, and the other on the principle of optimality in dynamic programming theory. Chapter 2 of the Arrow-Kurz book reviews both in mathematical depth. The former theory is for continuous time models, whereas the latter is for discrete time models.

9. In formal economics-speak, the objective function is the felicity functional justified at length in the Arrow-Kurz book. This is an interpersonal extension to society of the intrapersonal mandate that each person on his own will attempt to maximize his utility for what is at stake.

10. More formally, each trajectory is a so-called policy function indicating what decision is best at each "state" of the system as it evolves over time.

Chapter 3: Resolving the Entitlements Spending Crisis

1. K. J. Arrow, "Uncertainty and the Welfare Economics of Medical Care," *American Economic Review*, 1963, 53.
2. I refer here to the "equiprobability principle" otherwise known as the "principle of insufficient reason" in statistical decision theory. For a simple but axiomatic account of this principle, see Chapter 13 of R. D. Luce and H. Raiffa, *Games and Decisions* (New York: John Wiley & Sons, Inc., 1957).
3. Robert Wood Johnson Foundation, March 2010.
4. Kaiser Family Foundation, January 2010.
5. Association of American Medical Colleges, "AAMC Statement on the Physician Workforce, June 2006." www.aamc.org/workforce/work forceposition.pdf. Accessed October 1, 2007.
6. The report states in more detail: "When medical education was last expanded during the 1960s and 1970s, the number of first-year resident positions was increased by 10,000, bringing the class of first-year residents from 10,000 in 1960 to 20,000 by 1980. Over the next fifteen years, another 5,500 first-year positions were created, bringing the total to 25,500. But this growth ceased abruptly when, as part of the Balanced Budget Act of 1997, Medicare fixed the number of residency positions it would support at its 1996 level. This was done in order to freeze physician production because of a widely held belief in the mid-1990s that physician surpluses were developing, a view promoted by the Council on Graduate Medical Education (COGME) and endorsed by major medical organizations, and little change has occurred in the number of residency positions since then. However, rather than surpluses, increasing evidence of shortages has emerged. These shortages were projected by Cooper and Getzen a decade ago, confirmed in subsequent projections by both COGME and the Association of American Medical Colleges, and supported by declarations of shortages by more than 20 physician specialty societies and an equal number of state medical and hospital associations. Major medical organizations that had previously endorsed Medicare's cap have reversed their position, and numerous state medical and hospital organizations have joined the call for Medicare to lift the cap. Yet, the cap persists."
7. Email correspondence with the author's research assistant, Andrew Beasley, August 3, 2010.
8. For further statistical details, and for the sources of the statistics we have cited, please see D. Lynge, E. Larson, M. Thompson, R. Rosenblatt, and L. Hart, "A Longitudinal Analysis of the General Surgery Workface in the United States, 1981–2005," *Archives of Surgery*,

April 2008, 143. Also see Association of American Medical Colleges, "The Physician Shortage and Health Care Reform," 2009. Finally, see N. Bathia, D. Meredith, and F. Riahi, "Managing the Clinical Workforce" *McKinsey Quarterly*, March, 2009.

9. Because of its technical nature, I am glossing over the possibility of bypassing full-fledged supply/demand analysis for forecasting by utilizing the so-called "reduced-form" of a structural model. The problem here is that most reduced-form models in practice are invalid as they are not properly derived from their underlying structural model. Moreover, the ability to derive the former from the latter is virtually impossible when issues of structural change about the future arise. Structural models on the other hand lend themselves very naturally to these two sets of difficulties. This matter is discussed at length in H. W. Brock, "Arrow-Bayes Equilibria: A New Theory of Price Forecasting," in *Arrow and Ascent of Modern Economic Theory*, ed. G. Feiwel (New York: New York University Press, 1987).

10. The logic of supply and demand is deductive in a general equilibrium context of the kind originally introduced by Arrow and Debreu in 1954. So is its statistical counterpart in econometrics, namely the theory of identifiability. The classic axiomatic treatment of general economic equilibrium theory is *Theory of Value, an Axiomatic Analysis of Economic Equilibrium*, by Gerard Debreu, (New Haven: Yale University Press, 1959).

11. K. J. Arrow, "The Role of the Securities Markets in the Optimal Reallocation of Risk," in *Econometrie* (Paris: Centre National de la Recherche Scientifique, 1953).

12. H. Pardes, "The Coming Shortage of Doctors," *New York Times*, November 5, 2009.

13. The easiest way to understand why this is true is to calculate the trajectory of debt-servicing costs as a share of total tax revenues over the next 40 years under such an entitlements burden (and this does not include unfunded Social Security liabilities). Many analyses of the entitlements crisis fail to take future debt-servicing costs into account. The situation is completely unsustainable.

14. We assume here that the personal savings rate remains constant.

15. Strictly speaking, it is the portion of the outward shift in the supply curve due to productivity growth that makes possible increased living standards. We are going to say nothing further about this point since our focus is not so much on rising living standards as it is on the need to increase the quantity of health-care services while reducing total expenditures. For this purpose, what matters are the total outward shifts of the supply and demand curves, and not merely the productivity-driven share of the supply curve shift.

16. For a description and critical review of this system, see Jessica Keyes, "Putting the Expert into Expert Systems," *Artificial Intelligence*, March 1990.

17. *New York Times* op-ed page, September 15, 2010.

Chapter 4: Preventing Perfect Financial Storms

1. This "inclusion principle" is a mark of genuine scientific progress, as is well known in the philosophy of science. It is thus not surprising that the new theory of endogenous risk in economics is compatible with the insights of "behavioral finance," and can incorporate them within it. In my view, the new theory permits a synthesis of many of the alternatives to efficient-markets theory that have sprouted in recent years. But the new theory has an advantage the other theories do not: It is an analytically self-consistent and closed structure that permits falsifiable predictions about the future. That is to say, it is scientifically valid, as was the efficient-markets theory. But the latter theory did not explain or predict real-world levels of volatility.

2. While the role of correlated forecast mistakes in amplifying risk is intuitively obvious, it is extremely difficult to model in a suitably rigorous manner. See Mordecai Kurz, "On Rational Belief Equilibria," in *Economic Theory* (Berlin/Heidelberg: Springer Verlag, 1994) for a fairly simple treatment, and Kurz, *Handbook of Game Theory with Economic Applications* (Amsterdam: Elsevier Press, 1994) for a more advanced treatment.

3. For readers not familiar with the concept of a moral hazard, the term refers to situations where the act of obtaining insurance on some event changes the probability that the event will occur. If an insurer knows that the true probability of a disability such as a bad back is one in 300, and you obtain insurance against it, then you will have an incentive to pretend you have a bad back once you have insurance. What now are the odds of purported bad backs? Insurers are understandably reluctant to issue policies in these circumstances. This is an example of "the moral hazards problem" that leads to many "missing markets" that in turn make it impossible for honest people to obtain insurance at all.

4. There is little need for a formal justification of this precondition. Suffice it to say that classical finance postulates the existence of a complete set of hedging markets for an optimal reallocation of risk, as was demonstrated by Kenneth Arrow in his 1953 paper, "The Role of the Securities Markets in the Optimal Allocation of Risk." This paper is discussed in Chapter 3. The well-known fact that many hedges do not exist, and that hedging strategies often malfunction and break down, is sufficient to establish the validity of precondition 2.

5. Pricing Model Uncertainty is not explicitly identified as such in Kurz's own theoretical papers. Rather, it is scrambled up with other sources of endogenous risk, most importantly uncertainty about the "extended state space" central to his theory of rational beliefs. I myself have focused on this particular dimension of risk, partly because I have found it to be important in the minds of investors whom I have advised during the past two decades, and partly because I was able to demonstrate its importance at a theoretical level. The proof was presented as an invited paper at a Stanford University seminar in theoretical economics during the summer of 2009. It is based upon a complex theorem in the theory of games of incomplete information applied to "optimal exiting" in duopoly theory proven by D. Fudenberg and J. Tirole. I am indebted to my colleague John O'Leary for discovering their 1986 result and appreciating its relevance to Pricing Model Uncertainty. The basic intuitive idea at work here is summarized in the text. Importantly, it is required that the investors be motivated by *relative* (not absolute) performance for the theorem to hold true, as indicated in the main text. See D. Fudenberg and J. Tirole, "A Theory of Exit in Duopoly," *Econometrica* (1986), vol. 54, no. 4, 943–960.

6. See M. Kurz and M. Motolese, "Endogenous Uncertainty and Market Volatility," in *Economic Theory* 2001: 16, 497–544.

7. At the most fundamental level, the restrictive axiom here is that the environment is stochastically stationary, in the sense of that term within ergodic theory. In a stationary system, whereas things can change over time (for example, GDP output rises and falls with the business cycle), *the way things change cannot change over time.* Formally, the joint probability distributions representing forecasts are invariant across time. Classical theory also allows for "learning" of a restrictive type. The problem is that, for genuine learning to be possible, it must be assumed that some fixed truths exist that can be learned with enough data. In a nonstationary environment, this is not the case. Kurz deals with all these details, and in fact develops an important and useful halfway house between stationary and nonstationary systems known as "weak asymptotic mean stationarity" or more briefly "stability." I believe that Kurz's theory permits a satisfactory integration of both classical and behavioral finance. On the one hand, it retains the classical view that people are goal-seeking in their behavior ("weakly rational" in a sense), but that in seeking to maximize their risk-adjusted expected returns, they make mistakes because their forecasts are inevitably wrong. In other words, agents are weakly rational yet wrong. His theory of rational beliefs does not delve into why we are wrong when we make mistakes. Rather, it explains the implications of being wrong (for whatever reasons) for market volatility, and for the need for corrective policies.

8. We stress "subjective uncertainty" because, in at least one version of Arrow's early theory, there was no assumption that "all agents possess the same forecast—a forecast that is correct." This so-called rational expectations assumption arose later within the Chicago school of efficient-markets theory, and as indicated in the text, was an unfortunate mistake. To be fair, the introduction of this assumption was a necessary and important milestone in the evolution of economic theory. It helped clarify the previously fuzzy concept of "efficient markets." I view it as akin to Galileo's great advance in understanding the relation between mass and gravity. Galileo had to assume "friction-free physics" to obtain his result that balls of different sizes and weights hit the ground at the same time. It is not fair to criticize him for not incorporating friction, as he lacked the tools for doing so. The same applies to the work of Sargent and Lucas in developing rational expectation economics. They did not have the analytical tools for developing general equilibrium models with mistakes. What Kurz has achieved is to make possible *economics* with *mistakes*, just as Newton and his successors did by making possible *physics with friction*. We could finally model the reality that feathers and lead balls do not hit the ground in equal time during a windstorm. Indeed, feathers may rise upward given the right wind conditions!

9. R. J. Shiller, *Macro Markets: Creating Institutions for Managing Society's Largest Economic Risks* (New York: Oxford University Press, 1993).

10. Deep truths are often found in so-called "limitative theorems" of this kind (for example, the Heisenberg uncertainty principle in quantum theory, the Arrow impossibility theorem in preference aggregation theory, and the Godel incompleteness theorem in metamathematics). Kurz's result here on nonknowable probabilities recalls these and other discoveries of our epistemological limits.

11. Perhaps I am being a bit too pessimistic here. It is in fact possible to quantify endogenous risk in terms of Figure 4.2 in the following very elementary manner. First, for any given time period, assess the joint probability distribution over the four drivers shown in Figure 4.2. Next, assign a payoff (in this case the magnitude of distress from a Perfect Storm) to each of the events defining the domain of this joint distribution. Finally, integrate to arrive at a marginal distribution on "distress," and compute the mean value of this result. It will represent the expected degree of Perfect Storm distress. By performing this simple operation every few weeks, officials could track whether a Perfect Storm is becoming more or less likely.

12. To be fair, changes in policies of the kind seen in Figure 4.3 reflect not only a change in the philosophy of governance, but also a change in how "financial innovation" permitted investors to evade traditional regulations. For example, once the Chicago Board Options Exchange

was opened in 1973, individual investors could take speculative (option) positions in stocks without utilizing classical margin accounts. In the case of the reserve requirement, the advent of "sweep accounts" and of securitization revolutionized the ability of banks to create balance sheets of their liking. See the interesting essay by Paul Bennett and Stavros Peristiani, "Are Reserve Requirements Still Binding?," *Economic Policy Review* 8, no. 1 (May 2002).

13. Robert Shiller, "Margin Calls: Should the Fed Step In?" *Wall Street Journal*, April 10, 2000.

14. Remember that in a classical textbook economy, no one agent can harm or benefit another. As in Adam Smith's *Wealth of Nations*, no one can gang up on anyone else, and no one wheat farmer or group of farmers can impact the interest of any other. All players in this sense are "strategically independent" or "inert."

15. H. Jin, M. Kurz, and M. Motolese, "Economic Fluctuations and the Role of Monetary Policy," Chapter 10 in *Knowledge, Information, and Expectations in Modern Macroeconomics: Essays in Honor of Edmund Phelps*, P. Aghion, R. Frydman, J. Stiglitz, and M. Woodford, Eds. (Princeton, NJ: Princeton University Press, 2003).

16. It might be thought that agents could insure themselves against the extra risk caused by a dotted-line environment by utilizing appropriate hedging strategies in private markets. But this is not the case. Moral hazard arguments, in this context, imply that the requisite hedging strategies will not exist. For no rational agent will write a hedge against the societal costs imposed by binges of excessive optimism and leveraging that can lead to a Perfect Storm. This lack of hedges is an example of the "missing markets" problem in economics.

17. More specifically, between 1990 and 2010, the correlation between the CPI and the S&P 500 was -0.316, the CPI and existing house prices (average) 0.141, the CPI and gold -0.074, and between existing house prices and the S&P 500 index 0.143, for an average negative correlation of -0.025.

18. In terms of economic jargon, I am urging for greater "controllability" of macroeconomic policy in Jan Tinbergen's sense. The nation needs a new "target," namely asset prices, and to regulate these it will require a new "policy instrument," namely the proposed Department of Leverage. As is required by Tinbergen's principal theorem, the new instrument should be independent of the government's other instruments, namely fiscal and monetary theory, and there should be no "degeneracy" problems in achieving all three of the government's targets: full employment, consumer price stability, and asset price stability. See Jan Tinbergen, *The Theory of Economic Policy* (Amsterdam: North Holland Publishing Co., 1952). As the father of controllability

theory, and for other accomplishments, Tinbergen shared the first Nobel ever awarded.

Chapter 5: Bargaining Theory 101

1. Two other scholars also played an important role in developing a theory closely allied to the Nash-Harsanyi theory of bargaining: Lloyd Shapley of UCLA and Reinhard Selten of the University of Bonn. But their initial focus was more upon the axiomatic valuation theory of cooperative games than on bargaining theory *per se*.

2. As regards economics being a special limiting case of politics, the basic result here was proved in 1977 by the mathematician Robert J. Aumann of Hebrew University, one of several contributions that would earn him the Nobel Memorial Prize in Economic Sciences. [Technically, he did not utilize the actual Nash-Harsanyi theory but a "linearized" version of it known at the non-transferable utility (NTU)-value of a game.] Seen in this light, bargaining theory emerges as the master discipline subsuming both politics and, as a very special case, free market economics. This is the perspective I shall adopt throughout this discussion. I have never seen this viewpoint expressed within the political science community, especially amongst rational choice theorists. Indeed, I do not believe Aumann's contribution is either known or understood in that community which is unfortunate since his result puts matters into a new and important perspective. See Robert J. Aumann, "Values of Economies with a Continuum of Traders," *Econometrica* 43 (1975), 611–646.

3. Theoretical political scientists of the "rational choice" school may be quite unhappy with what I am writing here, so let me defend my argument. To be sure, rational choice models drawn largely from economics have made a grand foray into many branches of political science in recent decades. This began with the revolution within social choice theory inaugurated by Kenneth Arrow's celebrated impossibility theorem of 1950, and the subsequent rise of Public Choice theory. It proliferated from there in many directions. My problem lies with the kind of rational-choice models chosen, and in the inability of these models to achieve the insights into bargaining proper that the Nash-Harsanyi model alone permits. To explain this view, I must utilize a bit of academic jargon. The fundamental difference between the Nash-Harsanyi approach and that of voting literature models lies in the differences in their algebraic symmetry groups. Voting models (including traditional Shapley-Shubik and Banzhoff measures of "power") are invariant under monotonic transformations of the players' utility functions. This implies

that such models cannot incorporate considerations of the relative intensity of preference differences between players, for example, and hence cannot utilize the logic required to determine optimal threats and compromises in proper bargaining theory.

In contrast, the Nash-Harsanyi theory, and the closely related theory of axiomatic NTU valuation theory (for example, the Shapley values of games) requires players' preferences to be invariant under the more restricted group of linear transformations of the utilities. Accordingly, their models make possible a proper theory of bargaining which, by its very nature, entails issues of relative intensity of preferences, as Harsanyi, Aumann, Kurz, Shapley, and other scholars have noted. In this vein, John Harsanyi in 1962 was able to formulate a general n-person measurement-of-power index useful in all conflict situations, a power index that is derived from bargaining power, as it should be. I have never seen a paper in the RC political science literature that utilizes this remarkable index, much less that acknowledges its existence. See, in particular, John C. Harsanyi, "Measurement of Social Power in n-Person Reciprocal Power Situations," *Behavioral Science* 7, 1962.

Predecessor rational choice models could only measure power in voting situations, using interesting but limited concepts such as "swing vote power" and "blocking" power, as in the ordinal concept of the core of a game. But eyeball-to-eyeball bargaining proper cannot be modeled in such models. For a discussion of these issues, consider the arguments and references cited in Horace W. Brock, "To Each According to His Needs: An Axiomatic Characterization," in *Assets, Beliefs, and Equilibria in Economic Dynamics*, eds. Charalambos Aliprantis, Kenneth Arrow, Peter Hammond et al. (New York and Berlin: Springer Verlag, 2004). See also *Rational Behavior and Bargaining Equilibrium in Games and Social Situations*, John C. Harsanyi (New York: Cambridge University Press, 1977).

4. The fundamental paper in this regard is "A Simplified Bargaining Model for the n-Person Cooperative Game," by John C. Harsanyi, *International Economic Review* 4, 194–220, 1963. This paper synthesizes and unifies the different axiomatic valuation theories of Nash, Selten, and Shapley into a coherent whole.

5. These building blocks are analogous to those in a free-market model that consists of the producers (firms) and consumers, their preferences, their endowments, and market prices.

6. Nash introduced a set of reasonable axioms that a solution to the bargaining game must satisfy. He then proved that there is only one such solution satisfying these axioms. This is known as a "deductive proof" devoid of any behavioral interaction between the players. Harsanyi produced a "constructive proof" showing how the Nash solution results from a model of step-by-step human behavior during

the bargaining process. The two approaches are fully complementary, but very different in spirit. Both arrive at the same solution to the bargaining problem.

7. Mathematically, this point happens to be the outcome with the property that it maximizes the arithmetic product of the utility gains of the players above their threat payoffs. The product—not the sum!

8. See Horace W. Brock, "To Each According to His Needs: An Axiomatic Characterization," in *Assets, Beliefs, and Equilibria in Economic Dynamics*, eds. Charalambos Aliprantis, Kenneth Arrow, Peter Hammond et al. (New York and Berlin: Springer Verlag, 2004).

9. To express this more correctly, there will be a unique *set* of optimal threat strategies, the elements of which are equivalent with respect to the utility payoffs to the players. This is only true for two-person games.

10. I am deliberately sidestepping an important difficulty in bargaining theory that arises when players do not know the true strategy sets and payoffs of one another. This problem of "incomplete information games" was first addressed by John Harsanyi and Reinhard Selten in a bargaining context, and then later extended in an important way by Roger Meyerson of the University of Chicago, perhaps the leading game theorist of the next generation. In such games, each "player" is replaced by a set of potential "types" of players, one of which is the true one. Players then ascribe probabilities to the different types they could be playing against. Types may differ in terms of risk tolerance, or any other strategically relevant variables. The game is then played between these "types" rather than between the actual players. The original idea here, dating from 1966, was due to John Harsanyi. Much of this logic goes through, but in some cases matters become much more complicated. Based on my own research on "arbitration schemes," I believe it is appropriate to *approximate* a game of incomplete information with a game of complete information in many cases, and then to proceed as above.

11. See, for example, the excellent summary of these developments by Kathrin Hille and Jamil Anderlini, "Red Alert," *Financial Times*, June 3, 2011.

12. I am speaking of labor productivity here, not total factor productivity. As regards the latter, China has led the way in "factor stuffing" via its unprecedented investment program.

13. These statistics were cited in an article in the *Financial Times* on June 28, 2011.

14. Paul A. Samuelson, "Where Ricardo and Mill Rebut and Confirm Arguments of Mainstream Economists Supporting Globalization," *Journal of Economic Perspectives* 18, no. 3 (2004).

15. Robert Scott, Briefing Paper of the Economic Policy Institute, #260, March 23, 2010.

16. What gets funded annually by foreign investors is an amount equal to the size of the U.S. current account (trade) deficit. This funding is often referred to as the "net capital inflow" into the debtor country, in this case the United States. By the capital account = current account identity of international accounting, this capital inflow will and must always get funded by some subset of foreign investors. If some lose interest, others will take their place, typically at a lower and hence less risky value of the dollar.

17. *Financial Times*, July 1, 2011, 11.

18. Specifically, the equations characterizing the two games within the game are a set of simultaneous nonlinear equations that, when solved, yield solutions to both subgames.

19. In political science, there was the celebrated 1950 Arrow impossibility theorem, proving the impossibility of aggregating individuals' preferences into social preferences. In economics, there were the theorems showing the near-impossibility of aggregating the microeconomic behavior of individuals into the macroeconomic behavior of groups, for example, the Ando-Simon-Fisher theorems.

20. In bargaining, there are in fact supply-and-demand functions for the payoffs from the game known as "utilities." Lloyd Shapley in 1969 showed that an "equilibrium" supply = demand for utilities occurs when the payoffs to the players satisfied the two conditions of both efficiency and equity, properly defined. I extended this perspective much further in my doctoral thesis. See in particular Lloyd S. Shapley, Part 1 of "Utility Comparisons and the Theory of Games," in *La Decision: Aggregation et Dynamique des Ordres de Preference*, Ed. G. T. Guilbaud (Paris: Centre National de la Recherche Scientifique, 1969).

21. Invited paper presented at the 1978 annual meetings of the American Political Science Association in New York.

Chapter 6: Beyond Democratic Capitalism

1. See, in particular, his bestseller *Justice: What Is the Right Thing to Do?* (New York: Farrar, Strauss, and Giroux, 2009).

2. To make this summary complete, I could have added the "global" requirement of free and fair trade between all nations. But the most important points can be covered by restricting the analysis to the case of a closed economy without trade, as I have done.

3. See L. Hurwicz, "On Informationally Decentralized Systems," in *Decision and Organization*, eds. C. B. McGuire and R. Radner (Amsterdam: North Holland, 1972), 297–336. Also see L. Hurwicz, Nobel Prize lecture, "But Who Will Guard the Guardians?" A prerecorded version of the lecture was presented on December 8, 2007, at Aula Magna, Stockholm University.

4. Of course, the central planner needed the information conveyed by those "dual variables" or "shadow prices" associated with the mathematical programming problems that had to be solved for the central planner to determine who should produce/consume what.

5. He did not in fact get quite this far. What he did was to construct a new allocation system known as "the Greed Process." He then showed that it satisfied a few of the seven norms that can be satisfied by true capitalism. But by extension of the logic and mathematics that Hurwicz utilized, it is clear that virtually no other system does or can compare favorably with true capitalism. See L. Hurwicz, "On Informationally Decentralized Systems," in *Decision and Organization*, eds. C. B. McGuire and R. Radner (Amsterdam: North Holland, 1972), 297–336.

6. The concept of incentive compatibility is a deep one, and it is best understood by utilizing the concept of a noncooperative game. Think of a family of games, each parameterized by its incentive structure (represented mathematically). Suppose that all agents take those rules of the game as given, and optimize against them, each doing what is best for him or her under the circumstances. The outcome of each such game will be its Nash equilibrium, for example, a particular production of and allocation of resources. Now rank these outcomes in terms of their performance according to one or several of norms 1–7, for example, the size of the pie, the stability of the economy, or whatever. The incentive structure that induces the creation of the largest and best pie is said to be "most incentive compatible" or simply "incentive compatible" *with* the goal of efficiency, stability, or whatever the chosen norms might be.

7. The proof that the contribution principle will be satisfied in bargaining theory follows from the mathematical equivalence of the Nash-Harsanyi bargaining solution and the generalized Shapley value of any n-person cooperative game. This equivalence buys us our result because the Shapley value awards each player a payoff equal to the sum of his marginal contributions to various coalitions that he joins. Additionally, it was recently demonstrated that there can be no measure of relative contribution other than that of the Shapley Value, assuming certain reasonable axioms are to be satisfied. See H. Peyton Young, "Individual Contribution and Just Compensation," in *The Shapley Value*, ed. Alvin E. Roth (New York: Cambridge University Press, 1988).

8. R. J. Aumann and M. Kurz, "Power and Taxes," *Econometrica* 45 (1977), 1137–1161.

9. K. J. Arrow, "The Role of the Securities Markets in the Optimal Reallocation of Risk," in *Econometrie* (Paris: Centre National de la Recherche Scientifique, 1953).

10. R. J. Shiller, *Macro Markets: Creating Institutions for Managing Society's Largest Economic Risks* (New York: Oxford University Press, 1993).

11. This logic completely undermines the central point of Robert Nozick's fascinating refutation of Rawls and egalitarianism in *Anarchy, State, and Utopia* (New York: Basic Books, 1974). Nozick cites the example of the basketball player Wilt Chamberlain. "If 1,000,000 fans choose to pay 25 cents each for a ticket to watch him perform, then what claim does government have upon his earnings?" Our answer is that, by his own admission, Wilt rose to fame partly as a result of many lucky breaks: a coach who was obsessed by him, routine physical accidents that did not befall him, and so forth. Under ideal capitalist theory, he would have wished to insure himself against these various random events. Then, upon lucking out as he did, he would have forfeited to less fortunate competitors the premiums of his insurance contracts. But he never did: Markets for such transfers did not exist. The progressive tax levied upon his income can thus be viewed as a surrogate for the missing insurance premiums he would have paid had he obtained insurance and ended up being repeatedly lucky.

12. For early efforts to exploit this logic, see R. J. Zeckhauser, *Benefit Cost and Policy Analysis* (Chicago: Aldine Publishing Company, 1974), and H. W. Brock, "Social Choice, Distributive Justice, and the Theory of Games with Non-Linearly Transferable Utility," PhD Dissertation, Princeton University, 1975.

13. John Rawls, *A Theory of Justice* (Cambridge, MA: Belknap Press, 1971).

14. John C. Harsanyi, "Game and Decision Theoretic Models in Ethics," in *The Handbook of Game Theory*, eds. Robert Aumann and Sergiu Hart (New York: North Holland, 1992).

15. See H. W. Brock, "A New Theory of Social Justice Based upon the Mathematical Theory of Games," in *Game Theory and Social Science*, ed. P. Ordeshook (New York: New York University Press, 1978), 563–628. Also see "Game Theoretic Insights into Ethics Based on a New Theory of Justice," in *Game Theory, Social Choice, and Ethics*, Special Edition of *Theory and Decision*, ed. H. W. Brock (Amsterdam: Reidel Press, 1979).

16. In game theory terms, this "no agreement regime" represents the *non-cooperative* game played between the players deprived of the rule of law that makes most social cooperation possible. The payoff will be the Nash equilibrium strategy payoffs to all players from this Hobbesian noncooperative game.

17. See Rawls, op. cit., pp. 305–308, for an interesting discussion of the contribution principle and its relation to other moral norms. Also see Marx's "Critique of the Gotha Program" in *Karl Marx and Frederick Engels, Selected Works*, Vol. II (Moscow: Foreign Languages Publishing House, 1955). The paper by Charles Taylor was at that time not published, and

was given to me by Professor Bell in mimeographed form. It influenced me greatly.

18. One source of murkiness in the Rawlsian and utilitarian theories was the lack of a clear definition of the set of constitutions comprising the choice set of the stage 1 game. In my own original papers, this problem was explicitly addressed. Every constitution corresponds to a specific element in the space R of all possible strategy- and payoff-restrictions that can be imposed on the choice set of the Hobbesian null regime game. This latter set can be thought of as a "maximal set" of anything-goes strategies. Any constitution will correspond to a particular element of this set.

19. This is true because every competitive allocation awarded by the market is a Shapley value of the associated bargaining game. The same is true for all multilateral bargaining equilibria in political contexts whose Nash-Harsanyi bargaining solutions are always Shapley values. Recall that the Shapley value of any game is the *only* solution that satisfies the principle of remuneration in accord with relative contribution, as Peyton Young proved in his 1988 paper, referred to previously.

20. Note here how the concept of relative contribution is as *irrelevant* to distributive justice in the context of charitable giving as relative need is *relevant*. This reinforces my basic division of labor point.

21. In technical jargon, Rawls's theory requires simple ordinal comparisons of utility, whereas utilitarianism requires complete cardinal comparability of both the constant and the multiplicative term of the different agents' cardinal utility functions.

22. See "To Each According to His Needs—An Axiomatic Characterization," by H. W. Brock, in *Assets, Beliefs, and Equilibria in Economic Dynamics*, eds. C. D. Aliprantis, K. J. Arrow, P. Hammond et al. (New York: Springer Verlag, 2004). Mathematically, the solution to the equitable sharing of the pie problem based upon relative need is the generalized harmonic mean of the unique Nash bargaining allocation of a "pure" n-person bargaining game. Such a game can be associated with any distributive arbitration problem, such as the stage 1 game of my theory. The freedom from interpersonal comparisons of utility is inherited from the i-wise cardinal utility invariance of the Nash bargaining theory.

　　The basic insight is that a bargaining game that is "morally purified" by removing any elements of threat and coalitional power has the following property: The differences in each player's equilibrium share of the pie will be inversely proportional to the players' degree of risk aversion, with more risk-averse players being bargained down and receiving less. But relative risk aversion is shown to be equivalent to relative neediness. Thus, by "inverting" for every pair of players the shares of pie going to each via bargaining, you arrive at the fair, needs-based allocation. Mathematically, this allocation turns out to be the generalized harmonic mean of the Nash allocation.

The fundamental discovery here is that bargaining behavior forces a revelation of relative neediness, just as the ranking of lotteries under risk reveals an individual person's degree of risk aversion and hence his cardinal function in classical decision theory, as von Neumann first proved in 1947. My paper applies to a subset of all reasonable utility functions of the players, which is a limitation. This is the set of functions that never intersect one another when graphed in 0–1 normalization. But I sketch in Section 4.2 how the result can be generalized using a suggestion from Robert Aumann. Section 7, "Full Distributive Justice," of this paper restates and rectifies my original theory of 1978, incorporating this new analysis of relative needs.

23. This is because the Nash-Harsanyi bargaining allocation whose harmonic inverse satisfies stage 1 justice is in fact the Shapley value allocation of the pure *n*-person bargaining game played in stage 1. But the Shapley value is the fundamental criterion used for defining contribution justice in the stage 2 game. The realization that these two fundamental ethical norms are mirror images of one another is remarkable.

24. Equation 19 of section 6 of my 2004 paper (cited in endnote 22) establishes that the utilitarian distribution does not comply with the norm of relative need. Harsanyi's strongest argument that it did can be found in one of his last papers on the subject, "Von Neumann-Morgenstern Utilities, Risk Taking, and Welfare," in *Arrow and the Ascent of Modern Economic Theory*, ed. G. R. Feiwel (New York: New York University Press, 1987).

25. T. M. Scanlon, *What We Owe To Each Other* (Cambridge, MA: Belknap Press, 1998).

Appendix A: Supply/Demand Summary of the Patient Protection and Affordable Care Act

1. Please note that, while there is much detail in the Act regarding the expansion of public programs, tax changes related to health insurance, health insurance exchanges, and changes to private insurance, I do not review such matters in this document as they have little bearing on our main arguments.

Index